D0084414

Treatment Outcomes in Psychotherapy and Psychiatric Interventions

Mental Health Practice Under Managed Care
A Brunner/Mazel Book Series

S. Richard Sauber, Ph.D., Series Editor

The Brunner/Mazel Mental Health Practice Under Managed Care Series addresses the major developments and changes resulting from the introduction of managed care. Volumes in the series will enable mental health professionals to provide effective therapy to their patients while conducting and maintaining a successful practice.

Mental Health Practice Under Managed Care, Volume 6

Treatment Outcomes in Psychotherapy and Psychiatric Interventions

Len Sperry, M.D., Ph.D.
Peter L. Brill, M.D.
Kenneth I. Howard, Ph.D.
Grant R. Grissom, Ph.D.

BRUNNER/MAZEL, *Publishers* ● New York

Table 8.3 on page 213 and Table 8.4 on page 214 are reprinted by permission of the publisher and the authors. From M. Keatley et al., "Using 'Normative' Data for Outcomes Comparisons." *Behavioral Health Management* (1995), vol 15(3), pp. 20–21.

These tables are part of OUTCOME™ software provided by Evaluation Systems International, Inc. Boulder, CO (313) 443-2200.

Library of Congress Cataloging-in-Publication Data

Treatment outcomes in psychotherapy and psychiatric interventions/ Len
Sperry . . . [et al.].
    p. cm. — (Mental health practice under managed care ; v. 6)
    Includes bibliographical references and index.
    ISBN 0-87630-826-4 (paper)
    1. Psychotherapy.   2. Outcomes assessment (Medical care)
I. Series.
    [DNLM: 1. Psychotherapy—methods.   2. Mental Disorders—therapy.
3. Treatment Outcomes.   WM 420 T7845   1996]
RC480.T678   1996
616.89'14—dc20
DNLM/DLC
for Library of Congress   96-26029
                                                   CIP

Published by
BRUNNER/MAZEL, INC.
19 Union Square West
New York, New York 10003

Manufactured in the United States of America
10 9 8 7 6 5 4 3 2 1

ABOUT THE AUTHORS

Len Sperry, M.D., Ph.D., is Professor of Psychiatry and Behavioral Medicine at the Medical College of Wisconsin, where he directs the Division of Organizational Psychiatry and Corporate Health. He has been involved in managed mental health care services and outcomes management as a provider, teacher, researcher, and consultant since 1984. Board certified in both psychiatry and clinical psychology, he is listed in *Best Doctors in America, Midwest Edition* 1996–1997. Dr. Sperry has authored 24 books, including the *Handbook of Diagnosis and Treatment of the DSM-IV Personality Disorders, Psychopharmacology and Psychotherapy: Strategies for Maximizing Treatment Outcomes, Corporate Therapy and Consulting*, as well as over 200 articles.

Peter L. Brill, M.D., founder and Chairman of Compass Information Services, Inc., is a board certified psychiatrist with 25 years of experience. Dr. Brill is on the faculty of the University of Pennsylvania School of Medicine and is a Senior Fellow at the Wharton School of Business. He is also Clinical Associate Professor of Psychiatry and Behavioral Medicine at the Medical College of Wisconsin. Dr. Brill has served as Chair of the Committee on Occupational Psychiatry of the Group for the Advancement of Psychiatry, and a Fellow of the American College Occupational and Environmental Health.

Kenneth I. Howard, Ph.D., is Professor and Director of Clinical Programs in Northwestern University's Department of Psychology. Dr. Howard is among the world's most respected and accomplished researchers in the field of psychotherapy outcomes. He has authored over 150 presentations at professional conferences and in journal publications. Dr. Howard founded the Society for Psychotherapy Research (SPR), which is now the leading international organization in the area of psychotherapy outcomes. He is the recipient of numerous awards, and is one of only two individuals in the world to win all three of the top awards in the field: the *Senior Scientist Award* (NIMH), the *Distinguished Career Award* (SPR), and the 1996 *Distinguished Professional Contributions to Knowledge Award* (American Psychological Association).

Grant R. Grissom, Ph.D., is Vice President for Research and Development of Compass Information Services, Inc. and a national leader in directing applied social science research. Dr. Grissom has received more than 20 grants to serve as Principal Investigator for the Departments of Health and Human Services, Justice, Education, and Defense. He has directed a dozen major mental projects funded by the National Institute on Drug Abuse, the National Institute on Alcoholism and Alcohol Abuse, and the National Institute on Mental Health. All grants were peer-reviewed by independent scientists. His record of achievement has rarely been equaled, and places Dr. Grissom in the top rank of social science researchers.

MORE PRAISE . . . .

The authors of *Treatment Outcomes in Psychotherapy and Psychiatric Interventions* have provided us with a conceptual framework and specific methodologies to help us in attempting to cope with the economic demands of the 1990s. Throughout the book, there is an emphasis on concurrent outcome measures during treatment. There is also much attention to the combined employment of medication and psychotherapeutic approaches. I am pleased with this attention, and I believe that this book will be very helpful to my colleagues in their clinical practice during the managed care period and beyond.

Melvin Sabshin, M.D.
Medical Director
American Psychiatric Association

This book is an outstanding reference volume that combines research findings with clinical sense. It makes the case for ongoing outcomes assessment and management in the most persuasive manner of any volume currently available on managed health care. By shifting the focus of MCOs from "cost" to "value" and treatment from descriptive to prescriptive, the authors set needed directions for MCOs to follow.

Larry E. Beutler, Ph.D.
Director
Counseling/Clinical/School Psychology Program
University of California, Santa Barbara

Sound outcomes assessment is critical for patients, providers, and purchasers of mental health and substance abuse treatment. These very knowledgeable authors provide a thoughtful and important guide to this new field.

G. Richard Smith, M.D.
Professor of Psychiatry, University of Arkansas
Director, Center for Outcomes Research and Effectiveness

The authors describe an inspiring set of initiatives that demonstrate the unique and profound contribution the private sector can make in turning the tide toward more quality and outcome based valuation of behavioral health care services. They introduce a paradigm shift in outcomes management with use of concurrent measurement techniques to compare actual treatment progress for individual patients against predicted improvement curves. In so doing, they show convincingly how clinicians can use concurrent measurement to determine the need for adjustments in treatment strategy, and how systems of care can use this same approach to document and improve the overall effectiveness of their treatment services.

Tom Trabin, Ph.D.
Director, Research Division
Institute of Behavioral Healthcare
Portola Valley, California

Contents

To Patricia, Karen, Michele, and Gay for managing to care.

Foreword

Data which proves the efficacy of therapeutic interventions is the cutting edge of medicine as we move towards the twenty-first century. Outcomes studies are the most critical path to destigmatizing mental illness and bringing more individuals who require help into the care system. While research on outcomes systems is still in its infancy, the authors of this extraordinary volume are truly making headway in designing and defining simple, cost-effective, useful, and helpful outcomes measures to maximize the care of the mentally ill and substance abusing populations.

Beginning with the seminal work of Kenneth Howard, Ph.D. and the continuing efforts of all of the authors, they have developed methodologies that measure not only a single snapshot of the patient's care, but also provide continuous measurable and utilizable feedback for positively impacting the course of treatment. The research efforts of this group allows the clinician to change the intervention and measure the success or failure at any moment in the course of treatment. The evolution has been of the basic concept and a description of the techniques as well as the variables to measure different levels of severity are described clearly and directly in this book.

Their initial efforts to understand how psychotherapy works have been expanded to include varying levels of care for inpatient treatment outcomes, substance abuse treatment outcomes, psychopharmacological treatment outcomes, as well as mental health treatment outcomes in primary care settings. This outcomes system allows clinicians to view the progress of treatment over time and independent of the setting, the level of care, the intensity of the treatment, or the type of treatment. This system is not dependent on diagnosis, nor does it require extensive and sophisticated tools. Also, it has generated treatment prediction algorithms that have been tested and have demonstrated the capacity to combine the feelings and opinions and data from both the clinician and the patient. This combined information creates a reliable data set that is immensely useful for the clinician.

It is no secret that psychotherapy has been one of the most difficult interventions to measure and to predict either process or outcomes. Can we actually know what we're doing and whether it's working? Can we switch gears in a way that's flexible and allows the patient to get better with the shortest course of treatment and the greatest "bang for the buck." In these times of managed care and intense concern about utilization of scarce resources, it is imperative that we find a method to measure interventions and a method which allows us to know how we are doing at any given moment in the course of treatment. Clinicians have struggled with a stigmatizing, repetitive, antipsychotherapeutic diatribe based on false beliefs about what psychotherapy is and have always come up short on data regarding the efficacy of psychotherapy and other psychiatric interventions. An individual clinician in his/her office knows that psychotherapy works. They see patients who come in crippled, unhappy, anxiety-ridden, depressed and who finish treatment in a state of excellent mental health, in a state of enthusiasm, optimism and willingness to take risks. There has been no way to demonstrate this other than anecdotally and through the occasional confession from a successful patient that they have, in fact, had treatment and the treatment worked. At least until now.

On a recent trip to Mexico City, I had the pleasure of leading a delegation of 40 psychiatrists and their spouses to the home of the daughter of Diego Rivera, the famous artist. It was a very exciting occasion at which the hostess was more than cordial. She treated us all to drinks, hors d'oeuvres, and a tour of her home which had many beautiful paintings, a number of which had been painted by her father. At one point, as the leader of the delegation, I felt obliged to say something to express our thanks for the wonderful reception she gave us. I will always remember her response. She looked me in the eye and said, "I am the product of a successful analysis and I am very proud to have all of you in my home." Anecdotes, whether from celebrities or the average person who comes to see a clinician, continue to be insufficient.

Any outcomes measurement system must take into account the biopsychosocial paradigm in which all treatments become measurable. The combination and variation of treatment methods are less important than the attention paid to the initiation of appropriate interventions for specific diagnoses and an overall treatment plan which may include any and all settings and variations in intensity. The measurement of outcomes then, follows naturally as a final common pathway for testing the appropriateness and the efficacy of the treatment applied. The work of Sperry, Brill, Howard, and Grissom takes a process that they have developed and makes outcome work into a scientific endeavor that will grow as part of the armamentarium of the average clinician.

More importantly, in the enormous world of health care financing, proof that psychotherapy, psychopharmacology, and other interventions work is critical to funding not only through the government but private insurance as well. Throughout the country there is a small band of researchers who are trying to find the right and most effective way to carry out this research. This small volume is an important addition to the literature. It points us in the direction of an appropriate system of outcomes research which will finally prove what we have known about psychiatry as a science. This book will also help in the development of prescriptive treatments that are appropriate for given patients whose circumstances are known and in whom interventions can be measured. It represents a monumental step toward achieving the type of treatment outcomes system that will ultimately lead us to a new standard of effective and appropriate treatment for all patients.

Paul J. Fink, M.D.
Senior Consultant, Charter Fairmont Behavioral Health System,
Professor of Psychiatry, Temple University School of Medicine, and
Past President, American Psychiatric Association

Preface

Cost-effective, efficient, and efficacious treatment outcomes have become the norm for the provision of mental health services. This norm is very recent and represents a philosophy of treatment that is radically different from that in which most providers were trained. The result is that many providers are confused and concerned about the meaning and implications of this "paradigm shift" imposed on the profession. Some professionals view outcome systems as an intrusion into their practice pattern and as a breach of confidentiality. Others just want to get oriented to it. Both sides are asking basic questions such as: "What are treatment outcomes? How are they measured? and What are the implications for practice?" Unfortunately, the literature on outcomes research geared to providers is almost nonexistent.

This book addresses these issues and concerns. It is authored by professionals on the cutting edge of the treatment outcome frontier. It provides the reader with a "road map" through the theoretical and clinical roadblocks and checkpoints that providers will surely encounter on the way to treatment accountability. *Treatment Outcomes in Psychotherapy and Psychiatric Interventions* can serve as a survival manual for providers confronting the avalanche of changes in clinical practice today. First and foremost, this is a practical book that emphasizes clinical applications.

Several types of outcomes measures, outcomes monitoring systems, and outcomes management systems are described and illustrated. A rather complete listing of available measures and systems can be found in *The 1996 Behavioral Outcomes and Sourcebook* (Vibbert & Youngs, 1995). Among these is the COMPASS Treatment System (Vibbert & Youngs, 1995; Compass Information Service, 1995) which was developed and refined by a research group that includes the authors. This book is not intended to promote COMPASS, but rather to highlight a number of state-of-the-art treatment outcomes systems for various treatment options such as psychotherapy, inpatient therapy, and medication. This is a clinically oriented, practical manual geared to both the mental health provider and the case manager. It will also be of interest to students, benefits managers, consultants, and managers and executives of managed care organizations (MCOs).

The book is divided into two parts. The first three chapters of Part I describe the paradigm shift that has been occurring in health and mental health care, particularly regarding treatment outcomes. Chapter 1 describes how efforts to quantify the value and effectiveness of psychotherapy and psychiatric treatments began with measures of outcomes. First, it was patient satisfaction queries. These were soon followed by inventories and ratings of patient variables such as symptoms and functioning. In addition, some MCOs are also monitoring outcomes, and a few have attempted to manage the outcomes system. This chapter describes the evolution of these three phases and extends the challenge of establishing a truly comprehensive treatment outcomes system.

Chapter 2 describes how efforts to establish the most effective, efficacious, and efficient psychotherapy and other psychiatric treatments by means of the randomized clinical trial have been failures, while also being nonresponsive to the needs of patients, clinicians, and MCOs. Nevertheless, it is possible to standardize treatment and determine the type of patient who responds well to it. This chapter describes a self-correcting learning model that is based on a theoretical framework of the healing process—the dose response and phase models—that provides clinically relevant feedback to patient, provider, and case managers, while enhancing treatment outcomes.

Chapter 3 describes the paradigm shift in the provision of treatment. Until recently, psychotherapy and other treatments were essentially provider-centered. Often these treatments were limited to a single modality (i.e., individual psychotherapy or medication or couples therapy) and a single system (e.g., psychoanalytic or behavioral). There is mounting evidence that efficient and cost-effective treatments are prescriptive treatments: those tailored to patient variables such as symptom severity, level of functioning, or readiness for change, while integrating techniques from different psychotherapy systems, and combining modalities. The chapter briefly describes this paradigm shift in treatment formulation and selection, and reviews treatment strategies and guidelines for maximizing treatment outcomes.

The five chapters in Part II address how treatment outcomes are applied to clinical practice. Chapter 4 describes the use of measures of patient variables useful in tracking patient progress in outpatient treatment settings. A theory-based comprehensive measurement and monitoring or tracking system is detailed and illustrated with extensive case examples. Provider profiling and treatment system outcomes assessment are highlighted.

Chapter 5 addresses level of care, including treatment outcomes, in an inpatient psychiatric setting. Only recently have efforts to measure, monitor, and manage outcomes of inpatient treatment settings been undertaken. The chapter describes a state of the art measurement and monitoring system for guiding decisions on the necessity of inpatient admission, treatment selection, discharge, and aftercare planning.

Chapter 6 addresses treatment outcomes in substance use disorders. The chapter briefly reviews the changing status of detoxification, counseling, support group, and other treatment modalities for substance abuse/dependent patients. Guidelines for prescriptive treatment are briefly described. A system to measure, monitor, and manage outcomes is described and illustrated with cases.

Chapter 7 describes treatment outcomes in medication management. The use of medications alone or in combination with other treatment modalities has been shown to quickly and effectively ameliorate symptoms of major psychiatric disorders, as well as to modulate mood instability, impulsivity, and violence proneness in personality-disordered patients. The chapter provides specific treatment guidelines for the use of psychopharmacologic agents and a newly developed measurement/monitoring/management system.

Finally, Chapter 8 describes the value and application of treatment outcomes in both primary care and behavioral medicine settings. This chapter briefly reviews the cost savings that result when psychological treatments are made available to patients with medical and psychosomatic presentations who do not seek or want psychotherapeutic or psychiatric treatment. This is referred to as "medical-offset." The implications of utilizing behavioral health treatment outcomes in medical and behavioral medicine settings are described. A system for measuring and monitoring such treatment outcomes is illustrated.

Outcomes Terminology

While outcome measures are not new in mental health care, the notion that they could impact the delivery of behavioral health services is new. Ten years ago, only a small number of providers and clinical researchers were familiar with such terms as functional outcomes, outcomes monitoring, quality assessment, and cost-effectiveness analysis. Today, such terms are the coin of the realm among researchers, policy analysts, and payers. A relatively new journal, *Managed Care Quarterly*, devoted the entire 1995 spring and summer issues to the topic of "Outcomes Management." This journal is targeted to health care executives, policy analysts, and payers. The expectation is that now these readers should be conversant with outcomes terminology. Subsequently, behavioral health providers will also be expected to be conversant with outcomes terminology.

There are very few dictionaries or thesauruses that include outcomes terminology (Scriven, 1991), nor is there consensus on the meaning of key terms. For this reason, we thought it essential to specify the meaning of the outcomes terms that are used throughout the book. The glossary shown on page xx defines these commonly used terms.

Acknowledgments

The writing and production of this book have involved many individuals whom we would like to acknowledge. First, we express our appreciation to Richard Sauber, Ph.D., editor of the Mental Health Practice Under Managed Care Series, and Natalie Gilman, Editorial Vice President of Brunner/Mazel, for their support and encouragement of the project. Next, we need to extend heartfelt gratitude to our friend and colleague, Jennifer Lish, Ph.D. for her intellectual contributions to this text, particularly Chapters 5 and 8. We owe gratitude to Meghan Byrne, Heather Duncan, and Janet Eyles for their paper "Summary of Cost Offset Research," an internal document; to Laura Dietzen and Heather Duncan, members of the COMPASS ITC development team, for their assistance with Chapter 5; and again to Meghan Byrne, Project Director for the Integra "Matching" study, for her assistance with Chapter 6. The research reported in Chapters 2 and 4 was partially supported by grants R01 MH42901 K05 MH00924 from the National Institute of Mental Health. We are grateful for the participation of all of the members of Northwestern/ Chicago Research Program: Elizabeth Bankoff, Greg Kolden, Mark Kopta, Hans Kordy, Robert Lueger, Wolfgang Lutz, Michael Maling, Zoran Martinovich, Michael O'Mahoney, David Orlinsky, Stephen Saunders, and our many graduate and undergraduate research assistants. We especially wish to acknowledge the crucial role that Bruce Briscoe has played in all of our work. Furthermore, we want to thank Sally Matchner for her yeoman efforts throughout the entire time this text was taking shape.

Finally, we acknowledge the staffs of Integra, Inc. and Compass Information Services for their hard work and dedication, which has contributed to COMPASS in endless ways.

We could not have completed this book without the assistance of these colleagues.

Treatment Outcomes in Psychotherapy and Psychiatric Interventions

GLOSSARY OF OUTCOMES TERMINOLOGY

Clinical Outcomes: Outcomes that describe the physical and psychiatric signs and symptoms of a disease or disorder.

Cost–Benefit Analysis: The analysis of costs and benefits of treatment expressed in the same unit of measure, usually monetary units.

Cost-Effectiveness Analysis: The analysis of the benefits and outcomes of treatment expressed in nonmonetary measures, such as symptom reduction, increased life functioning, treatment compliance, or quality of life.

Effectiveness: The determination—in naturalistic settings—that a treatment has a beneficial effect. It is also the outcomes for average or typical patients treated in common practice settings by average or typical providers. Effectiveness compares actual with optimal practice.

Efficacy: The determination—usually through clinical trials—that a treatment has beneficial effects. It also refers to the outcomes for specific groups of patients treated under optimal treatment conditions by highly qualified providers. Efficacy defines optimal practice.

Functional Outcomes: Outcomes that describe levels of patient functioning in such areas as work, family, health and grooming, intimate relations, self-management, and social relations.

Outcomes: Outcomes are outputs or posttreatment effects. Three types can be distinguished: immediate outcomes, end of treatment outcomes, and long-term outcomes as noted in follow-ups.

Outcomes Evaluation: Evaluations that focus on outcomes rather than on process or inputs.

Outcomes Management: The use of monitoring data in a way that allows learning from experience. Usually, this results in reshaping or improving the administrative and clinical processes of services provided. Patient profiling and provider profiling are additional aspects of outcomes management systems.

Outcomes Measurement: Quantification or measurement of clinical and/or functional outcomes during a specific time interval. Measures include changes in symptoms, functioning, quality of life, and/or patient satisfaction.

Outcomes Monitoring: The use of periodic measurement or assessment of treatment outcomes over time compared against expected outcomes in order to alter treatment, compare treatment interventions, or make attributions about what produced change. Typically, feedback of data to the provider serves as the basis for modifying the plan and course of treatment.

Process: Process is what happens between inputs—such as treatment initiation—and outputs—such as treatment termination. Process can also refer to any characteristics other than input or output variables.

Process Evaluation: Evaluation of treatment that focuses on variables between input and output, although it may include input variables.

Quality Assessment: The evaluation of the reasons actual and optimal practice differ, and whether this gap can be narrowed by improving treatment delivery.

Part I

The Paradigm Shift in Treatment Outcomes

1

From Outcomes Measurement to Outcomes Management

Mental health treatment is entering a new era. There is increasing emphasis on quality and accountability of mental health treatments based on outcomes measurement. In this chapter, we describe how the changing health care scene will force competition based on value. Next we discuss why demonstration of value to payers requires the use of outcome information. However, measuring outcome is not easy. There are many clinical and practical problems to be overcome. We describe an approach to the solution of these problems. We then highlight the evolution of three phases of the use of outcomes information: measurement, monitoring, and management systems. Last, we discuss what we believe will be the ultimate solution to the complexity of documenting and improving treatment, which we label the predictive system.

THE MENTAL HEALTH ENVIRONMENT

Over the past two decades, the enormous increase in health care expenditures has become a major issue confronting U.S. policy makers and business leaders. Spending on health care has been growing faster than the economy, rising from 8% to 14% of gross domestic product from 1975 to the early 1990s. Mental health care costs have grown even faster—doubling from $150 per employee to over $300 between 1987 and 1992.

One of the main forces pushing up the cost of mental health care is the increasing demand for services among employees. Frequent downsizings by corporate employers trying to become more competitive have raised stress levels of American workers, whether they are the ones laid off or those who have remained on the job, shouldering greater responsibilities and putting in longer hours. Meanwhile, traditional institutions such as the family are no longer offering the support systems that they once provided.

In the Business and Industry Needs Assessment survey (developed by Integra, Inc., 1992), nearly half of 8000 employees tested in 35 organizations were shown to be experiencing behavioral problems. This survey, which was funded by the National Institute on Drug Abuse, measured 12 behaviors, including work stress, job impairment from alcohol and other drug use, work dissatisfaction, anxiety, and depression. Over 47% of employees in the survey were found to be suffering from one of these five problems, with almost 13% of the survey participants suffering from two or more. Results showed 21% of employees experiencing high stress and 18% meeting the criteria for high anxiety, with 11.5% to 12.5% shown to be problem drinkers. Indeed, a major factor accounting for the increase in mental health care costs has been the rise in inpatient treatment for alcohol and drug abuse.

When Diagnostic Related Groups (DRGs) were instituted, providing for a fixed payment by diagnosis, psychiatric and substance abuse diagnoses were not included. For the rest of medicine, DRGs ended the cost-plus era (i.e., the era in which the more that was spent, the more the hospital was reimbursed). DRGs worked to keep costs down and tended to limit the profitability of inpatient facilities. However, since psychiatric and substance abuse diagnoses were excluded, insurance companies continued to reimburse hospitals for their per diem costs and doctors for patient visits, no matter what they charged. With the rest of medicine controlled by DRGs, an opportunity now existed in mental health and substance abuse that resulted in the rapid growth of inpatient treatment. As a result, inpatient costs skyrocketed, rapidly pushing up the percentage of the medical dollar spent on mental health. Indeed, in many corporations it rose from under 8% to higher than 20% of all medical expenses.

At the same time, state legislatures began to license more and more mental health professionals, which included social workers, marriage and family counselors, and nurses. Insurance companies reimbursed these professionals, who seemed to offer a cheaper alternative to treatment than did doctoral level psychologists and psychiatrists. This was intended to hold down reimbursement costs but instead, the demand for treatment accelerated and with it, the costs.

Finally, some states began to pass laws mandating coverage of substance abuse and in some cases making it equal to other medical conditions. This additional coverage, coupled with an enormous need for substance abuse treatment, rapidly accelerated the growth of costs in this area.

In the past, corporations assumed a relatively passive attitude toward these rising costs, relying on indemnity insurance, which paid for therapy sessions and other services on a cost-plus basis. But as costs continued to escalate and corporations found themselves under increasing financial pressure, they began the search for cost-containment plans.

This presented an opportunity for managed care companies and led to the entry of HMOs and carve-out firms into the mental health field. Initially, these firms concentrated on reducing inpatient health care costs by using a variety of approaches to case management. Through utilization review, they began to challenge providers who were recommending continued treatment for some of their patients, especially those who had been in long-term therapy. Through managed access, HMOs and carve-out firms (firms that contract to provide mental health services separate from other medical services) established barriers that made it more difficult for patients to obtain care—for example, patients were required to receive permission from a case manager before visiting a clinician. The managed care companies also tried to contain costs by altering benefits— raising copayments and deductibles, and so on.

Next, managed care companies developed networks of clinicians who discounted their fees. This was made easy because of the oversupply of providers. However, managed care firms feared that clinicians would make up for the drop in income per session by extending the number of sessions. Therefore, the managed care organizations began to profile providers on their average number of sessions per case and on whether they were "managed care friendly." What did this mean? Sessions per case translates into dollars per case. If a provider used "too many" dollars per case on the average, he or she would be dropped from the network. "Managed care friendly" meant such things as whether the clinician too often argued with the managed care firm over the number of sessions. The power had clearly shifted to the managed care firm, which could reduce care by simply saying "No." Some carve-out managed care firms did little to limit outpatient care except to ask clinicians to provide long treatment summaries, which deterred them from requesting more sessions. Other firms simply allowed for very few sessions on the average. Unfortunately, no objective measures of quality counterbalanced these cost reduction measures. There was no universally accepted or scientifically sound method of determining how much of what type of care was needed.

Many managed care contracts were initially for administrative services only. There was no additional compensation to these firms if they saved the employer money and no risk if they overspent in authorizing care. Gradually, at-risk arrangements began to develop and capitation rates became the standard in the managed health care field. HMOs and carve-out firms now found themselves required to provide adequate levels of care to patients for fixed annual fees set by the payers, with enough money left to pay overhead expenses and make a reasonable profit.

Meanwhile, capitation rates kept going lower and lower, under pressure from large corporations as well as from partnerships between corporations and insurers who were trying to drive down costs. With all the competing HMOs and carve-out firms in the field, mental health care had gradually become a commodity, driven by price. Since price was the only element that could be measured at that time, it was also the only one that would be rewarded. As yet, there were no adequate measures for other elements of care, such as rates of patient improvement or cost-effectiveness.

Managed care firms and provider networks found themselves operating in a new environment, and many of them began to fear that they would eventually be driven out of business as capitation rates continued to go lower and lower (Figure 1.1).

Price cannot be the only driver. Among gasoline stations, for example, only 20% of customers have been shown to make purchases solely on the basis of price (IBH Keynote Address, 1995). Other factors include the location of the station, how well-lighted it is, cleanliness, or whether it has a convenience store. Customers make buy-

FIGURE 1.1

Competition Will Drive Capitation Down

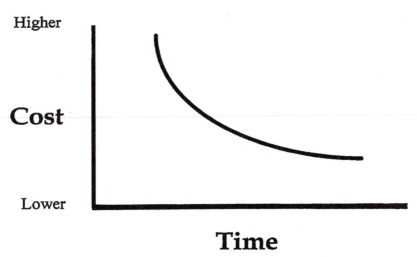

ing decisions based on perceived value. To a certain extent, the concept of perceived value can be determined only in a circular fashion. Features such as the location of a station, for instance, are thought to have value because they persuade customers to buy, or to buy at a higher price.

These same forces have begun working in the managed mental health care field. Today, many companies are looking for ways not only to reduce costs but also to maintain or improve quality of care—in short, achieve value for their health care dollar. Value in mental health care is a very tricky concept. The first essential question is: Value to whom? Value may mean different things to the patient, his family, the clinician, the corporation, the community, the government, and society at large. Each may represent a different constituency that perceives very different values from different aspects of mental health care. For example, when a family has a member who is suicidal, the fact that a treatment site is open 24 hours per day may be of enormous value. On the other hand, the community may place a high value on treating substance abuse patients who have been involved in thefts. Value as perceived in the present may beg the question of how a decision made today may impact the future. For instance, failure to receive two extra sessions of treatment this month may result in long-term disability in the future.

The complexity of the value problem initially caused payers to shrink from making any differentiation in terms of clinical quality and to simply make purchases based on price. However, the benefits managers of many companies became dissatisfied with the performance of their current managed care vendors and decided to re-enter the market to find a more effective approach. These managers began to grasp that while the determination of values and clinical quality is complex, it cannot be ignored simply because of its complexity.

For example, the benefits manager at one large steel company decided to sever a three-year relationship with a managed care firm after receiving a substantial number of complaints from employees about the quality of care. He wanted greater consistency of treatment and more accountability, not just lower costs. At a major pharmaceutical company, the director of corporate benefits recognized that the only way to cut costs without reducing the quality of care was by the "efficiencies offered by carefully monitoring the results of treatment."

More and more employers are looking for an effective approach to achieving cost-effectiveness by monitoring outcomes in mental health care treatment. This would also offer managed care companies an opportunity to compete on the basis of quality as well as cost. But finding accurate measurement tools to evaluate the effectiveness of treatment has proven to be extremely difficult.

One reason is the complex mix of levels and types of care, as well as of diagnoses. Due to the stringent efforts of managed care companies, inpatient hospital stays have been reduced and the resulting costs substantially lowered. However, inpatient care has often been replaced by a more complicated matrix of treatments. This includes: (1) different levels of care—ranging from residential, to full- and part-time day care, to regular outpatient sessions with a clinician; (2)

different types of care, such as individual or group therapy, medication, or shock therapy; and (3) an entire range of illnesses that these treatments are supposed to alleviate. How can anyone managing this kind of mental health system measure the cost-effectiveness of a particular treatment for a particular patient? There appear to be far too many variables.

For example, should patient A receive individual therapy combined with medication in addition to full-time day hospital treatment? It would be cheaper to move him into partial day care and group therapy. But how do we measure the impact of these changes on the patient? If the change in treatment didn't work, was it the partial day care or the group therapy or both that were not helping? What's more, which measurements are we using to determine whether the patient is getting better or worse? And are these measurements valid?

Thus, determining cost-effectiveness is extremely complex. But in the absence of any valid measurements, managed care companies were faced with the dismal prospect of continuing to compete only on cost. Some of these companies even tried to reduce costs further by buying up networks of providers, setting standards for them, and subcapitating. Meanwhile, provider groups had been attempting to deal with capitation through vertical and horizontal integration to prevent cost shifting (e.g., from outpatient to inpatient). Eventually, the provider groups began to recognize that they could eliminate the managed care companies and deal directly with payers themselves. However, whether it is a managed care company trying to cut costs by passing on a subcapitation rate to a provider group or a provider group contracting directly with a payer, the problem is the same: Will all the competition be solely on the basis of price, or will it be on value?

One final note about organizations that compete solely on price: When price is the only basis of competition, then the pressure to decrease profits is relentless. A buyer constantly tries to shop the cheapest price, which drives down the organization's profits. However, when an organization competes on value, then profit margins are not as subject to a profit squeeze. The purchaser is then making a decision to buy on value and not necessarily pushing an organization's profits downward.

The problem remains though, that to compete on clinical value, a method of determining clinical quality must be found that is accurate and accepted by the field. To better understand this, one must appreciate outcomes research and its evolution.

EVOLUTION OF OUTCOMES RESEARCH

Traditionally, providers and managed care companies have measured the quality of their programs by three different methods: structure, process, and patient satisfaction. *Structure* refers to the elements of the mental health treatment program, the credentials of its providers, and whether they are sufficient to provide the services offered. For example, does the program provide substance abuse treatment, or is there a medical doctor on staff to administer medications? While a patient may be unable to receive the necessary treatment unless a program has the proper structure, there is no proof that these structural elements are directly related to the patient's improvement. Thus, the patient may be prescribed a specific medication, but it may not be treating his illness effectively.

The second criterion for measuring the quality of a program has been how well its *processes* are executed. For instance, how many rings of the telephone occur before an intake employee answers it? How long does it take from the time of referral to the time a patient receives an appointment with a provider? Clearly, these things are important. After all, a patient may feel more satisfied if he has rapid access to care, and certainly he cannot receive care without this access. However, there is no proof that the rapidity of access has any impact on the outcome of treatment.

The third measurement of quality has been *patient satisfaction.* This includes such measures as how well the patient thought she was treated by the therapist and how much she thought she improved during therapy. While patient satisfaction is important, it is not an accurate assessment of treatment outcomes. Indeed, while a variety of studies have tried to show that greater satisfaction is associated with greater symptom reduction, these experiments have contained methodological flaws (Vuori, 1987.) For example, by the time treatment ends, most patients have forgotten how sick they were at the beginning of therapy, so they don't really know how much they have improved. The healthier a patient is at the beginning of treatment, the more he thinks he has improved by the end of it and the more satisfied he is. But the patient's satisfaction may have little or no relationship to actual improvement. Other variables that may impact patient satisfaction include the amount of prior psychotherapy, the duration of the current problems, the perceived importance of treatment, and the patient's level of confidence that treatment will be successful.

Indeed, patient satisfaction has previously been found to be a poor measure of clinical improvement. For example, Attkisson (1982) showed that symptom improvement explains only 10% of the variance in patient satisfaction. And according to a study conducted by COMPASS® (1995)—the designers of an outcome measurement tool that will be discussed later in this book—the relationship between clinical improvement and reported satisfaction was not statistically significant, either for patients still in treatment or for those who had completed treatment.

Clearly, none of the traditional quality measures are sufficient to explain what really works and at what cost. Yet answers to these questions are essential for mental health professionals if they are to be able to choose among the myriad levels and types of treatment available to deal with such a broad range of illness. Without outcomes, it is impossible to determine what worked and what didn't. Outcomes are necessary to find out whether an individual patient improved or whether a new type of treatment worked better than the one before it. Outcomes are the only quality measure with sufficient weight to counterbalance cost. When the field is able to say such things as, "A 20% reduction in benefits left 10 more people unable to work full time," it will have come a long way toward finding the right amount of capitated coverage and an effective way for systems to compete on value.

Outcomes measurements begin to provide some of these answers. They yield three broad types of benefits.

1. The first of these benefits concerns the identification of effective treatments. This requires pretreatment and posttreatment assessment of a patient's status to determine the changes that occurred as a result of treatment. Aggregation of these data across all patients who received a specific treatment is the basis for this first-stage evaluation process.

2. Following years of research, the authors have developed a measurement system involving assessments of patients on multiple occasions concurrent with treatment (COM-PASS®). This approach makes possible a second-stage benefit: immediate feedback to clinicians and case managers that enables them to identify those patients who are improving adequately, those who have improved to the point where treatment may no longer be necessary, and those whose lack of progress or determination suggests that their treatment should be changed. In short, a concurrent outcomes measurement system enables us to alter treatment outcomes.

3. On the horizon is the possibility of a third-stage system of prescriptive care. While it is now possible to accurately identify patients who are unlikely to benefit from their current treatment, clinicians cannot yet determine the specific treatment intensity or modality that has the highest probability of yielding a positive outcome. The current stage-two method is important in improving the cost-effectiveness of care, making it possible to avoid wasting money on treatment that does not produce positive outcomes. But the authors believe it will soon be feasible to identify the specific changes most likely to move the unimproved patient onto a more positive growth path—that is, to determine whether the introduction of medication, the involvement of a spouse or family in treatment, the transfer to a different therapist and different type of therapy, or some other alteration in treatment is most likely to result in the patient's recovery. In short, there will be a *predictive expert system* of treatment. This will be another quantum leap in improving cost-effectiveness, provider networks, and patient outcomes by continually applying what is learned from experiences with prior patients to treating similar cases.

THE DIFFICULTIES OF MEASURING OUTCOMES

If outcomes measurement is so important to the management of health costs, and in particular to applied mental health, why hasn't it been undertaken sooner? The reason is that there are tremendous scientific and practical problems in knowing what to measure and how to measure it.

High Rates of Spontaneous Remissions

Approximately 40% (Beitman, 1993a, Lambert & Bergin, 1994) of outpatients would probably improve to some extent without therapy, given enough time. Therefore, it is very difficult to determine which methods of treatment actually benefit specific patients. When seeing improvement in his or her patient, a clinician might be inclined to conclude that it was due to some element of treatment. However, maturation and general life experience no doubt account for significant improvements. Thus, it is very difficult to separate spontaneous improvement from the impact of treatment.

A Variety of Divergent Clinical Approaches

Providers use a wide range of approaches, each one claiming to provide a sound basis for effective treatment. But the clinician's own approach may actually prevent him from accurately measuring the real outcome of treatment. It's as if you wanted to measure the impact of a sport, such as baseball, on physical fitness. You might make the assumption that the better an athlete hits the ball or plays the outfield, the fitter he or she must be. But this assumption might be totally incorrect. What's more, it tells you nothing about whether the athlete might be more or less fit if she ran two miles every day instead of playing baseball.

The same holds true in mental health. Therapist A, a cognitive therapist, for example, might believe that changing a patient's cognition is the way to improve his mental health, so he would measure only change in cognition. The patient's cognition may change, but what does this say about whether the patient is actually getting better? It may bear a great deal of relation to overall improvement, some relation, or none at all. There is no way to be sure. Therapist B, an analyst, may believe that making unconscious material conscious is the answer. Therapist C may believe in a third approach—working on the patient's coping skills. If therapist A can show the patient's change in cognition on a scale, therapist C would argue that the scale doesn't measure coping skills. The variety of approaches to treatment all carry different assumptions of what the "etiology" of the condition is and, therefore, what is important to measure. This problem led the National Institute of Mental Health to convene a conference on outcomes measurement that produced a consensus set of measures so lengthy that they were never used. The fact that effective measures are difficult to find, however, doesn't eliminate the problem. In order to determine outcome, it is necessary to have a rationale for what is important to measure.

A Variety of System Levels for Intervention

The study of different therapies doesn't explain at which system level intervention actually occurred. There is a broad continuum of system levels, which adds enormous complexity to outcomes measurement. For example, suppose a woman comes into therapy suffering from severe depression and says that she is unhappy with the role she's playing in her marriage and the support she's receiving from her husband. Where could the clinician intervene? He could give the woman an antidepressant, which works at the molecular level. He could propose individual therapy, where he might be focusing on her intrapsychic conflicts, her interpersonal relationship with her husband, her role in society, and whether or not she should return to work, or some combination of these. He might also decide to treat the couple—instead of the individual patient—or treat the woman or the couple in a group therapy setting. At the present time, there is no generally accepted method for making these decisions.

A Variety of Factors Within System Levels

At every system level, there exists a number of key elements that may impact a patient's improvement. For example, suppose a clinician believes that a patient's family climate or work environment may be significant. How does he know which elements to measure? How does the clinician know that these are the most important ones to correlate with overall improvement? How does he know that his method of measuring them is accurate? These issues complicate the task of outcomes measurement even further.

A Variety of Improvements to Measure

It's easy to compile hundreds of ways to measure improvement. For example, a patient's self-esteem may improve as a result of therapy, but he may show little improvement in his family relationships. Or his marriage may improve, but he may still have severe anxiety attacks. Or the patient's depression may be alleviated, but she may still have difficulty coping with all the changes that are occurring in her work environment. Which is the better outcome?

Diagnoses Are Not Diseases

Generally, in medicine a disease includes symptoms, a decrease in functioning, and a pathogen that causes the illness. In mental health, the etiology of illness is relegated to various theories of causation (e.g., Freudian, Jungian, cognitive.) In mental health, diagnoses are problematic—indeed, they explain only about 4% of variations in illness—so DRGs have not been used in the field. In the absence of definitive information about etiology, clinicians are reduced to classifying illnesses solely on the basis of characteristic symptoms. This is as though internists only used the diagnosis "chest pain disorder" for both gastro-esophageal reflux disease and coronary artery disease. If this were the case, diagnosis would be a poor guide to treatment selection.

This is currently the case for psychiatric illness. For example, a clinician treating three people with major affective disorder (depression) might prescribe the same antidepressant. One may improve significantly, one may remain the same, and one may get worse. The differing responses to treatment of patients with the same diagnosis greatly complicates the task of outcomes measurement. In addition, not only are the DSM diagnoses problematic, we also know that the lengthy Structured Clinical Interviews for Diagnosis (SCIDs) required for reliable diagnosis are rarely used by practicing clinicians. Frequently, there is only random agreement between the SCID diagnosis and the clinician's diagnosis after seeing the patient. With no consistency of diagnosis among clinicians, it becomes even more difficult to measure and compare the impact of various treatments.

Accounting for Different Interventions

Psychotherapy research has shown that different clinicians who believe they are practicing the same form of psychotherapy, cognitive, for example, actually use different interventions (Lambert & Bergin, 1994). Since we cannot be certain what types of treatment are being utilized, even if they're called by the same name, measuring the outcomes of these interventions won't yield much useful data about specific interventions.

Experiments with Limited Value

Outcomes measurement is often conducted in experimental settings, but these may bear little or no resemblance to the real world of actual treatment. For example, researchers may decide to test the effect of Prozac on patients under 30 who are first-time sufferers of depression and have no other comorbid psychiatric disorder. Seventy percent of them may show improvement. But the patients in this model may not accurately reflect the population that most clinicians see in their practice. First, patients often don't take the medicine, or take it irregularly, in actual clinical practice. Second, the selection criteria are so specific in the clinical trial that when the same medicine is applied to a broader spectrum of problems and patients, it may have a very different effect. First-time depression in women, for example, may be a very different condition from third-time depression with anxiety in men. We may make a faulty assumption when outcomes are generalized from a specific population to a wider clinical one. Further, the clinician's feelings about the treatment may have an enormous effect. Whether or not the clinician believes strongly in the medication affects the patient and thus the results. These and other differences have led the field in defining the difference between effectiveness and efficacy. Efficacy is the potential benefit of a treatment under controlled conditions: Does it have the potential to work? Effectiveness is how well it works in actual clinical practice. In addition, experiments may take several years to conduct and during that time the treatment may have become outdated due to factors such as the discovery of a new drug, a change in the diagnosis, or changes in society itself.

When to Measure Outcomes

This presents an especially difficult problem. Do clinicians measure outcomes at the completion of therapy? Six months later? A year later? By this time, many other factors may have intervened, such as developmental changes in the patient, life accidents, etc. These will affect the accuracy of outcomes measurement.

Determining Cost-Effectiveness

Another problem that hampers outcomes measurement is determining the actual cost-effectiveness of applied mental health. A primary reason is cost shifting—that is, decreasing costs in one area, such as mental health expense, while increasing it in another area, such as medical costs. Suppose a corporation decides to reduce the behavioral health care coverage for employees from 80% to 40%. The company may save money in the mental health area, but what about the costs elsewhere? How many more workers are going to their family doctors with stress-related problems? How much more turnover or absenteeism has occurred as a result of reduced coverage? Most companies do not have a central pool of information that enables them to make connections between such things as cost cutting, disability, and turnover.

Most studies of this complex issue suffer from methodological weaknesses or limited generalizability. However, cost-offset literature generally suggests that a medical offset exists for mental health care.

It has been well documented that a relationship exists between mental health status and immune system status. This may account for some of the findings. For example, a study by the Group Health Association of Washington found that patients who were treated for mental health problems had 30.7% fewer visits to physicians in specialties other than psychiatry and that their usage of laboratory tests and x-rays decreased by 29.8% (Gotcher & Redfield, 1988.) And another study involving the Blue Cross–Blue Shield federal employees health plan showed that a group of patients who began outpatient psychotherapy following diagnosis of chronic medical disease used 56% fewer medical services during the third year after diagnosis than a group with the same diseases who received no outpatient psychotherapy (Sharfstein et al., 1984.)

A variety of studies also show that mental health treatment can lower organizational costs. For example, The Midwestern Study (1991) of workforce populations found that addiction resulted in a 335% increase in absenteeism, 235% increase in disciplinary actions, and 120% increase in sick benefit claims. These negative performance indicators were reduced by over 50% following addiction treatment. Another study (Yu et al., 1991) showed that successful treatment for substance abuse significantly reduced medical care costs in a workforce population. A treated group showed a 48% decline in medical care averaged over two years of posttreatment compared with a group that refused treatment and showed a 116% increase in health care costs.

Practical Problems

In addition to the scientific problems associated with conducting outcomes measurements, there are also a variety of logistical obstacles to overcome. For example, the task of collecting outcome data must be *administratively efficient.* It can be very time-consuming for therapists and patients to fill out questionnaires evaluating the effectiveness of treatment, so this process must be made as simple as possible.

Of course, administrative efficiency involves more than just the way questionnaires are designed. Monitoring and evaluating treatment requires a large sum of money for developing the questionnaire forms, training people to administer them, preventing gaming among therapists and patients, providing MIS support to process the data, interpreting the reports, and communicating the information to patients and providers, as well as providing incentives for them to participate in it.

Clinicians have traditionally regarded their work as part science and part art. They often resent measurements as an intrusion into their field—as an attempt to quantify what cannot be quantified. So clinicians (as well as patients) must be convinced that there is immense practical value in outcome studies or they won't cooperate with them. Therefore, researchers must be able to demonstrate that outcomes measurements will reduce costs and lead to shorter treatment as well as to more successful outcomes. What's more, this research must solve the problems faced by other constituencies besides providers and patients, including large corporations, managed care systems, the self-insured population, and the government.

OUTCOMES AS LEARNING

What to Measure

Over the course of almost two decades, we have begun to overcome many of the problems that stood in the way of developing outcomes measurement. Take the issue of what to measure. In the past, discussing the benefits of psychotherapy often seemed similar to attempting the same conversation about the blessings of religion. They were very broad and often highly subjective. What should be measured? The improvement in a patient's self-esteem? Symptom reduction? Improved work functioning? There were an endless number of measures. As a result, it seemed almost impossible to narrow the list to a manageable size and create a measuring device that would be easy for patients and clinicians to use.

When one is addressing the outcomes problem, it is important to define the criteria of the solution. We believe that the following criteria are essential to consider.

1. Not everything can be measured at the outset. No one will fill out a questionnaire of such length. More is often less.

2. A perfect solution is not possible. The field must be satisfied with successive approximations as it learns more. From the discussion in the previous section, it should be obvious that the field of outcomes confronts many complex and difficult obstacles. Therefore, there are only two choices: Do nothing and wait for the perfect solution or work through successive stages of improvement. The latter is the only possibility. Therefore, no approach will be above criticism. Rather, the key question is whether the approach offers the possibility of continued, incremental improvement.

3. It is essential to start with the most important things to measure first. Important must be defined by various constituencies, not simply by what clinicians think is important. Major constituencies, in addition to the clinician, are the patient, the family, the employer and the payers. (The family becomes a more critical constituency in substance abuse and in chronic, persistent mental illness.) For outcomes measures to be useful in determining quality, they must be broadly accepted by the several constituencies—that is, a generally agreed upon method for determining "truth." Since there is no absolute measure of the truth, societies must agree to it, just as juries agree over a defendant's guilt or innocence.

4. The outcomes measure must not be limited to a specific form of treatment. The reason should be obvious from the previous section regarding the problems of outcomes measurement. Any measure that is biased toward one form of treatment will be unacceptable to the others.

5. The outcomes measures must have immediate practical uses that build in value. The costs in terms of clinician and patient time must be reflected in an equal amount of practical value. Otherwise, patients and clinicians will not provide the needed information with any regularity. The outcome measures must also continually increase in value to keep the system vigorous.

6. The system must be based on established science that is theoretically sound. The problem of multiple measures with no underlying theory is that, while they measure much, in a sense they measure nothing since they offer no possibility of integration and knowledge development.

Only recently have breakthroughs been reported in this area. First, Compass Information Services, Inc. discovered that it was not necessary to measure all the benefits of mental health care, just a few of them. Then they conducted a series of focus groups with benefits managers, clinicians, and state and federal department heads involved in mental health and substance abuse. From the payers (corporations and government), it was learned that the cost of care was a major concern to them. But equally important was what they were buying for their dollars. They wanted to be able to tell whether an individual needed therapy in the first place and, once in treatment, whether the patient was really improving. What did they mean by improvement? (1) Did the employee experience an enhanced sense of well-being? (2) Were his symptoms significantly alleviated? (3) Did he function more effectively on the job, in his family, and in various social relationships?

Enhanced well-being contributed to the patient's positive attitude, which translates into higher morale and higher job satisfaction. The alleviation of symptoms would reduce problems such as absenteeism, poor job performance, alcohol abuse, and overall medical expenses, while improved functioning on the job contributes to greater productivity. In short, these were highly practical outcomes with clear benefits to payers and, therefore, ones that they would be willing to support. Focus groups with clinicians yielded similar results. A search for the common denominator across different clinical approaches yielded three measures: improvement in well-being, decreased symptoms, and improved functioning. These same measures coincided with the goals of most patients in treatment who wanted to feel better about their lives, reduce their symptoms, and function more effectively.

Meanwhile, the scientific foundation for this approach was being developed through the conduct of one of the largest studies ever attempted in the field of psychotherapy (Howard et al., 1986). While other studies had used smaller samples, this one included over 1000 patients who were being treated by 80 psychotherapists. The study lasted over a period of 10 years, supported by a grant from the National Institute of Mental Health. It was designed to test a dose/response, stage-based model of change. The study was based on concurrent outcomes measurement. During the course of therapy, the investigators received both self-reports from patients and reports from the clinicians that enabled them to measure changes as they occurred. They found that most improvement took place during the patient's initial therapy sessions, with the increments of change declining as treatment continued and patients approached a normal range. Nevertheless, these later changes were very important.

The study also demonstrated a stage-based model of change. The stages are: remoralization, or restoration of hope; remediation, or improvement of symptoms; and rehabilitation, or improvement of functioning. They occur sequentially, with each stage a prerequisite for the next.

In the remoralization stage, the patient usually improves his sense of well-being. The decision to seek help, the process of finding a clinician, and the initial sessions of talking with the clinician usually restore the patient's hope. This generally occurs within four sessions. Indeed, if there has been no improvement in this time, it may be a warning sign that therapy is not progressing successfully and perhaps the treatment, the provider, or both should be changed.

Since well-being, symptoms, and functioning behave in just the manner predicted by phase theory, Howard's model not only provided a theory to tie the measures together but also an immediate practical benefit to measurement. Treatment that failed to progress properly was quickly visible.

When to Measure: Concurrent and Pretest/Posttest Measurements

In the past, outcomes measurement has usually meant measuring a patient's status at the end of treatment and comparing it to his condition when therapy commenced. By contrast, Howard's study (Howard et al., 1986) relied on concurrent outcomes measurements, which enabled his team of researchers to detect changes as they occurred. Why is this type of outcomes measurement so important? Let us illustrate with an analogy from the medical field.

Suppose a patient has a diagnosis of lung cancer. His physician follows a series of protocols for this type of cancer that include chemotherapy, radiation, surgery, or some combination of them. The patient undergoes a course of treatment, his condition is evaluated by the physician over a number of months, and the physician also monitors the patient's survival over a period of 5 to 10 years. Based on the experience of this patient and thousands of others, medicine learns more about which treatments are most successful. But learning is slow because the feedback cycle takes such a long time.

Now, someone develops a blood test to determine if cancer cells are still present in the body on any particular day. Tests run on a series of patients demonstrate that the presence of these cells means that the cancer will return; however, if all of the cells are eliminated, the disease will not come back. Instead of just following protocols, a physician can now monitor a patient daily or weekly to discover whether any cancer cells are present. If the physician is using chemotherapy and the cells are not eliminated, he can immediately switch to another form of treatment. Care is now more individualized.

What should be obvious about this discussion is that outcome is feedback. No learning takes place in individuals or in a field without feedback. Further, the rate of learning is often largely controlled by the frequency and utility of the feedback cycle. If cellular information were available in cancer treatment, not only would the individual patient benefit and the clinician learn faster, the entire field would learn faster. In this sense, outcome is learning. The same will be true for mental health—properly constructed concurrent systems will greatly accelerate learning in the field of mental health and substance abuse.

A major problem with pretest/posttest measurement is that it fails to give information in either a timely or specific fashion. Since, by definition, the information is obtained after treatment is completed, it can be used only to change systems or protocols of care. Often the differences in effectiveness of different treatments are too small to be distinguished in clinical practice.

Consider three units of a hospital with slightly different protocols: Unit A has a 72% improvement, Unit B has a 70% improvement, and Unit C has a 68% improvement. The first problem to be considered is whether the mix of patients in each of these units is the same. Without random assignment, which is almost never practical in real clinical care, there is no way to fully control for case mix.

Second, even if the differences are real, they may be due to non-specific factors such as personnel mixes, and not to the treatment protocols. Third, the full variation between the protocols, if real, is only 2%. There is more within-unit variation than between-unit variation. That is, the patients are almost certainly more widely different in their responses to the same treatment than the treatments are different from each other.

How will this information be used to learn? The initial question to ask clinicians at any treatment site using pretest/posttest information in regular clinical practice is, "What improvements or changes have you made by implementing this information?" Be prepared for a lot of excuses. The reason is clear: pretest/posttest information occurs too late and is not specific enough. Quality improvement can often only be done one case at a time.

The second problem with pretest/posttest measurement is a little more subtle. Since there are only two points of data collection per case, a great deal of information is lost regarding the path of that case. Path is defined as the combination of treatment and effect through the clinical process, and after. Treatments vary during the course of most care—with combined treatments, combined medications, and changes in treatments because of improvement or lack of effect. To measure all of these events only at the end certainly provides data insufficient to produce learning.

One criticism of concurrent measurement is that it alters the conclusion of the study (i.e., per the Heisenberg Uncertainty Principle—

observing a phenomenon changes that phenomenon.) This concern would be valid if the only purpose of measurement were scientific documentation. However, the real purpose of outcomes measurement is to improve the quality of care. If measuring the care and feeding back the information accelerate improvement, then its real purpose has been achieved.

By using concurrent outcomes, clinicians, instead of simply measuring outcomes, could manage them. Concurrent measurement provides evaluation not only at the beginning and end of treatment (like pretest/posttest measurement), but also at various intervals during the course of therapy itself. A clinician would relate this information to the care and make changes if necessary.

How would this work in mental health? In a National Institute of Mental Health collaborative study, the efficacy of alternative treatments for depression was evaluated in a large, multisite, randomized controlled trial. When patients' symptomatic and functional status prior to treatment were compared to their status after treatment, the study found that three alternative treatments for depression (namely, psychopharmacological management with imipramine, cognitive-behavioral psychotherapy, and interpersonal psychotherapy) were equally effective. However, when the time course of improvement was evaluated using a concurrent measurement approach, it became apparent that psychopharmacological treatment using imipramine produced gains much more rapidly than either form of psychotherapy. This difference could be of tremendous importance to a patient at high risk of suicide, for whom it is vitally important that the level of depression be lessened as quickly as possible. The clinician could immediately switch this patient to imipramine, producing quicker results. In addition, the cost of treatment could be reduced.

Concurrent outcomes measurement enables care managers to make sound judgments about each individual case. They can determine whether treatment is producing improvement at the expected rate, whether a deterioration in patient status is occurring and treatment should be changed, how ill an individual patient is at a particular time, and when a patient's status has returned to the normal level. This type of care requires a large normative database that is easily accessible on-line. The database can be compiled from concurrent outcomes measurements of thousands and thousands of patients in real-world clinical settings rather than from patients who participated in experimental studies, as in the past. It can determine the true effectiveness, in actual clinical use, of multiple combined treatments, applied in a systematic, sequential fashion to all patients, including those who have been excluded from randomized clinical efficacy trials because of medical illness or other factors. The goal is to improve the clinician's ability to select the specific treatment or combination of treatments that will be most effective for each patient.

A MULTILEVEL PROCESS

What has been described here is a multilevel process of data development with enormous potential for advancing the entire field of mental health care. As mental health and outcomes move into the world of data, they join a much larger trend. In *The Third Wave*, author Alvin Toffler (1980) explains that the world is currently experiencing a revolution as large as the agricultural and industrial revolutions. According to Toffler, the transition to automation with computers will transform society and the way work is done.

Outcomes data have the potential to revolutionize mental health treatment. To realize this potential, the data must be transformed into information, and information into knowledge. Data are merely numbers having no inherent utility or significance. Data provide information only when presented in a meaningful context. Knowing that your daughter scored 43 on a math test tells you nothing. However, if, you also know that the class average was 25, the data (her score) become meaningful information about her math performance. Knowledge implies the ability to combine information with past experience to take effective action. Suppose your daughter's math score is improving relative to the class over the last year. Further, if her class is the best in the state, that knowledge might influence her choice of college.

Figure 1.2 maps the increasingly sophisticated uses of databases, measurement, outcomes, and computers. It defines three levels of functional usage: outcomes measurement, outcomes monitoring, and outcomes management. These demonstrate the increase in value to the field as data are transformed into information and information into knowledge.

Outcomes measurement is the quantification of outcome. The data are used to assess outcomes and can be used to compare services and programs. Measurement can be pretest/posttest or concurrent, but the data are reported only after the case is closed and never used on a single case to alter treatment. The reason is that the information is available only after the treatment has ended. A conclusion using this type of measurement might show that 72% of Program A patients improved, while 70% of Program B patients improved. Except in special circumstances of controlled studies with random assignment, outcomes measurement has all the problems described earlier in the pretest/posttest section of this chapter. Differences in comparison groups may or may not be valid, and the utility of the data is limited. Adequate case mix adjusting improves the delimitation of real differences, but doesn't help with practical use.

Outcomes monitoring represents a higher level of usage for information. The goal of outcomes monitoring is the comparison against a standard of expected results to determine if progress is being made as anticipated. In other words, outcomes monitoring is used to monitor change over time and alter treatment when it is not proceeding well. It can be used in single cases, then summed and risk-adjusted to compare one program with another. Outcomes monitoring can be accomplished only with repeated measures, and the information must be available during the treatment.

Outcomes management is defined differently here than it is by many others in the field. While the information is used to manage a case, treatment is affected only in those cases that fail to meet expectations. The goal of outcomes management is the accumulation and use of information in a way that allows learning from experience. The data are used to reshape care delivery. Table 1.1 lists multiple usage of the information. For example, it is possible to profile providers by assessing improvement per session for a particular diagnosis (see Figure 1.2).

This information can even be corrected for case mix. Then selective referral can direct certain patients to a clinician who is highly effective with their particular diagnosis. Thus, the entire care system is now altered by the availability of new information.

Together, outcomes measurement, monitoring, and management reflect the movement of the field from data to knowledge. Since knowledge is the accumulation of experience to aid in decision mak-

FIGURE 1.2

Therapist Comparison

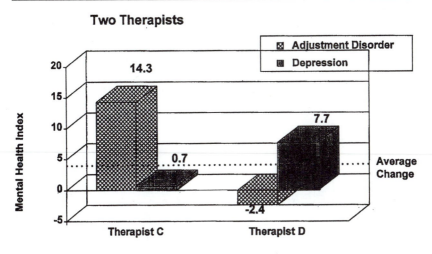

Amount of Change in Percentile Scores Per Session

ing, outcomes management qualifies as knowledge. Pretest/posttest measurement, as mentioned previously, is just too weak a data source to function adequately in the development of knowledge systems.

PREDICTIVE SYSTEMS

Science is based on developing hypotheses that are quantifiable and can be disproven; what's more, scientists should be able to replicate their results again and again. In chemistry or physics, for example, scientists know that a hypothesis is true if it repeatedly produces the same results under the same conditions. However, it is not possible to replicate in astronomy. The universe is expanding and the planets and stars are never in exactly the same place as they were in previous observations. And yet, astronomy is considered a science because it is highly predictable. Therefore, for science, predictability can be the standard when replication is not possible.

Replication is also a problem in the field of geology—after all, scientists cannot create the same earthquake over and over again. The

TABLE 1.1

Uses of Outcomes Information

Goals	Use of Data	Examples of Level or Type of Use	Measurement Frequency	When Information Available	Example of Conclusion
Measurement: —Quantification	Assess Outcome	—Service —Program	—Pre/Post —Concurrent (Repeated)	After Treatment Only	72% Improved in Program A 70% Improved in Program B
Monitoring: —Comparison with Expectation	Comparison Against Expected Results Over Time To Alter Treatment	—Single Case— Change in Treatment for Failing Case —Program Comparison of Programs	—Concurrent (Repeated)	During Treatment	The Patient Should Be At The 65 Percentile After 6 Sessions.
Management: —Accumulation and Use of Information in A Way That Allows Learning From Experience	Reshape Care Delivery	—Provider Profiling —Prediction of Path —Level of Care Determination —Program TQM	—Concurrent (Repeated)	During and After Treatment	Therapist D is 3 Times More Effective with Depression Than Average (See Figure 1.3)

Copyright, All Rights Reserved. Compass Information Services, Inc. 1995.

28

best they can do is study different quakes under different conditions. But if they examine enough of them and begin to amass enough data about the conditions under which the quakes occur, they can begin to make predictions about what may cause future quakes. As predictability increases, the scientific understanding of earthquakes is assumed to increase. The field is considered to be moving from description to a quantitative science. There is also a practical value in being able to accurately predict quakes. Thus, prediction can be a valuable union of science and practice.

Mental health is similar to geology. Since society is not the same as it was five years ago, the conditions that caused a specific illness cannot be replicated as suggested by Toffler and others; changes in these conditions are occurring at an ever-accelerating rate, altering forever the causal circumstances in which psychological problems enlarge. Many examples can be given. The social context and stressors relating to marital difficulties have changed radically in each of the last three decades. Mental illness occurs in a sociocultural context. As individuals and as a society, we are powerfully affected by changes in the economy, crime rates, educational systems, divorce rates/family stability, and the myriad social and interpersonal phenomena that shape our lives. New sociocultural conditions arise that cause stress, and the stress may be exhibited in different ways by various patients. Therefore, it is impossible to replicate the conditions that prevailed in clinical tests on patients suffering with stress conducted as recently as five years ago. Clinicians may not even want to rely on the same drug that was used to treat those patients because something better may have been discovered. For example, the multistage study of the treatments for depression described above focused on tricyclics, which have now been replaced largely by SSRI medications.

Toward Diagnosis

Medicine reasons backward from what type of treatment patients received and what the results were to what their illnesses must have been. This is the way diagnoses are developed. In mental health, clinicians can now begin to gather outcome data that will enable them to describe common sets of patients with common treatments and common outcomes (common paths). These are clinically useful diagnoses. They provide an opportunity to treat each case on a more individualized basis, with a higher probability of success and at substantially lower cost.

But, what is there about mental health treatment that is worth predicting and how can it be done? Clinically, the most valuable would be prediction of path. What is path? Path can be defined as the continuous series of positions or configurations assumed in any motion or process of change by any moving or varying system. The patient's path will be the normal course of the condition and its response to a variety of treatments over time. As the field learns to predict the path of a patient in advance, it will be moving toward becoming a true clinical science.

The long-term goal is to develop mathematical models that would enable a clinician to predict from a patient's course early in therapy his ultimate response to treatment. When patients enter treatment, their functioning has declined as their symptoms worsened, due to an external or internal event, or both. For example, a patient may have lost his job (external event) or is going through midlife crisis (internal event). Some of these patients will adapt and return to baseline (path B, Fig. 1.3), while others will experience growth as a result of treatment (path A, Fig 1.3). But a few patients will decompensate (path C, Fig 1.3).

Ideally, clinicians would be able to tell, from the first assessments, which patients are likely to deteriorate and conclude treatment in worse symptomatic and functional status than when they began therapy. These are the 20% of patients who use 80% of the mental health dollars. If treatment doesn't help them soon enough, they will deteriorate no matter how much money is spent on them. In this sense, long-term chronic and deteriorating mental illness may be very much like cancer. It is possible to treat cancer with early detection and effective treatment, but once the disease has progressed beyond some point, it is highly unlikely that one will achieve a cure. Being able to predict early in treatment which patients are likely to follow this atypical downhill course would enable clinicians to deflect them from that path by a special, intensive intervention. This may result in a higher proportion of patients concluding treatment in a substantially improved state at a much lower cost to the health care system.

FIGURE 1.3

Predictive System

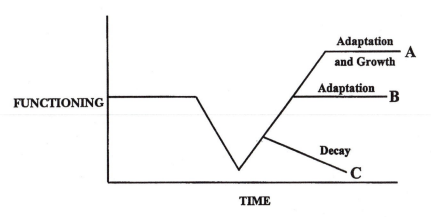

Predictive systems rely on an accumulation of background data about a large number of patients. This might include their current condition upon entering therapy, their treatment history, their motivation for seeking therapy, and chronicity of the presenting problem, as well as current age and marital status. The database also includes interventions that were identified as seeming to have a high probability of success, along with concurrent outcome measurements on the effectiveness of these interventions for various types of patients. (See Figure 1.4.)

Consider the problem of identifying and interviewing in cases at high risk for deterioration. By comparing after a few initial sessions an individual patient's background data and status with others in the database, a clinician can make a hypothesis about whether this patient is likely to deteriorate and what intervention has the highest probability of working effectively. Once this type of intervention is implemented, progress can be monitored in relation to other similar cases and an evaluation made to determine the impact of the intervention on the patient's path. If the patient is not improving by

FIGURE 1.4

Effectiveness of Intervention

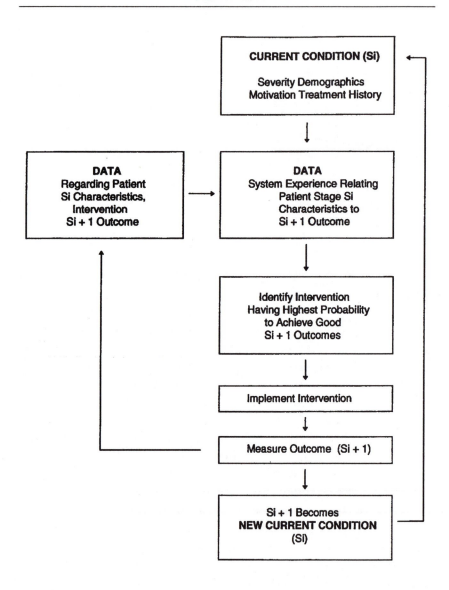

comparison to other, similar cases in the database, then another type of intervention can be implemented and the same process followed again. This represents an enormous leap forward in the field of applied mental health. This type of combination of a database coupled with course and intervention constitutes a "predictive system." The predictive system is a database organized and structured to allow for continuous improvement in the ability to predict path.

Building a Predictive System

What specific elements are necessary for a predictive system? First, an accurate method of measuring the progress of patients in treatment. Concurrent outcome measurement is critical, since it provides intermediate points in the path and a rich enough data source to support the calculations that are necessary. Second, there must be a population that is contained within a system of care. Patients who go elsewhere for their care would introduce enormous error into the system, since there would be no measurement of their condition after they left the system. Third, the system must be able to use the data to alter patient care. Therefore, the care system must be dedicated to the use of information and knowledge systems and be willing to alter care. Simply to have the information and not use it would inhibit the ability to predict. It is vital to have determined a path, to alter care, and to quantify any resulting alteration of the path.

Last, the system must have sufficient computer capability, as well as a commitment of capital sufficient to support the project until it bears fruit. Indeed, the prediction of path has become a realistic possibility only with the advent during the past decade, of economical computing systems and their capacity for storage and analysis of vast quantities of data.

Obviously, the longer the time in the future, the greater the uncertainty about the relationship between an intervention and its outcome. First, some additional illness may strike or the current illness may not truly have been cured. For example, patient A receives six weeks of treatment and improves substantially. Three weeks later, he is just as symptomatic as he was upon entering treatment. Most clinicians would conclude that the original problem was never fully resolved. How long after treatment would the second event have to occur to be considered an independent problem? No one currently knows. It probably depends on the condition. Is it going to be necessary to do lifetime follow-up to determine if the patient really improved? How will an independent problem be ruled out? The field again must work through successive approximations.

Initially, an attempt might be made to predict six months posttreatment. When reliable probabilities exist for six months posttreatment, it may not be necessary to measure cases six months posttreatment. In many instances, the certainty of what a patient's condition will be at this juncture may be so high that it will be necessary to measure only at the cessation of treatment. The same argument applies to the connection between six months and one year, and so on. The field will need to build models of the natural course of conditions during and after treatment and use prediction to document their accuracy. This is a large agenda for the first half of the twenty-first century.

SUMMARY

This chapter has attempted to demonstrate the importance of outcomes for the determination of value and quality in managed care. Only by improving methods of determining outcomes can a competitive arena be created that is based on something other than price. Next, this chapter presented some of the scientific and practical problems inherent in determining outcomes in mental health, as well as some of the principles that might lead to their resolution. The problem of outcomes is inextricably linked to the movement from data to information to knowledge. Finally, because of the complexity of human beings, computers will be necessary to gather and use sufficient information to solve the relationship between patient, treatment, and outcomes.

2

From Clinical Trial Outcomes Research to Clinically Relevant Research on Patient Progress

In 1952, the British Psychologist Hans Eysenck published a paper in which he seriously challenged the efficacy of psychotherapy. His claim that psychotherapy was no more beneficial than spontaneous remission received wide attention and stimulated the development of more rigorous psychotherapy outcomes research. For some 40 years, the major focus of such research was to document unequivocally that psychotherapy works. These efforts have been summarized in several statistical reviews (e.g., Lipsey & Wilson, 1993; Shapiro & Shapiro, 1982; Smith, Glass, & Miller, 1980) of the hundreds of outcomes studies that have been completed during this period. The verdict: **psychotherapy works.**

Therapists and patients, however, never had any doubt about the efficacy of psychotherapy. Despite Eysenck's challenge, therapists continued to maintain their practices and patients continued to seek such treatment for a variety of psychological disorders. In other words, in response to Eysenck, outcomes research was initiated and pursued for scientific rather than clinically practical reasons—that is, outcomes research was never intended to be very relevant to practice. This lack of relevance was further underscored by the compromises of generalizability that were necessary to carry out such research. For, in order for the findings of psychotherapy outcomes research to be generalizable to actual practice, patients, therapists, therapies, and treatment settings must be representative and outcomes measures must be clinically relevant. Instead, outcomes research used scientifically rigorous methodology, which required that treatments, patients, and therapists meet study requirements (e.g., inclusion and exclusion criteria) rather than be representative of practice situations.

The randomized clinical trial (RCT) has been the recommended model for outcomes research in psychotherapy. The RCT is most useful for addressing questions regarding the sufficiency of an intervention: "Can this treatment produce this desirable effect in this type of patient?" However, several problems arise when such methodology is applied to patient populations.

First, the process of random assignment to treatments does not represent the process through which patients enter and persevere in treatment.

Second, because of the multitude of uncontrolled, potentially causally relevant, independent variables, the sample size in a particular study is never sufficient to ensure that random assignment will equate groups with regard to possible confounds. Thus, even when statistically significant outcome differences between treatments are obtained, we cannot be sure that these differences were a result of the causal influence of the selected independent variables rather than of confounding with other variables.

Third, when within-cell variation exceeds measurement error, there are reliable differences among patients within treatments, that is, some patients are responding differently to the same treatment (Lyons & Howard, 1991).

Fourth, although patients may be randomly assigned to treatment conditions, therapists almost never are, with the result that outcome findings reflect therapist-by-treatment packages in which therapist characteristics are neither well controlled nor well described. As typically implemented, this research design does not permit the attribution of outcome findings to treatment effects alone.

Fifth, statistically significant findings (and effect sizes) are rarely large enough to eliminate overlap between the outcomes of patients in the comparison groups (see Howard, Krause, & Vessey,

1994). Thus, there will almost always be some patients in the inferior treatment that achieve better outcomes than some patients in the superior treatment, and vice versa.

Sixth, in conducting research with patients, it is virtually impossible to avoid missing data (attrition) because patients routinely fail to provide complete information at all data points and routinely fail to complete treatment regimens as defined by the investigator. Missing data, therefore, always compromise random assignment and, thus, the clinical trial is often reduced to the status of a poorly designed quasi-experiment.

Seventh, and last, the inclusion/exclusion criteria of a study make it difficult for the practitioner to know the extent to which a particular patient in his or her practice is of the same type as a patient who would have qualified for the study. For example, few practitioners use structured diagnostic interviews and/or psychometric instruments to evaluate their patients, so a study based on carefully diagnosed patients will perforce have limited generalizability to situations in which diagnoses are not made reliably.

An alternative approach to the RCT would be to standardize a treatment and determine the type of patient who responds well to this treatment (e,g., see Howard, Krause, & Lyons, 1993). This systematic exploratory approach would entail a self-correcting learning model that continuously incorporates the response to treatment of new patients in order to clearly determine the relevant patient group. The main problem with this approach is that it is unlikely that we could ever standardize a treatment in such a way that it could be delivered in the same way by the same therapist across patients, by different therapists, or in different settings.

No matter what the methodology, clinical research has to be judged ultimately on the basis of its informativeness. To this end, we recommend the adoption of a more systematic exploratory methodology and a greater emphasis on the generalizability and the constructive replication of findings.

A systematic exploratory, quasi-naturalistic approach is an outgrowth of the case study method, which has had such a tremendous impact on the practice of psychotherapy. This methodology entails the systematic use of objective data, continuous assessment, a model of problem stability, diverse and heterogeneous samples of patients, and clear evidence of an effect that can be measured for its magnitude and used to modify treatment processes. A case-based method that realizes all of these features can address a variety of potential confounds. But how are we to systematically describe these cases?

A MODEL OF RELEVANT PATIENT CHARACTERISTICS

Our standard diagnostic system has not been very useful for categorizing patients. In addition to the obvious problem of depending on more or less arbitrary and seemingly ever-changing diagnostic categories and criteria, most clinicians are unwilling or unable to obtain the required training or to spend the time necessary to arrive at a reliable and valid diagnosis for a patient. Therapists are usually confronted by a patient who is quite upset—anxious, frustrated, depressed—and must deal directly with this presentation. At this level, what do we need to assess?

We recommend a model that specifies five factors: presentation, pattern, predisposition, perpetuants, and readiness for treatment (Sperry et al., 1992).

1. Presentation. Refers to a description of the nature and severity of the individual's psychiatric presentation. It can include symptoms, past history, and course of the illness. Presentation is similar to the descriptive formulation component described in Chapter 1. As such, it lends itself to being specified in DSM-IV (American Psychiatric Association, 1994) diagnostic language.

2. Pattern. Refers to the predictable and consistent style or manner in which a person thinks, feels, acts, copes, and defends the self both in stressful and nonstressful circumstances. It reflects the individual's baseline functioning. This pattern has physical, psychological, and social features, such as a sedentary and coronary-prone life style, dependent personality style or disorder, or collusion in a relative's marital problems. Pattern also includes the individual's functional strengths, which counterbalance dysfunction. One way of specifying pattern is with DSM-IV Axis II personality traits or disorder terms.

3. Predisposition. Refers to all factors that render an individual vulnerable to a disorder. Predisposing factors usually involve physical, psychological, and social factors. Physical or biological factors include genetic, familial, temperament, or medical patterns, such as family history of a major psychiatric disorder, an organ inferiority, family history of substance abuse, a difficult or slow-to-warm-up child temperament, or cardiac disease or hypertension. Psychological factors might include dysfunctional beliefs or convictions involving inadequacy, perfectionism, or overdependence, which might further predispose the individual to a medical disorder, such as coronary artery disease. Other psychological factors might involve limited or exaggerated social skills such as lack of friendship skills, unassertiveness, or overaggressiveness. Social factors could include early childhood losses, inconsistent parenting style, overly enmeshed or disengaged family of origin, or a family constellation characterized by dogged competitiveness or emotional surveillance. Subcultural, financial, and ethnic factors can be additional social predisposers.

4. Perpetuants. Refer to processes by which a patient's pattern is reinforced and confirmed by both the patient and the patient's environment. These processes may be physical, such as impaired immunity or habituation to an addictive substance; psychological, such as losing hope or fearing the consequences of getting well; or social, such as colluding family members or agencies that foster disordered behavior rather than recovery and growth.

5. Readiness for Treatment. Refers to the patient's desire for and capacity to make therapeutic changes. Readiness involves three components: treatment expectations, treatment willingness, and treatment capability (Sperry, 1995b). Though related, each of these three are relatively independent markers of readiness. Patients can have high, low, or ambivalent expectations for change, and these expectations may be realistic or unrealistic. Generally speaking, patients with moderate to high realistic expectations of change do change more than patients with unrealistic or minimal expectations (Sotsky et al., 1991).

Treatment willingness reflects the patient's potential or likelihood for change. Normative stages or levels of change have been noted in psychotherapy and psychopharmacotherapy (Prochaska & DiClemente, 1986; Beitman, 1993). The stages are: precontemplation—denial of need for treatment; contemplation—acceptance of need for treatment; decision—agreeable to take responsibility and collaborate with treatment effort; action—taking responsibility and collaborating in change effort; and maintenance—continuing effort and avoiding relapse. Knowledge of treatment willingness or stage of change is critical in predicting treatment outcomes because patients who have accepted the need for treatment, decided to co-operate with treatment, and have made efforts to change and maintain change are more likely to have positive treatment outcomes than patients that do not (Beitman, 1993).

Treatment capability reflects the degree to which patients are capable of controlling or modulating their affects, cognitions, and impulses. As such, they are psychologically available to collaborate in treatment in contrast to patients who are continually parasuicidal or engage in treatment sabotage or escape behaviors (Sperry, 1995b).

Patterns traditionally have been the focus of instrumentation in psychological assessment and the basis for a comprehensive psychiatric interview. Clinicians who can effectively elicit and articulate information on pattern as it is distinct but complementary to predisposition, perpetuants, and treatment readiness are cognitively aided in both case formulation and treatment planning.

In assessing a patient's condition it is important to measure the kind and severity of symptoms, the kind and pervasiveness of vulnerabilities, and the likely reoccurrence of the environmental stressors.

Moreover, as we described in Chapter 1, an illness can be conceptualized as having four attributes: subjective distress, symptoms, disability, and the presence of a pathogen. So, when assessing the extent of the patient's presenting psychopathology, it is important to assess each of these facets.* It should also be kept in mind, however, that these criteria may be differentially important to the stakeholders in any treatment: (1) Patients—the people who received the treatment; (2) Therapists—the people who deliver the treatment; (3) Clients—the people or institutions who request the treatment (e.g., parent, court, school, spouse, employer); (4) Managers—people who decide on the allocation of treatment resources (e.g., sessions); (5) Sponsors—people or institutions paying for the treatment; and, (6) Researchers—people who scientifically investigate the

---

*The assessment of subjective distress, symptoms, and disability is relatively straightforward. However, pathogens tend to be theoretical constructs (e.g., unconscious conflicts, dysfunctional thinking, conditions of worth, unfinished business) that are quite theory-specific. Consequently, in what follows, we shall not be concerned with the assessment of the putative causes (pathogens) of distress, symptoms, or disabilities.

TABLE 2.1

Outcomes Perspectives and Outcomes Criteria

| Perspective | Distress | Criteria | | Pathogen |
		Symptoms	Functioning	
Patients				
Therapists				
Clients				
Managers				
Sponsors				
Researcher				

treatment. Table 2.1 depicts the matrix formed by these evaluative criteria and evaluative perspectives.

THE DOSAGE AND PHASE MODELS

The dosage model of psychotherapeutic effectiveness (Howard, Kopta, Krause, & Orlinsky, 1986) demonstrated a lawful linear relationship between the log of the number of sessions and the normalized probability of patient improvement. Figure 2.1 shows this dose–response relationship based on a meta-analysis of 15 studies that reported relevant data (using a variety of outcome measures for about 2300 patients). As can be seen, the effective dose 50 (the amount of treatment needed to achieve 50% improvement) was 6 to 8 sessions. The modeled relationship shown in Figure 2.1 also shows that about 15% of patients would achieve improvement by just making an appointment to see a therapist (the extrapolated "percent improved" value of session zero.

This dose–response function was shown to be different for different syndromes of pathology (e.g., Borderlines require a higher treatment dose than do Depressives). Subsequent work (e.g., Horowitz, Rosenberg, Baer, Ureño, & Villasenor, 1988; Howard, Lueger, Maling, & Martinovich, 1993; Howard, Orlinsky, & Lueger, 1995; Kopta, Howard, Lowry, & Beutler, 1994; Maling, Gurtman, & Howard, 1995) has provided evidence of the differential responsiveness of various symptoms and syndromes to psychotherapy.

The dosage model gave rise to the following three-phase conception of psychotherapy (see Howard et al., 1993).

FIGURE 2.1

Dose–Response Relationship Based on a Meta-Analysis of Data from 15 Studies (Adapted from Howard, Kopta, Krause, & Orlinsky, 1986)

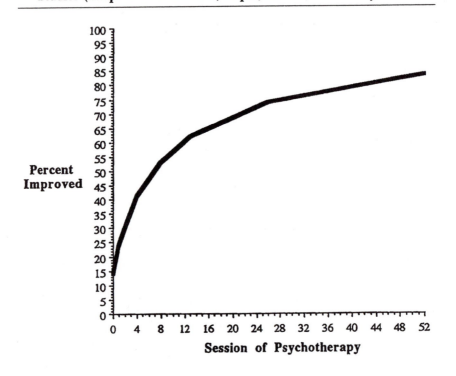

1. Remoralization. (Frank, 1973; Frank & Frank, 1991). Some patients are so overwhelmed that they become demoralized and feel that they can barely hang on. This experience is so pervasive and of such intensity that the patient's ability to mobilize personal coping resources is severely disrupted, and he or she begins to feel things are slipping out of control. This state of pervasive upset responds to a variety of interventions (medication, vacation, emotional support, etc.) and will, in less severe cases, usually abate substantially in the period between making an appointment with a therapist and the completion of a few sessions of supportive or crisis-oriented psychotherapy. For some patients, this reduction of distress will allow them to mobilize their own coping resources in a way that leads to resolution of current life problems. Other patients move on to a second phase of therapy.

2. Remediation. A second phase of therapy is focused on remediation of the patient's symptoms, symptoms so upsetting that they
led the patient to seek professional help. During this second phase,
treatment is concerned with refocusing the patient's coping skills in
a way that brings symptomatic relief. For many conditions, this phase
usually lasts three or four months (about 16 sessions), but it can be
shorter or longer depending on the number and severity of symptoms. At this point many patients terminate treatment, but some will
find that the problem(s) that brought them to therapy have been encountered repeatedly in their lives (e.g., instability in employment,
problematic interpersonal relationships) and are probably the result
of long-standing psychological or behavioral patterns (habits, character) that are maladaptive or that hinder the achievement of their
life goals (e.g., finding a satisfying career, forming a long-lasting intimate relationship). These patients move on to the third phase.

3. Rehabilitation. A third phase of treatment is focused on un-
learning troublesome, maladaptive, long-standing psychological or
behavioral patterns and establishing new ways of dealing with various aspects of life (prevention, rehabilitation). This phase of therapy
may last many months or years, depending on the accessibility and
malleability of these maladaptive patterns, and on the treatment
model applied.

Research has demonstrated that these phases are sequentially causally dependent: remoralization > remediation > rehabilitation
(Howard et al., 1993). Figure 2.2 shows the dose–response relationship of three phase criteria—subjective well-being, symptomatic distress, and life functioning. For this graph, each criterion was modeled for a group of patients who succeeded in treatment. As can be
seen, subjective well-being shows a relatively quick response to treatment, symptoms respond more slowly, and functioning responds
even more slowly in these successful treatments.

To the extent that these phases are distinct, they imply different
treatment goals and, thus, the selection of different outcome variables. This model also suggests that different interventions will be
appropriate for different phases of therapy and that certain tasks
may have to be accomplished before others can be undertaken. Also,
there is an implication that different therapeutic processes may characterize each phase. For example, remoralization might be accomplished through the use of encouragement and active empathic lis-

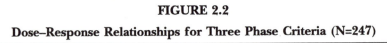

FIGURE 2.2

Dose–Response Relationships for Three Phase Criteria (N=247)

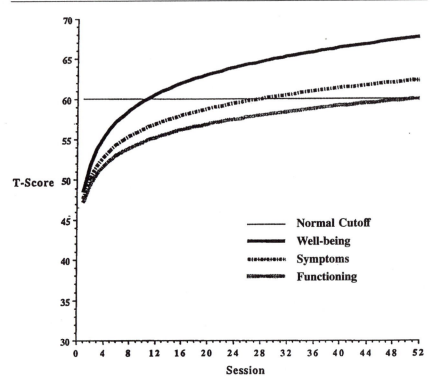

tening; remediation may be accomplished with the use of homework assignments, interpretations or clarifications; assertiveness training may be useful for rehabilitation, and so on.

Most importantly, however, these phase constructs are theoretically neutral and can be applied by any practitioner to the treatment of any patient. Feedback regarding the status of the patient with regard to these criteria could be used to shape a particular treatment episode—that is, to focus interventions on particular goals.

A GENERIC MODEL OF PSYCHOTHERAPEUTIC PROCESS

In the evaluation of the outcome of a treatment, it is important to consider the therapeutic processes that promote a beneficial result of that treatment. On the basis of extensive reviews of the process-outcome literature, Orlinsky and Howard (1986) developed a conception of therapeutic process that they used to organize the research literature and that could be applied to any treatment.

According to the generic model (Orlinsky & Howard, 1987),* every treatment can be characterized in terms of (1) the therapeutic contract, (2) therapeutic interventions, (3) the therapeutic bond (relationship), (4) treatment compliance, and (5) immediate outcomes of the therapeutic encounter.

The Therapeutic Contract

The therapeutic contract defines the purpose, format, terms, and limits of a treatment. It specifies what the treatment is, what and whom it is for, and who is to be involved in it. The times and places, duration, and frequency of meetings must also be specified, and a limit may be set in advance on the overall number of sessions. Finally, some agreement must be reached as to the fee that the patient or the patient's sponsor will pay for the therapist's professional services. An example of process-outcome research in this area would be an investigation of the differential effectiveness of group and individual psychotherapy.

Therapeutic Interventions

Therapeutic interventions comprise the transactions that are carried on under the terms of the therapeutic contract. This includes the determination of medical necessity and diagnosis. Complementing this diagnostic aspect are the ameliorative techniques that are applied to the patient's problems. Various schools of psychotherapy have developed on the basis of proposed strategies and techniques for resolving patients' problems. Nowadays, of course, many clinicians seek to broaden their base of practice and enhance their effectiveness with patients by drawing their diagnostic understanding and a repertory of technical interventions from diverse schools of practice. An example of research in this area would be an investiga-

---

*What follows is a somewhat adapted version of the original model.

tion of the differential effectiveness of cognitive and interpersonal psychotherapy in the treatment of patients suffering from Major Depressive Disorders.

The Therapeutic Bond

The therapeutic bond is an aspect of the relationship that forms between patient and therapist as they implement the therapeutic contract by engaging in therapeutic interventions. The therapeutic bond extends beyond patient and therapist roles to include personal qualities of the relationship that forms between the participants. Three aspects of the therapeutic bond may be distinguished: (1) therapeutic alliance, (2) empathic resonance, and (3) mutual affirmation.

Therapeutic alliance reflects the degree to which each participant is invested in carrying out his or her therapeutic role. Empathic resonance refers to the ability of the participants to effectively and meaningfully communicate. Mutual affirmation involves a sense of respect and trust that develops between the patient and therapist. These aspects of the therapeutic relationship have received a great deal of research attention and it is now well established that they are important determinants of treatment outcomes.

Treatment Compliance

The fourth process component is the patient's degree of treatment compliance—openness to and compliance with therapeutic tasks. An example of process-outcome research in this area would be an investigation of the determinants and consequences of completing homework assignments.

Immediate Outcomes

"Insight" is the most familiar example of an immediate treatment outcomes in psychodynamically oriented psychotherapies, but other common in-session outcomes include problem resolution, conflict management, reduction of anxiety, control of maladaptive behaviors, dispelling irrational attitudes, and so on. These immediate manifestations of helpful impacts within therapy sessions are the theoretical basis for change in the patient's life and personality outside of therapy. An example of process-outcome research in this area would be an investigation of the effect of experiencing relief in a session and functioning better at work.

CONCLUDING NOTE

There are three fundamental questions that can be asked about any treatment (intervention): (1) Can it work? (2) Does it work? and (3) Is it working? Answers to any of these questions, of course, are dependent on what it means for a treatment or intervention to "work."

Clinical scientists tend to focus on the first question—"Can we demonstrate that this intervention produces better results (outcomes) than a presumably inert (control) condition?" The preferred method for addressing this question is the randomized experiment, a method in which the emphasis is placed on internal validity and attempts to ensure the comparability of the treatment and control groups. Patients are included according to highly specific inclusion/exclusion criteria and experimental conditions are clearly specified and closely monitored (e.g., controlling for number of "sessions," monitoring the integrity of interventions). Evaluation is based on the comparison of pretreatment and posttreatment assessments.

Service researchers tend to focus on the second question—"Does this intervention produce beneficial results as it is administered in clinics and offices?" The preferred method for addressing this question is the systematic, naturalistic experiment, a method that emphasizes external validity and attempts to ensure the generalizability of findings to other clinical settings and patient groups. Assignment to comparison groups (e.g., successful cases versus failure cases, patients who attend many sessions versus patients who attend fewer sessions) is not random and, thus, comparison groups may differ on many variables in addition to the variable that has been selected for study. Consequently, because of threats to internal validity, any observed results are subject to multiple interpretations (alternative plausible explanations). Quasi-experiments require constructive replication to test these plausible alternative hypotheses. Again, however, assessments are made only at two time points (beginning and end of treatment).

Finally, practitioners are most concerned with the third question—
"Is this patient's condition responding to the treatment that is being applied?" From the practitioner's point of view, the patient has
sought amelioration of some (treatment-appropriate) condition, and
it is the practitioner's job to provide a treatment that will provide
this amelioration. In this context, it is not sufficient for the practitioner to know that a particular treatment can work (efficacy) or that
the treatment usually works (effectiveness). The practitioner needs
to know whether the treatment is working for this patient. The task
of research is to provide valid methods for systematic, relevant feedback about the patient's condition (assessment of progress during
the course of treatment, not the assessment of outcomes after the
termination of treatment).

The major advantage of a systematic naturalistic research approach is that, in addition to specifying an orderly pattern of response to treatment, it is possible to develop a system for clinical
feedback regarding the status and progress of each case (as described in Chapter 1). This feedback can be used in supervision and
case management, as well as in making treatment decisions. In this
way, the clinical relevance of research can be transformed from a
general conceptual issue into a practical clinical application.

The dosage, phase, and generic process models are particularly
appropriate for this latter task. We shall exemplify this application
in Chapter 4.

3

From Generic Treatment to Prescriptive Treatment

The clinician or health care system committed to maximizing outcomes will also be committed to prescriptive treatment. What is prescriptive treatment and how does it differ from generic treatment? Not too long ago, generic treatments were the only treatments. They were essentially provider-centered, and usually limited to a single modality such as long-term, insight-oriented psychotherapy or ongoing medication monitoring. Until recently, such generic, one-size-fits-all treatments were considered normative. Similarly, clinicians were skeptical or even hostile about combining treatment modalities such as individual psychotherapy and group therapy, or medication and psychoanalytic psychotherapy. Nevertheless, a commitment to prescriptive treatment is essential in clinical practice that incorporates outcomes monitoring and management.

This chapter describes prescriptive treatments, which are treatments characterized by being tailored or patient-centered and integrative. Prescriptive treatment is the result of a series of treatment selection decisions that often involve combining treatment modalities. The chapter begins with an overview of prescriptive treatments and a description of an integrative, prescriptive treatment system model. This is followed by a discussion of practical treatment guidelines for combining various treatment modalities to optimize treatment outcomes. The chapter concludes with an illustration of an outcomes tracking and monitoring system utilized in managed care settings.

PRESCRIPTIVE TREATMENT

A number of research efforts over the past several years have provided encouraging responses to Gordon Paul's query: "What treatment, by whom, is most effective for this individual with that specific problem under which set of circumstances?" (1967, p. 111). Paul's call for specifying the conditions under which an intervention will be effective is consistent with the notion of prescriptive treatment. Prescriptive treatment has been defined as "the prescription of a highly specified, thoroughly evaluated treatment regimen in order to ameliorate a highly specified, thoroughly assessed complaint" (Acierno, Hersen, & Ammerman, 1994). Application of prescriptive interventions to psychiatric disorders has long been utilized by psychopharmacologists. Lately, psychotherapists have also begun utilizing the prescriptive approach.

Successful implementation of focused prescriptive treatments requires the focused assessment of (a) symptoms and level of functioning (psychopathology), (b) predisposing factors (vulnerabilities), (c) perpetuating factors, and (d) readiness for treatment. Thorough assessment across each area permits the informed selection of those treatments found to be most effective in treating specific disorders. Exclusive assessment of a single factor, such as presenting symptoms, ignores the existence of diagnostic subtypes and increases the likelihood of inappropriate or ineffective treatment.

The assumption of homogeneity across patients sharing the same symptom presentation is equally problematic (Beutler, 1979). Wolpe (1977) refers to this unfounded assumption as "the Achilles heel of outcomes research in behavior therapy." Assumptions of homogeneity are problematic in that conclusions reached regarding the efficacy of a particular treatment are meaningless when one is not fully aware of the nature of the disorder treated.

As a result of ongoing research on empirically derived treatments, several prescriptive treatments currently exist for well-defined diagnostic entities such as depression for which specific treatment guidelines have been issued (American Psychiatric Association, 1993). While exceedingly potent, prescriptive interventions have highly specific indications. Therefore, highly focused initial and ongoing assessment is necessary. Initial assessment would include presenting symptoms and levels of functioning, predisposing factors, perpetuating factors, and treatment readiness, while ongoing assessment would include symptoms, levels of functioning, and treatment readiness. Measurement across each of these factors facilitates the informed selection of the most effective treatments.

Assessment along only one factor, to the exclusion of others, disregards important information and thereby increases the possibility that an inappropriate or ineffective treatment will be selected. Indeed, several investigators have reported that patients who manifest similar symptoms often differ in predisposing, perpetuating, or readiness factors and will respond differentially to treatment (Hersen & Ammerman, 1994).

Empirically derived and validated psychopharmacological and psychological interventions with demonstrated effectiveness across several areas of psychopathology are continually being reported. Psychopharmacological approaches have been shown to alleviate the distressing aspects of endogenous major depression, bipolar disorder, several anxiety disorders, bulimia, insomnia, and the positive signs of schizophrenia. Additionally, successful prescriptive psychological interventions exist for almost every anxiety disorder, nonendogenous depression, insomnia, sexual dysfunction, substance use disorders, pain, and the skills deficits typically found in schizophrenics (Hersen & Ammerman, 1994; Sperry, 1995b).

AN INTEGRATIVE THERAPEUTIC TREATMENT SYSTEM MODEL

Psychotherapy and psychiatric treatments are exceedingly complex phenomena that can be extraodinarily difficult to conceptualize and seemingly impossible to research. Thus, theoretical models can be quite useful in mapping these phenomena in a manageable fashion. The following model of an integrative and prescriptive therapeutic treatment system has been useful in conceptualizing both the process and outcome variables involved in the provision of psychotherapy and psychopharmacology services in outpatient settings with adults. The model incorporates the case formulation model described by Sperry (1988, 1992), Howard's phase model of psychotherapy (Howard et al., 1993), and a modification of Beitman's model of the treatment process in psychotherapy and psychopharmacology (Beitman, 1984, 1991). Figure 3.1 illustrates this systems

FIGURE 3.1

Treatment System and Subsystems: Input, Process, and Outcome

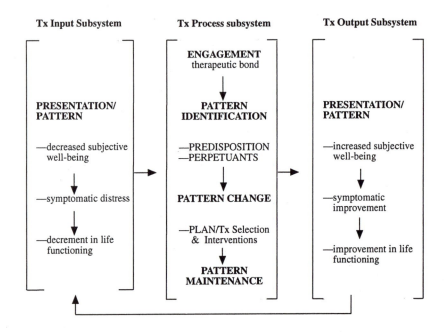

model with three treatment input subsystems: (1) the pretreatment variable of "presentation/pattern"; (2) a treatment process subsystem with variables of "engagement," "pattern identification," "pattern change," and "pattern maintenance"; and (3) the treatment output subsystem with the posttreatment variable of "presentation/ pattern." The feedback arrow from the treatment output system to the treatment input system indicates that outcomes monitoring data can influence and alter the treatment process.

Case Formulation Model

The case formulation model involves seven dimensions for articulating and explaining the nature and origins of the patient's presenting problem and subsequent treatment. The dimensions are: presentation, predisposition, precipitants, pattern, perpetuants, treatment readiness, and treatment plan (Sperry, 1988; 1992). Five of these dimensions are germane to the integrated therapeutic treatment system model. They are: presentation, pattern, predisposition, perpetuants, and readiness for treatment. These have been previously described in Chapter 2.

Phase Model of Psychotherapy

The phase model has been described in detail in Chapter 2 of this book. Central to the phase model is that the development of psychopathology proceeds from a decrement in life functioning to the expression of symptomatic distress, which, if it persists, leads to demoralization and a sense of helplessness. It is this significant decrement in well-being that leads individuals to seek professional help. Positive psychotherapeutic outcomes typically entail progressive improvement in subjective well-being first, followed by reduction in symptomatology, with lasting changes in life functioning occurring more gradually.

STAGES OF THE TREATMENT PROCESS

The phase model also suggests that different change processes—requiring certain types of interventions—are appropriate for different phases of treatment and that different therapeutic processes characterize each phase. The presumption is that effective outcomes require a focus on changing phase-specific problems (Howard et al., 1993). Beitman's (1984, 1991) effort to articulate the developmental change processes in psychotherapy and psychopharmacotherapy nicely complements the phase model. Beitman's model articulates four stages of the treatment process: engagement, pattern search, change, and termination. These stages have been modified and incorporated in the Integrative Treatment System Model (Figure 3.1). The modified stages are: engagement, pattern identification, pattern change, and pattern maintenance.

Engagement

Engagement is the principal therapeutic process in the early phase of treatment. Engagement requires the patient to trust, respect, and accept the influence of the provider. The building of trust and respect results in psychological connection and commitment. The provider's empathic stance toward the patient is essential in establishing a working therapeutic relationship or therapeutic bond. Engagement is a prelude to psychotherapy and psychopharmacotherapy; until it is achieved, formal treatment should not proceed. One indication that engagement has been achieved is the patient's willingness to follow the ground rules of therapy. Engagement also involves a socialization process, which culminates in a formal or informal treatment contract and includes elements such as fee, length of sessions and duration of treatment, education about the treatment process, and negotiation of treatment expectations, goals, and role behaviors. For instance, analysts encourage their patients to free associate; cognitive-behavioral therapists assign homework assignments; and existential therapists emphasize the value of here-and-now experiencing.

A critical task of the engagement stage is to assess the patient's readiness and motivation for treatment. Low readiness for treatment will be reflected in treatment resistance and noncompliance in various ways: missing or coming late for appointments, failure to take medication or complete intersession assignment, or minimal or no progress in treatment. If the patient does not possess sufficient treatment readiness, the provider's task is to focus on the readiness issue before proceeding with formal psychotherapy or psychopharmacotherapy. Predictably, transference and countertransference issues emerge in the engagement stage in subtle and not so subtle ways.

Pattern Identification

Pattern identification involves the elucidation of the patient's disordered psychological pattern, which reflects the style and manner of thinking, acting, feeling, coping, and defending self. Various assessment strategies are utilized at this stage, including personality testing and the elicitation of early recollection or core schemas. To the extent that the provider understands and appreciates the predisposing factors and perpetuating factors unique to the patient, interpretations, cognitive restructuring, behavioral interventions, or supporting the patient's defenses will tend to be more focused and efficacious.

Pattern Change

The purpose of defining underlying psychological patterns is to change them. Among these common change factors are increasing insight, decreasing maladaptive behaviors, modifying dysfunctional cognitions, reducing painful affects, and enhancing self-management and interpersonal skills (Perry, Frances, & Clarkin, 1990). The process of change involves three tasks: the disordered or maladaptive pattern is relinquished; a more adaptive pattern is adopted; and the new pattern is generalized—thoughts, feelings, and actions—and maintained.

Pattern Maintenance

As the new pattern becomes fixed in the patient's life, the issue of preventing relapse and recurrence needs to be addressed. As formal treatment sessions become less necessary, the issue of termination becomes the therapeutic focus. The elements of the termination process are relatively predictable when contrasted with the wide range of possibilities inherent in the pattern identification and change stages. Patients—and providers—often have difficulty with separation. New symptoms or old ones may appear, prompting requests for additional sessions. Presumably, when difficulty with separation or abandonment is noted in the maladaptive pattern, treatment will have focused on this issue.

TREATMENT SELECTION

According to Perry, Frances, and Clarkin (1990) the process of treatment selection, no matter how divergent in theory or style, has five inherent axes that must be considered. These axes are: setting, format, time, approach, and somatic treatment issues.

Setting. Refers to the place in which treatment occurs: inpatient, outpatient clinic or private office, day hospital, or a residential treatment center.

Format. Indicates the context of treatment and is a function of who directly participates in the treatment: individual, group, family, couple, medication monitoring, or some combination of these modalities, such as: individual—medication; individual—group;

individual—couple; medication—group; or even individual—couple—medication, and so on.

Time. Refers to the length and frequency of sessions as well as the duration of treatment. Duration of treatment might be brief or long-term, time-limited, open-ended, or discontinuous. Sessions might be scheduled two or more times per week, weekly, biweekly, monthly, bimonthly, or less often.

Approach. Refers to the treatment orientation and treatment methods and strategies utilized by the provider. These range from dynamic to cognitive-behavioral to psychoeducational or supportive.

Somatic. Perry, Frances, and Clarkin (1990) indicate that a specific treatment approach that deserves separate consideration is somatic treatment. Typically, somatic treatments include psychotropic medications or electroconvulsive therapy, but also can include other prescribed medication, nutritional counseling or an exercise prescription, or even referral for psychosurgery.

The provider also has a metadecision that overrides the consideration of these five components. That is, should any treatment be provided or should "no treatment" be the recommendation of choice? Frances, Clarkin, and Perry (1984) inidcate the types of patients at risk for negative therapeutic reaction in comparison to those at risk for no response to treatment. They also describe the relative indications for the "no treatment" option.

TAILORED AND COMBINED TREATMENT

So what is combined treatment and how is it related to tailoring and integrated treatment? Tailoring refers to modifying or adapting a particular modality and/or therapeutic approach to the patient's needs, styles, and expectations. A sartorial analogy might help to distinguish combining, integrating, and tailoring. A man could go into a clothing store to purchase a grey business suit. He could randomly choose a suit from the rack. There is a small chance it would fit perfectly, but more likely it will be a poor fit. The individual whose size is usually 40 long could look through the racks and try on 40 longs that might fit quite well, but need some minor fitting work by a tailor—partial tailoring. He could also go to a store for a fitting and have a suit completely custom made—total tailoring. Now the suit could be pure wool or pure silk, or it could be a blend of wool and silk. This blended fabric would be analogous to integrating treatment. Analogous to combined treatment would be the purchase of a blue sports jacket that might be worn with the slacks of the grey suit for a more casual look (Sperry, 1995).

Combined treatment refers to adding modalities, such as individual, group, couple, or family, either concurrently or sequentially, while integrative treatment refers to the blending of different treatment approaches or orientation, such as psychodynamic, cognitive, behavioral, interpersonal. Combining treatment modalities is also referred to as multimodal treatment. Finally, tailored treatment refers to specific ways of customizing treatment modalities and/or therapeutic approaches to "fit" the unique needs, cognitive and emotional styles, and treatment expectations of the patient.

Treatments delivered in combination can have an additive, and sometimes synergistic, effect. It is becoming more evident that different treatment approaches are differentially effective in resolving different types of symptom clusters. For example, in major depression, medication is more effective in remitting vegetative symptoms, while psychotherapy is better at improving interpersonal relations and cognitive symptoms (Frances, Clarkin, & Perry, 1984). Furthermore, the additive effect of medication and psychotherapy has been established for both major depression (Rush & Hollon, 1991) and agoraphobia (Greist & Jefferson, 1992).

While combined treatment refers to combining different modalities of treatment (i.e., individual group, marital and family therapy, day treatment, or inpatient) either concurrently or sequentially, integrative or tailoring treatment is different. Integrative treatment refers to blending various treatment approaches (i.e. psychodynamic, cognitive, behavioral, interpersonal, and medication). Recently, clinical investigators have advocated integrative treatment for borderline personality disorder (Stone, 1993; Linehan, 1993). Cognitive behavior therapy represents the integration of two therapeutic approaches: cognitive therapy and behavior therapy. The specific type of cognitive-behavior therapy developed by Linehan, dialectal behavior therapy, is an integration of various cognitive-behavioral intervention strategies and Zen practice (Heard & Linehan, 1994). Stone (1993) prescribes blending psychoanalytic, behavioral, cognitive, and medication intervention or approaches in the treatment of the borderline patient.

What are the indications, contraindications, and treatment guidelines for these various modalities? Unfortunately, these questions cannot presently be answered with the kind of research-based clinical precision that providers and utilization reviewers typically require. For now, this chapter translates and extends the current clinical research data regarding these questions. The following sections describe specific indications, contraindications, and treatment guidelines for prescriptive treatments, combining individual therapy and medication, group therapy and medication, family therapy and medication, individual and family therapy, and individual and group therapy.

GUIDELINES FOR COMBINED TREATMENTS

Combining Individual Psychotherapy and Psychopharmacotherapy

Of all the combined treatments, combining individual psychotherapy and psychopharmacology is the oldest, the most described, and the most widely practiced. Rather consistently, studies have shown that patients treated with medication and some form of individual therapy—be it psychodynamic, behavioral, or cognitive—show greater improvement than patients given medication alone. Whether the effect is additive or synergistic, the combined treatment mode effects both biological diatheses and psychosocial diatheses. Thus, while an anxiolytic may suppress panic attacks, individual interventions reduce phobic avoidance. And, where a neuroleptic suppresses delusions and hallucinations, individual interventions encourage socialization and facilitate reality testing. The end result is that patients are less anxious and depressed, are better able to concentrate, feel more accessible to psychological interventions, and, hopefully, can lead better and more productive lives (Karasu, 1982). Chapter 7 provides specific guidelines for combined treatments with anxiety disorder, depression, bipolar disorder, schizophrenia, and the personality disorders.

Combining Group Therapy and Psychopharmacotherapy

Combining groups intervention with medication is one of the more common combined treatment modes. More than two-thirds of group therapists recently surveyed reported that medicated patients were members of their outpatient psychotherapy groups (Stone, Rodenhauser, & Borkert, 1991). The most common diagnoses of these patients were mood disorders, followed by personality disorders, anxiety disorders, and schizophrenia. It should be noted that this study did not survey group therapists involved with the increasing number of medicated patients in skill-oriented groups, rehabilitation groups, or medication groups in day hospitals or outpatient clinics. Group therapy is particularly effective in improving self-esteem, modulating emotional reactions, and developing appropriate interpersonal and social skills. On the other hand, medication can ameliorate anxious, depressive, manic, psychotic, and disorganized thinking and suppress pathological ruminations, compulsions, and impulsivity (Sussman, 1993).

Psychotropic medications have greatly expanded the population for whom group therapy is now available, and have also expanded the theory and practice of group therapy itself. Other survey data suggest that dynamically oriented group therapists have been slower in their acceptance of this treatment combination than group therapists of other orientations (Rodenhauser & Stone, 1993). Finally, this combined treatment has broader applicability than combined family therapy and psychopharmacology, since not all patients have families that are available and willing to participate in the treatment process.

This form of combined treatment is indicated in at least four circumstances: (1) to ensure medication compliance; (2) to increase the patient's social skills and/or social involvement; (3) as an adjunct or as the main focus of aftercare treatment—following discharge from an impatient treatment setting. In all of these instances, combining group with medication is indicated. And (4), when symptoms interfere with patient involvement in a group in which they are already members. This is less common than the first three indications. Nonetheless, medication can greatly ameliorate certain target symptoms, allowing the patient to be more emotionally accessible to the therapeutic process of the group. There are relatively fewer contraindications for this combined mode than for combining individual and group therapy since patients treated for certain target symptoms (impulsivity, aggressivity, extreme hypersensitivity, etc.) may become more accessible to psychological intervention. Linehan (1987) reports that lower functioning, chronically parasuicidal patients diagnosed with borderline personality disorder can respond to structured group therapy.

Prior to initiating the combined format, the clinician should perform a comprehensive evaluation of the patient in terms of Axis I and II diagnosis, level of functioning, social and interpersonal skills, extent of social support network, target symptoms, and indications for combined group therapy and psychopharmacology.

The group therapy format includes heterogeneous and homogeneous groups (Frances, Clarkin, & Perry, 1984). Heterogeneous groups tend to be comprised of patients who differ widely in presenting diagnosis, target symptoms, level of functioning, socioeconomic status, and personality style. Heterogeneous groups are also characterized by their focus on interpersonal relations in a wide variety of contexts and tend to be ongoing, open-ended groups where members can join and "graduate" at various points. Homogeneous groups, on the other hand, tend to be composed of patients with similar diagnoses. For example, an eating disorder group or a medication symptom management group are homogeneous groups. These groups are more likely to focus on a specific target symptom and condition, to be more directive than heterogeneous groups, and to be time-limited rather than long term and ongoing.

1. Group Therapy Referral. Refer lower functioning patients with medication-modifiable target symptoms and/or noncompliance/nonadherance issues to homogeneous combined treatment groups, and higher functioning patients on medication who have minimal social skills to a heterogenous group. Generally, homogeneous groups are better suited to patients with chronic medication noncompliance or other nonadherence issues, who have difficulty in social functionings and/or experience persistent symptoms (i.e., dysphoria, anxiety, referential thinking, or hallucinations). These patients may be a good "fit" for a medication and/or symptom management group.

On the other hand, heterogeneous groups may be more appropriate to higher functioning patients on medication whose trait symptoms are well controlled and who have at least minimal social skills. Not surprising, heterogeneous groups are more likely to be found in private practices and other outpatient settings. Accordingly, not all patients in heterogeneous groups will be on medication, and so issues of medication noncompliance may not likely be a common topic of discussion, although the issue of treatment compliance is likely to be ubiquitous. However, issues about the meaning of medication and the fantasies associated with compliance could be the focus of discussions. Some patients on medication may resist discussing medications, while others will openly flaunt their medication and the "specialness" of having a "real" doctor—the prescriber—also caring for them (Rodenhauser & Stone, 1993). Fantasies of being controlled or losing control because of medication may be reflected in resistance to group process. Similarly, problems regarding intimacy are often projected onto the medication themselves (Zaslav & Kalb, 1989).

2. Medication. Introduce medication prior to the introduction of group therapy. Most often, acute target symptoms preclude the patient's accessibility to the therapeutic process—whether individual or group—and so medications are usually begun first. Whether the referral is for a heterogeneous or homogenous group, the patient must be relatively stable. Some patients, particularly those who are exceedingly shy or dependent, may need to be gradually introduced into the group modality and thus a few individual sessions may be necessary to encourage and socialize the patient to make the transition to the group modality. Sometimes, a few concurrent individual and group sessions are needed before the prescribing clinician is able to reduce individual sessions to a medication monitoring mode.

3. Collaboration Issues. Attend to the potential collaboration issues. Despite the encouraging finding of the Rodenhauser and Stone (1993) and Stone, Rodenhauser, and Markert (1991) studies about the increasing acceptance of medicated patients in groups run by nonprescribing clinicians, there is considerable potential for splitting and countertransference. The conduct of group therapy and the management of medication each requires considerable expertise. Clinicians in both instances need to appreciate the therapeutic potential as well as the adverse reactions attendant to this combined treatment (Sussman, 1993).

Although the prescribing clinician may be involved in a medication management group, a symptom management group, or other homogeneous group, it is quite unlikely that the prescribing clinician will be leading a heterogeneous group. Therefore, issues of collaboration can be paramount. Ideally, the prescribing clinician can refer medicated patients only to groups and group therapists who share similar views about this combined treatment and have a previous track record of working collaboratively with medicated patients. When this is not possible, it is the prescribing clinician's responsibility to assess the potential group therapist's attitudes about medication and receptivity to collaborative relationships, which can be expected to be fraught with splitting and projective identification.

Combining Family Therapy and Psychopharmacotherapy

The first generation of controlled studies of the efficacy of combined family therapy and medication is currently underway. Although largely focused on schizophrenia, some trials have studied combined treatment of mood and eating disorders as well as panic disorders and agoraphobia. This type of combined treatment is particularly valuable in suppressing symptoms, educating the family about the psychiatric disorder, improving family communication and problem-solving skills, and resolving dynamic and systemic issues created by the disorder (Glick, Clarkin, & Goldsmith, 1993). This section briefly describes medications/contraindications and two treatment guidelines.

This combined treatment is indicated for many instances of both specific symptoms of an individual family member and the family problems and interactions that accompany these conditions. Specific indications are: (1) to enhance medication compliance; (2) amelioration of psychiatric symptoms of the identified patient that delimit or preclude full participation in a family therapy; and (3) to reduce relapse and recurrence of the psychiatric disorder. An obvious contraindication is when either of the two modalities is in itself effective. A relative contraindication includes previous failure or current stalemate in family therapy.

Prior to initiating the combined treatment format, the clinician must make both a psychiatric (i.e., DSM-IV) diagnosis and a family systems diagnosis (Beavers & Hampson, 1990). Without such a combined diagnostic formulation, neither the appropriate medication, nor family intervention(s) will be prescribed or implemented. Furthermore, the clinician must be aware of the side effects of the medication and the family therapy, as well as their interaction (Glick, Clarkin, & Goldsmith, 1993). The following steps are vital to ensuring effective treatment:

1. Set specific outcome goals, particularly regarding target symptoms, for both modalities based on which symptoms are medication responsive and which are family intervention responsive. Without such a delineation of target symptoms, it may be impossible to determine which modality—or combination—is effective. Typically, these target symptoms are disabling anxiety, vegetative symptoms of depression, positive symptoms of schizophrenia, impulsivity, aggressivity, and affective instability.

2. Initiate treatment with the medication modality and add the family modality when the patient is stabilized. This guideline will hold for the majority of patients who are experiencing acute, debilitating psychiatric symptoms. For example, the psychotic patient who is paranoid may not be able to tolerate family sessions until being stabilized by medication. Before that, the patient might be too suspicious of the clinician or of other family members to benefit from treatment.

Combining Individual Psychotherapy and Family Therapy

Individual psychopathology and family dysfunction are nearly always interdependent. Interpersonal and intrapsychic dynamics reciprocally interact between each person and his or her family and social contexts. Various clinical reports and research studies combining individual therapy with either marital or family therapy have been published since 1966. This section describes five indications for this format and three treatment guidelines. Obviously, the combined treatment assumes that the individual family of origin or nuclear family is available and willing to be involved in treatment.

This combined treatment is indicated when the presenting problems include one or more of the following: (1) an adult whose symptoms are being triggered or reinforced by marital or family dysfunction; (2) a highly pathological level of marital discord; (3) sexual dysfunction; (4) a child or adolescent with a psychiatric disorder or significant symptom; and (5) a highly pathological level of parent–child conflict (Sanders & Feldman, 1993). Relative contraindications for this combined format include: (1) the adult's presenting problem does not have a significant etiology in or effect upon the family system; (2) strong motivation to be seen alone, such as adolescents who insist they have personal problems for which they will seek only individual help.

Individual and family modalities can be combined in two different ways. Either treatment can shift sequentially from one modality to the other or the two modalities can occur concurrently. Feldman (1992) describes sequential integration and "concurrent" integration that can be either symmetrical—equal emphasis on each modality—or asymmetrical—emphasis on one modality over the other. Sanders and Feldman (1993) advocate that the same clinician provide both modalities. However, two clinicians may be better utilized in the following circumstances:

1. An individual therapy relationship has been firmly established prior to the plan to add marital or family therapy.
When the presenting complaints are predominantly interpersonal, begin with marital or family therapy. When the presenting complaint is predominantly intrapsychic, begin with individual therapy. Afterward, the other modality is added. This is the sequential strategy and is more commonly employed than the concurrent strategy. In utilizing the sequential strategy, marital or family therapy is more often added to individual therapy than vice versa (Sanders & Feldman, 1993).

2. The number or severity of the presenting problems is usually high.
When the degree of individual and family interactional dysfunction is equally high and there is little resistance to either modality, begin both concurrently. This is the symmetrical, concurrent strategy. With couples, this means the partners are seen conjointly one week and then individually the next. In conjoint session they work out relational issues, while in individual sessions treatment focuses on dysfunctional cognitions, family-of-origin issues, or intrapsychic dynamics. With families, the entire family has a conjoint session, and later that week the identified patient has an individual session (Sanders & Feldman, 1993).

3. A family member is extremely resistant to "sharing" his or her therapist with other family members.
When family interactional dysfunction is manifestly greater than intrapsychic dysfunction, or vice versa, or there is a great resistance to individual sessions, begin with primary emphasis on the modality not resisted. Later, the other may be added. This is the asymmetrical, concurrent strategy. Assuming that both modalities are being utilized, the primary modality is scheduled weekly, while the secondary modality might be biweekly or monthly (Sanders & Feldman, 1993).

Combining Individual Psychotherapy and Group Therapy

Combined individual and group therapy is one of the oldest and most effective of all treatment combinations. While often considered simply an amalgam of individual and group therapy, it is a separate approach in its own right. It has its unique indications and contraindications, mechanisms of action, and technical issues (Porter, 1993). Over 100 publications on this combined format have appeared since 1949. This section will briefly describe mechanisms of action, indications-contraindications, and general treatment guidelines.

The mechanism of action of this combined format has both additive and magnifying effects for both individual therapy and group therapy. Porter (1993) notes that additive effects for individual therapy include one-to-one corrective emotional experiences and deep intrapsychic exploration. Additive effects for group therapy include exploration of multiple transferences and provision of a context to risk new behaviors. The magnifying effects of individual therapy include prevention of premature dropout from group therapy and in-depth exploration of material from group sessions. Magnifying effects of group therapy include prevention of premature dropout from individual therapy and analysis of transference resistance from individual sessions.

The consensus on this combined format is that it is appropriate and may be the outpatient treatment of choice for: (1) personality disorders—except the antisocial and severe narcissistic, borderline, paranoid, schizoid, and schizotypal personality disorders; (2) most impulse control, sexual, and substance abuse disorders; (3) most mood and anxiety disorders; and (4) stable psychotic conditions. Specific contraindications are acutely suicidal individuals, those who are extremely shy, those with focal neurotic symptoms who have no personality disorders, and patients for whom combined treatment is a resistance to treatment already occurring (Porter, 1993).

Combined individual and group therapy can be initiated in three ways: beginning with individual and then adding group therapy, beginning with group and then adding individual therapy, or simultaneously initiating both modalities. Generally, the third option is uncommon. Similarly, this combined format can be ended in three ways: terminating individual before group therapy, group before individual, or both simultaneously. Commonly, the two modalities are provided by different clinicians. When two clinicians are involved, the issue of collaboration between group therapist and individual therapist in terms of goals and focus must be negotiated. Lipsius (1991) offers three specific guidelines to achieve a balance as well as to maximize the synergy between the two modalities.

1. Start individual therapy for most patients and then add the group component.
The exceptions to this guideline are patients who have an intense fear of close one-to-one relationships and need the anonymity of a therapeutic group as a prerequisite to individual therapy, and those with a long history of previous individual therapies with limited results.

2. When appropriate, invite the patient to relate individual and group session material and assist with interpretations that are helpful in integrating the patient's therapeutic experience.
Specifically, Lipsius (1991) suggests that both clinicians inquire if what the patient experiences in one treatment modality relates to what he or she is experiencing in the other modality. He believes that this approach identifies intermodality resistances that when resolved result in the vital process integration of previously incompatible parts of the self. Moreover, it prevents premature terminations of either or both modalities.

Transference splitting is the main technical issue faced in this combined format. Common among patients with dependent and histrionic styles is positive transference in individual sessions counterbalanced with negative affect in the group setting. Among patients with schizoid and paranoid styles, the reverse is common. Porter (1993) contends that the presence of transference splitting represents the emergence of a tendency that otherwise might erupt outside the treatment setting with greater self-destructive consequences. He recommends supporting these patients in fully expressing their feelings in whatever modality they appear. The absence of certain feelings in the other modality can then be addressed, which initiates a process of reversing the split and facilitating integration.

3. Terminate the individual modality before the group modality. There are a few exceptions to this general guideline. When difficulty with separation is the central issue, ending both modalities simultaneously is preferable for patients whose treatment is reasonably complete. Terminating group therapy first is preferable when the patient has completed much in the combined modalities but still experiences transference difficulties within the individual modality (Porter, 1993).

Other Combined Treatment Modes

While combining two treatment modalities may be sufficient for many patients and circumstances, there are other patients and circumstances in which three or more modalities may need to be combined. The most common of such combined modes involves individual therapy, medication, and either group or family sessions. At this time, there has been very little written or researched to offer specific indications or guidelines on such multiple combined modalities. Occasionally, in the following chapters, such multiple combined treatment will be mentioned.

TRACKING AND MONITORING TREATMENT INTERVENTIONS: AN ILLUSTRATION

Tracking and monitoring the treatment process—including treatment goals, focus, and interventions—is an essential component of treatment selection and outcomes management. Since brief and time-limited treatments are, of necessity, focused treatments, it stands to reason that providers should be encouraged to provide focused treatment. Tracking and monitoring not only provides critical data for predicting treatment outcomes, it can also **influence** the process of treatment and, subsequently, the outcomes of treatment.

Central to Howard's phase model of psychotherapy (1993) is the level of patient functioning. It is perfectly reasonable to assume that cost-effective and efficacious psychotherapy and other psychiatric treatments should focus on changing level of functioning. The COMPASS Outpatient Treatment Assessment System has items involving six categories of presenting problems and current life functioning—family functioning, health and grooming, intimate relationships, self-management, social relationships, and work functioning. Any one of these areas of functioning—functional deficits—can be construed as a reasonable treatment target or focus of treatment. For instance, a patient with low functioning in intimate relationships probably should be accorded treatment focused on intimate relationships, whereas someone whose principal deficit in work functioning items should be offered therapy primarily focused on work issues and work functioning.

COMPASS elicits patient and therapist evaluations of six areas of functioning for which treatment could be focused. Providers using the COMPASS System can choose to utilize this information in their treatment planning and selection process. The System tracks "functional focus of treatment" as one of the five Current Treatment Selection areas. Providers simply check the area of functioning on which they are focusing treatment. Presumably, this task heighten's the provider's awareness of focusing treatment on specific functional deficits.

There are a number of value-added benefits of the COMPASS Predictive System. It could correlate duration of treatment, change in mental health index, and/or changes in current levels of functioning with treatment focus, treatment format, frequency of treatment, or medication, as well as with specific treatment methods employed. For instance, data on treatment format can be correlated with presenting problem or diagnosis, making it possible to answer questions such as: "Should medication be recommended for a married patient with moderate levels of depression?" "Should the psychotherapeutic treatment of a depressed client who primarily endorses work-functioning items be individual or couples therapy?" and the like. Such data will be essential in developing prediction equations to specify the optimal indications for single versus combined treatment formats, the relative efficacy of treatment methods.

Currently, a number of empirically based treatment guidelines are being derived from the expanding COMPASS database. The guidelines and treatment recommendations can suggest an optimal treatment plan for a divorced female with panic attacks, for example. Given data on demographics, clinical characteristics, and her overall level of life functioning, it is possible to specify the treatment she might be accorded: whether it should be individual or group treatment and whether a cognitive approach is likely to remit symptoms more quickly than a dynamic or supportive therapy if she cannot tolerate or refuses medication.

Another value-added benefit of the COMPASS Outpatient Treatment Assessment System involves case management. The provider, utilization reviewer, or case manager can quickly and rationally review treatment process (i.e., treatment selection) along with treatment outcomes. This provides an assessment of the "fit" between the patient's current life functioning and the provider's treatment focus and treatment methods. For example, when a case manager finds that the client's functional deficit in the work domain is not being addressed because the provider is focusing on social or intimate relationships with a dynamic or supportive therapy, the case manager can reasonably recommend that work functioning be addressed.

Five types of treatment selection information are incorporated into the COMPASS System. They are treatment focus, format, methods, modalities, and medications. As noted earlier, of these five, treatment focus will have major predictive value. Table 3.1 illustrates these components.

Case Example

The following case illustrates the importance and value of having a specific treatment focus. The client was a 28-year-old female, never married, who was referred to an Employee Assistance Program (EAP) program with a history of anxiety and life difficulties over 2 to 3 months. She received an initial diagnosis of Anxiety Disorder without history of panic. She stated: "I've been having problems everywhere lately. My parents and I aren't getting along like we used to, my boss and I are not communicating well, and I am just experiencing a lack of satisfaction in my life. I feel tense and anxious a lot of the time, but it's worse on workday mornings."

TABLE 3.1

Revision of Provider Tracking Sheet

CURRENT TREATMENT SELECTION

☐ **Check here if** *no* **change in #1–5 since last tracking**

1. **Functional Focus of Treatment:** (check primary focus)
   ☐ work ☐ family ☐ self-management ☐ intimate relationship ☐ other
   (_____)

2. **Session Frequency:** (check one) ☐ 1/wk ☐ 2/wk ☐ 2/month ☐ 1/month
   ☐ other (_____)

3. **Treatment Format:** (check primary modality)
   ☐ individual ☐ group ☐ family ☐ couple ☐ ind & Rx ☐ Rx & group
   ☐ Rx & couple ☐ ind & group ☐ ind & couple ☐ ind & family
   ☐ Rx & family ☐ other (_____)

4. **Treatment Method:** (check primary method)
   ☐ dynamic ☐ cognitive ☐ behavioral ☐ supportive ☐ psychoeducation
   ☐ other (_____)

5. **Medication (Rx):** (list all *and* check any new Rx started since the last tracking)
   ☐ 1) _____
   ☐ 2) _____
   ☐ 3) _____
   ☐ 4) _____

The patient was referred to a psychologist and after an evaluation—which included the COMPASS Outpatient (OP) instrument—treatment began. According to the EAP guidelines, the patient was eligible for five sessions. However, when the psychologist called to have her exit the EAP and enter fee-for-service treatment, the case manager expressed alarm. The patient's mental health index had fallen from the normal range to 50% during the course of those five sessions. (See Figure 3.2.)

The provider had utilized analytically oriented therapy to explore the nature of this patient's problems and to uncover underlying causes. The case manager pointed out that "work" was the highest peak in the presenting problems and inquired whether the psychologist had explored that area. The provider promised to explore the area further and six additional sessions were approved. The results of the next two tracking administrations showed further deterioration. The case manager continued to press for an exploration of the

FIGURE 3.2

Mental Health Index and Clinical Assessment

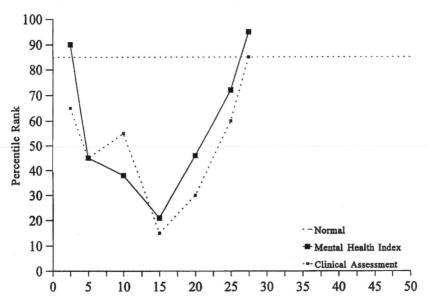

work situation and change in direction of the therapy. Finally, at 15 sessions, the case manager insisted the patient see a consultant who specialized in work-related problems for an outside opinion. The consultant and the case manager convinced the provider to alter the direction of the therapy toward problems at work and the patient improved rapidly over the next few sessions.

CONCLUDING NOTE

There is no question that psychotherapy and other psychiatric treatments have become more and more prescriptive and tailored to the patient's needs, expectations, and styles. At the same time, treatment outcomes management systems have become the norm for mental health care. This chapter has emphasized the link between tailored and prescriptive treatments and decisions about combining treatment modalities have been described.

This chapter completes Part I. Chapters in Part II cover clinical application of outcomes measures in outpatient, inpatient, substance abuse, medication management, and primary care settings.

Part II

Treatment Outcomes in Clinical Practice

4

Outpatient Treatment Outcomes

In Chapters 2 and 3 we presented the argument that practitioners need to know the progress of each patient during the course of treatment. We asserted that, "The practitioner needs to know whether the treatment *is working* for this patient. The task of research is to provide valid methods for systematic, relevant feedback concerning the patient's condition." We also presented the phase model of psychotherapy, a model that specifies the assessment of specific illness-relevant criteria. In the present chapter we shall show how these recommendations have been translated into a practical system for guiding outpatient treatment and give some clinical case examples.

Managers of mental health outpatient treatment have been at a loss to determine the medical necessity for treatment or the effectiveness of the treatment given to any specific patient. In the absence of this information, managed care organizations have had to take refuge in the draconian policy of simply setting session limits—limiting costs since they cannot evaluate benefit. They have decided to let the provider determine the need for the initiation of treatment (i.e., the therapist can determine if this patient needs treatment), but not to allow the provider to determine whether the patient continues to need treatment.

In the main, this distrust of psychotherapists is justified. Therapists are not trained to think of their patients as suffering from an illness. Rather, therapists view their patients as needing help in overcoming distress (and symptoms) and attaining a reasonable level of mental health (better and more comfortable functioning). In this sense, therapists view therapy as very long-term and are willing to provide treatment so long as the patient is motivated and willing to work on psychological problems. Indeed, it is quite rare for therapists to initiate the termination of treatment. Termination is usually determined by the patient on the basis of an informal cost-benefit analysis—"Is continuing in treatment likely to produce enough benefit to offset my financial and personal costs?"

At the same time, therapists are left to their own impressions of the amount of benefit the patient is realizing though therapy. This is akin to a physician impressionistically evaluating the blood pressure or white blood count of a patient. Since no "lab report" or x-ray has been available, the therapist has no alternative information on which to base his or her determination of treatment need. What is needed is a method for determining the "medical necessity" for treatment. This would allow for a rational system for deciding when to initiate and terminate treatment. What also is needed is a system of feedback that would provide information to the manager, therapist, and patient regarding the progress of the current treatment. This latter information would help to guide changes in focus or modality of treatment (e.g., addition of medication, group therapy). In what follows, we show how Compass Information Services, Inc. has adapted the dosage, phase, and generic process models to provide such information.

OPERATIONALIZATION OF PHASE MODEL CONSTRUCTS

As described in Chapter 2, the phase model proposes three stages of psychotherapy: remoralization, remediation, and rehabilitation. The criteria for each of these stages are subjective well-being, symptoms, and life functioning, respectively. Each of these criteria has been operationalized and measures have been standard scored (T-scores: mean = 50, s.d. = 10) on the basis of the pretherapy scores of a large group of patients, with a higher score indicating better mental health.

Subjective Well-Being

In keeping with the vast literature on well-being and quality of life, the content sampling for this scale includes both positive and negative affect (Diener, 1984; Watson & Tellegen, 1985), and health and

FIGURE 4.1

Subjective Well-Being: Frequency Distributions for Patients (N=6569) and a Community Sample (N=979)

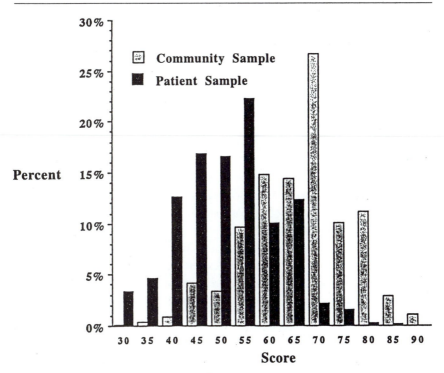

contentment (Cowen, 1991; Viet & Ware, 1983). The four items include the dimensions of distress, energy and health, emotional and psychological adjustment, and current life satisfaction. Structured responses are provided for each item. The internal consistency of the Subjective Well-Being scale is .79, the test–retest reliability is .82.

The Subjective Well-Being scale correlated .79 with the 22-item General Well-Being Scale (Dupuy, 1977), .51 with a 10-item measure of positive affect, and –.70 with a 10-item measure of negative affect (Watson & Tellegen, 1985), .73 with the total score of the SF-36 (Stewart, Hayes, & Ware, 1988), and .76 with the five-item mental health index of the SF-36 (Ware & Sherbourne, 1992). Figure 4.1 shows the frequency distributions of T-scores based on a sample of normals and a sample of patients at the initiation of treatment. Scores below 60 characterize the patient sample.

Current Symptoms

Much of clinical research has included a self-report symptom check-list adapted from (or used in its entirety) the Symptom Checklist-90R (SCL-90R, Derogatis, 1977). The SCL-90R was based on the Hopkins Symptom Checklist (see Derogatis, et al., 1974a,b). The response categories of the SCL-90R inquire into how much distress each symptom has caused and yields nine factorially derived scores, as well as a variety of summary scores.

Because of the growing interest in empirically based diagnosis, Compass Information Services devised a completely new symptom checklist. From clinical diagnoses based on 140 Structured Clinical Interviews for the DSM-III (SCID), it was found that 74.3% of out-patients had at least one of the following six Axis I diagnoses: Adjustment Disorder, Anxiety, Bipolar Disorder, Depression, Obsessive-Compulsive Disorder, Phobia. Of those patients who qualified for *any* DSM Axis I diagnoses, 92.0% had one of these six diagnoses.

Using the Diagnostic and Statistical Manual for Mental Disorders (DSM-III-R, American Psychiatric Association, 1987), we listed the signs and symptoms for these six diagnoses and also the diagnosis of substance abuse and recast them as a 40-item patient self-report symptom checklist. There are at least three questions for each diagnosis; however, the higher the prevalence of the diagnosis, the greater the number of questions pertaining to that diagnosis.

Like the SCL-90R, the Current Symptoms scale employs a 5-point, fixed-response format. However, in keeping with DSM-III-R, the response categories reflect the frequency of experiencing each symptom in the past month.

The Current Symptoms scale had an internal consistency of .94. The three–four-week test–retest reliability for the total score was .85. Table 4.1 gives the reliabilities of the Current Symptoms subscales.

The total score on the Current Symptoms scale (CS) correlated .91 with the total score of an abbreviated (47-item) version of the SCL-90R. We examined, in some detail, the concurrent validity of the Depression subscale of the CS. The Depression subscale correlated .68 with the *Center for Epidemiologic Studies of Depression Scale* (CES-D) (Radloff, 1977) and .87 with the *Beck Depression Inventory* (Beck, Ward, Mendelson, Mock, & Erbaugh, 1961). Using the Structured Clinical Interview for Diagnosis (SCID) (Spitzer, Williams, &

TABLE 4.1

Reliabilities of Current Symptoms Subscales

Subscale	Internal Consistency	Test–Retest
Adjustment Disorder	.80	.79
Anxiety	.80	.80
Bipolar	.60	.74
Depression	.88	.77
Obsessive-Compulsive	.74	.83
Phobia	.60	.73
Substance Use	.84	.65

Gibbon, 1988), 13 patients diagnosed with depression were compared to 15 patients with other Axis I disorders. SCID-diagnosed Depressives' CS mean Depression score was nearly a full standard deviation higher than the mean for all patients. The mean Depression score for Depressed patients was significantly ($t_{(26)}$ = 2.94; p < .01) above that of patients with other DSM-III-R Axis I diagnoses. Figure 4.2 shows the frequency distributions for the total score on this checklist for normal and patient samples. As can be seen, T-scores below 60 again characterize the patient sample.

Current Life Functioning

In the Current Life Functioning scale (CLF), the patient is asked to report the degree to which his or her emotional and psychological problems are interfering with functioning in six life areas. The intent of this scale is to assess the extent of disability caused by the patient's emotional and psychological condition. A variety of inventories, including the Social Security Disability Guidelines, were examined and self-report items were generated to cover the range of disabilities. Factor analyses of these items suggested the same six dimensions that were identified from presenting problem data. The 24 items in this scale are categorized into these six life areas so that there are at least three questions per area. The *family*, *intimacy*, and *social* questions inquire about the patient's interactions with others and carrying out his/her responsibilities to these people. The *health* items address the patient's health habits and hygiene, and the *work* items refer to the patient's workplace interactions and ability to com-

FIGURE 4.2

**Current Symptoms: Frequency Distributions for Patients
(N=6583) and a Community Sample (N=574)**

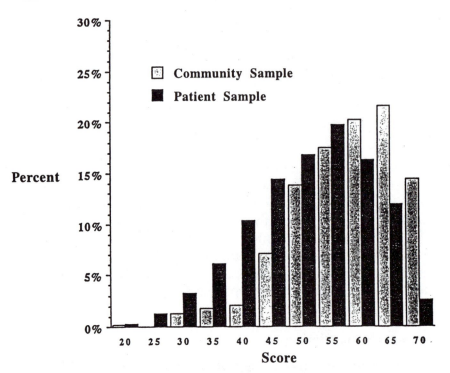

plete tasks. *Self-management* items assess the patient's control over, conceptions of, and satisfaction with himself or herself.

Based on a sample of patients prior to treatment, the internal consistency (alpha) of the total score of the CLF was .93. The three–four-week test–retest correlation was .76. Table 4.2 shows the reliabilities for the Current Life Functioning subscales.

Figure 4.3 shows the frequency distributions for the total score on this questionnaire for normal and patient samples. As can be seen, T-scores below 60 again characterize the patient sample.

Mental Health Index (MHI)

The MHI consists of the combination of Subjective Well-Being, the Current Symptom total score, and the Current Life Functioning to-

TABLE 4.2

Current Life Functioning

Subscale	Internal Consistency	Test–Retest
Family Functioning	.77	.42
Health and Grooming	.78	.79
Intimate Relationships	.71	.49
Self-Management	.80	.75
Social Relationships	.84	.68
Work, School, Household	.85	.77

FIGURE 4.3

**Current Life Functioning: Frequency Distributions for Patients
(N=6625) and a Community Sample (N=495)**

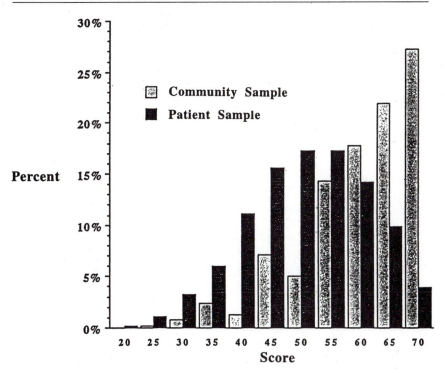

tal score. The MHI has an internal consistency of .87 and a three–four week test–retest stability of .82. Figure 4.4 shows the frequency distributions for the total score on this index for normal and patient samples. T-scores below 60 again characterize the patient sample.

FIGURE 4.4

**Mental Health Index: Frequency Distributions for Patients
(N=6591) and a Community Sample (N=493)**

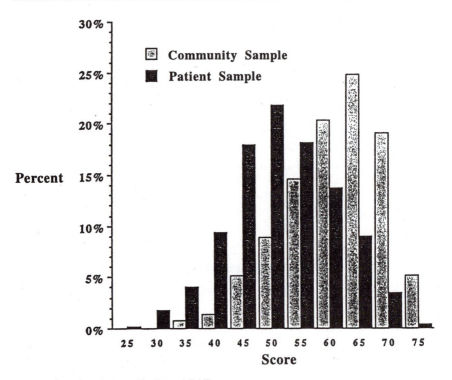

Clinical Assessment Index (CAI)

In addition to the phase measures based on patient self-reports, the clinician also rates the patient's condition.

The therapist answers two questions assessing the patient's subjective well-being—emotional and psychological adjustment and amount of distress.

The patient's symptomatic condition is assessed by the *Global Assessment Scale* (GAS) (Endicott, Spitzer, Fleiss, & Cohen, 1976), a rating of "the patient's lowest level of current functioning" using "a hypothetical continuum of mental health-illness." This scale, which is similar to Axis V of the DSM-III-R, consists of ten 10-point intervals, which correspond to a description of a patient's general functioning, on a 1–100 rating continuum with 100 representing superior status. The clinician is asked to categorize the patient into one of these intervals by providing a specific numerical rating within the range. For example, if the clinician believes the patient belongs in the lowest interval, 1–10, he or she must indicate where in that range the patient falls: 1, 4, 7, and so on.

Several studies have assessed the reliability of this measure. Endicott et al. (1976) conducted five studies (on samples that were primarily comprised of inpatients) resulting in test–retest reliabilities ranging from .69 to .91. Clark and Friedman (1983) found that the GAS test–retest reliabilities ranged from .74 to .78, decreasing as the length of time between assessments increased. In a study of chronic outpatients, interrater reliabilities for the GAS were obtained after four different training sessions involving either previously trained mental health professionals, untrained mental health professionals, or a mixture of trained and untrained clinicians. These interrater reliabilities ranged from .66 to .92, with greater reliabilities associated with the trained clinician groups (Dworkin, Friedman, Telschow, Grant, Moffic, & Sloan, 1990). Based on our sample, the test–retest correlation (two–three week interval, rated by different clinicians at each time point) was .68.

The *Life Functioning Scales* were devised to assess the patient's status in each of the six life areas included in the patient self-report Current Life Functioning questionnaire—Family Functioning, Intimate Relationships, Social Relationships, Health and Grooming, Work Functioning, and Self-Management. Each of the six domains is rated on a dimension ranging from 0 to 100, with increments of five marking the scale. Each scale has five descriptive anchors, with each anchor occupying one-fifth of the dimension space. Anchors range from "Severe Impairment, Virtually Unable to Function" on the low end (0–20), to "No Impairment, High Level of Functioning" on the high end (80–100) of the functioning dimension. Five behavioral examples, each of 20 to 50 words, are provided with each of the five levels to help standardize the labeled levels of functioning. Raters are asked to "circle the number (from 0 to 100) that best applies to the patient's level of, for example, Family Functioning."

The intercorrelations of ratings of the six domains ranged from .36 to .67. The sum of the ratings for the six life areas had an internal consistency of .86 and a test–retest (two–three week interval, rated by different clinicians at each time point) correlation of .77. Corrected item–total correlations ranged from .55 to .66. This indicated the presence of an overall dimension of functioning, but also indicated that there was meaningful content heterogeneity across the domains. Each of the separate domains and the sum of the six domains of life functioning were correlated with the GAS. The summed domains correlated .74 with the GAS; the separate domains correlated with the GAS in a range from .47 to .67. This further indicated convergence of the underlying dimension with another global measure of functioning.

The **Clinical Assessment Index** (CAI) is based on clinicians' ratings of the patient's subjective well-being, the Global Assessment Scale and the sum of Life Functioning Scales. The CAI has an internal consistency of .84 and a (two–three week interval rated by different clinicians at the two time points) test–retest stability of .77.

Therapeutic Bond

The system also includes an assessment of the therapeutic relationship based on the generic model conception of the therapeutic bond (Orlinsky & Howard, 1987). As described in Chapter 2, the bond has three theoretical components: working alliance, empathic resonance, and mutual affirmation. Working alliance has to do with the effort the patient and the therapist put into implementing their respective roles. Empathic resonance relates to the patient's perception that the therapist understands him/her, and mutual affirmation pertains to an open, caring regard and trust between the patient and the therapist. Originally, a 50-item Therapeutic Bond Scale (Saunders, Howard, & Orlinsky, 1989) was developed to assess these three components. Based on item–total correlations, we selected the best four items for each of the three-bond constructs. The sum of the 12 items correlated .81 with the 50-item Therapeutic Bond Scale. The internal consistency of this scale was .88 and the test–retest correlation (session one to session three) was .62.

CASE EXAMPLES

As we have emphasized, in order to be relevant to practice, research results must be interpretable in a way that allows application to the single case. Using the assessments presented above, we developed a system for assessing (tracking) a case in a manner that can inform therapists, supervisors, and patients about the efficacy and direction of a psychotherapeutic treatment. At its most general level, the system monitors each treatment by using three measures—the Mental Health Index, the Clinical Assessment Index, and the Therapeutic Bond. All of these measures are normed to a large sample of psychotherapy patients at intake and are expressed as T-scores (with a mean of 50 and a standard deviation of 10).

The following cases are from the Northwestern Memorial Hospital's outpatient clinic. This university-based clinic serves a large urban catchment area, is a primary training site for clinical psychologists and psychiatrists, and was the site for the NIMH-sponsored research (Howard, Orlinsky, Saunders, Bankoff, Davidson, & O'Mahoney, 1991) on which the assessment system was initially based. Complete clinical records were available on study patients (and informed consent for their use in research was obtained from patients and therapists).

A Shorter-Term Success

This patient was a single woman in her late twenties. She was employed full time, but felt that she was working at a dead-end job. She stated that she wanted to earn a college degree, but admitted to a lack of motivation to "move ahead in life." She stated that she wanted to discover whether or not she really did have a problem.

The patient reported that her parents had a shaky relationship. She described her father as "cool and stupid." She stated that she "adores" her mother and did not understand how she put up with her father. The patient had few friends, with no close male friends, and felt that she had never had a satisfying intimate relationship.

She considered her boyfriend to be a very stable and energetic person with a strong personality. She felt that he was not very supportive and told him that she saw him as distant and unfeeling. He responded by telling her that he was a strong person and she was weak, and that perhaps therapy would help strengthen her and reduce her negative thinking.

In the intake interview, the patient alternated between alert, task-oriented thought processing to very slowed, depressed cognitive functioning that included some suicidal ideation. She reported a pattern of bingeing with alcohol and marijuana to "self-medicate" her

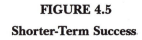

FIGURE 4.5

Shorter-Term Success

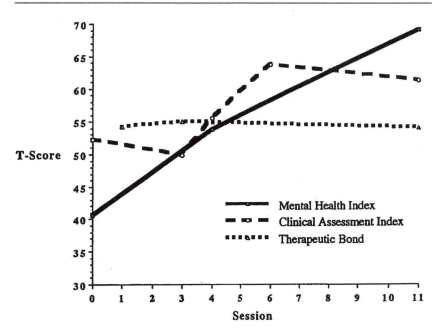

depression. The intake diagnoses were Adjustment Disorder; Narcissistic Personality Disorder; Alcohol Abuse; Cannabis Abuse. Her diagnosis based on the Structured Clinical Interview for DSM-III-R (SCID: Spitzer et al., 1988) was Adjustment Disorder.

Therapy was conducted by a married female clinical psychology predoctoral intern. Her therapeutic orientation was eclectic psychodynamic with an emphasis on object relations and self-psychology. She had previously seen only 6 to 10 patients in individual psychotherapy.

Figure 4.5 shows the course of therapy for this patient. As can be seen, the therapeutic bond was stable and slightly higher than average. By the end of this 11-session treatment, from both the perspective of the therapist (Clinical Assessment Index) and of the patient (Mental Health Index), the patient was assessed as functioning in the normal range (a T-score above 60) by session 7.

At discharge, the therapist wrote that, "Treatment was focused on helping the patient to look at the underlying feelings of the childhood experiences that she talked about. . . . Direct empathic verbalization of such feelings on the therapist's part were met with defensiveness. . . . An ego-supportive approach . . . proved to be more successful. That is, the patient was supported in her own exploration of her experiences and affects. This helped the patient to internalize a self-reflective stance. . . . However, she also became aware . . . that her problems were more pervasive and deeper than she had thought. She 'decided' not to continue exploring them at this point." The therapist rated the patient as 'slightly improved,' 'slightly distressed,' and as getting along 'fairly well; has her ups and downs.' "

A Shorter-Term Failure

This patient was a young, divorced female. She was well educated and appropriately employed. At intake, she stated she had been dating a man for over two years. "We have an overall good understanding and communicative relationship. Lately, he has been pressuring me to make a commitment. I can't seem to decide what is right for me to do. I don't think I want to make that commitment right now, but I'm confused as to why I feel this way. I wonder that if after such a long relationship I don't want to make a commitment to this man, if I ever will. I also worry that past events (my divorce) are scaring me away. My current situation in a job with a heavy workload and an intense study schedule continues to make me feel like I don't have enough time for myself."

The patient is an oldest child. She described her father as "not a real bright person, old fashioned attitudes, and lesser educated than my mom." Her father had a drinking problem while the patient was growing up, but had been sober for the last several years. She described her mother as "very intelligent, level headed, loving if somewhat protective . . . she can be phony sometimes and try to shy away from what's really going on. She would rather nobody know what's going on with her. She was always there for me but I don't think I ever really felt like I was in touch with her." She stated that she was closer to her mother than to her father while growing up. In high school she was "not popular" and did not feel close to anyone in her family. She recalled often feeling depressed. She had had suicidal thoughts, but never had plan or intent. She saw college as a "chance for a fresh start" and as a time when she was much happier.

After less than a year of marriage, her husband informed her that he was moving out. She stated that she knew there were problems in their relationship, "but they were things I thought we could work out." Shortly after the divorce, her ex-husband married another woman. About one year later, this woman left him.

She described her current boyfriend as "a sensitive person, nice almost to a fault, masculine looking, somewhat smaller physically than my idea of the most attractive man." The clinical intake diagnosis was Interpersonal Problem. Based on the SCID, her diagnosis was Adjustment Disorder.

The therapist was a young, married, male clinical psychology predoctoral intern. According to the therapist, in the early sessions of psychotherapy the patient resolved that she was not ready to get engaged and was unsure of her investment in the relationship with her boyfriend. Therapy focused primarily on working to understand the patient's general sense of unfulfillment, which was manifest in her ambivalence both about her relationship and about her choice of a career. With regard to both of these, she complained of a recurrent sense of boredom and a recurrent desire to move on to a new job and a new relationship.

The therapist provided the following case formulation. The patient's ambivalence about both her relationship with her boyfriend and her career appeared to mirror an underlying struggle between obedience and defiance that was characteristic of her somewhat compulsive, conforming personality style. The patient described a pattern of parental overcontrol to which she adapted for the most part by compliant, good behavior. This adaptation, however, took its toll when in adolescence her own internalized restrictions in combination with those imposed by her parents served to inhibit and restrain her strivings to achieve a sense of autonomy and self-competence.

The patient felt liberated and excited about her life at college. Unfortunately, during college and throughout her adult life, her most intensive efforts to break free of the restrictions she had internalized have ultimately led to disappointment or loss. In the wake of these efforts she has attempted to compromise in recent years by choosing a "risk averse" profession and staying involved in a rela-

FIGURE 4.6

Shorter-Term Failure

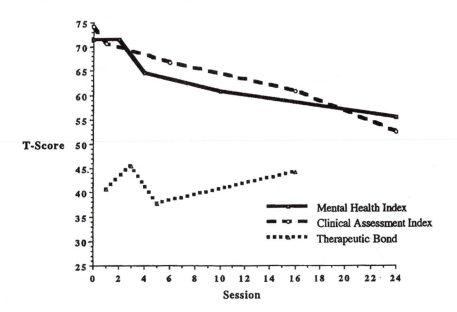

tionship that is "comfortable" but often frustrating and unfulfilling. These choices ultimately proved to be unsatisfactory and have resulted in considerable ambivalence about her direction in life, as well as in a sense of being somewhat ungrounded.

At discharge, the therapist stated that the patient ". . . responded well to psychodynamic, insight-oriented therapy which focused on understanding her current ambivalence and sense of unfulfillment in terms of the adaptations she had made during childhood and adolescence." The therapist stated that the patient chose to discontinue therapy (after 24 sessions) because she could see another therapist free of charge in another setting under her company's insurance program.

Figure 4.6 shows the course of therapy for this patient. As can be seen, the therapeutic bond was somewhat unstable and very weak. From the perspectives of both the therapist (Clinical Assessment Index) and the patient (Mental Health Index), the patient's condition worsened over treatment.

However, at the time of discharge, the therapist reported that the patient had achieved substantial clarification of the nature of her dissatisfactions. The therapist reported that the patient made progress in dealing with surface problems but that, at a deeper level, she was likely to experience angry, defiant urges to assert herself and break free of the restrictions she has imposed upon herself. The therapist rated the patient as "moderately improved," "slightly distressed," and getting along "fairly well; has her ups and downs."

A Longer-Term Success

This patient was a middle-aged, divorced male. He was employed full time in a professional capacity. The patient had two children, none at home. He was socially active, particularly with male friends.

The patient presented for therapy with the dominant complaints of depression, loneliness, and a general disappointment about the course of his life. He wanted a better understanding of himself and an opportunity to learn new coping strategies to meet life stressors.

The patient reported that his parents had always been emotionally distant. He characterized his father as having a bad temper and his mother as critical and unaffectionate. He believed that he was the least favored of his siblings. He described himself as a rebellious adolescent and felt that he never received positive attention from his family.

The patient was experiencing several symptoms of depression, such as feelings of hopelessness and overeating. He was emotionally constricted (except when drinking alcohol), had difficulty maintaining long-term relationships, had abused alcohol over an extended period of time, and had a history of sporadic abuse of marijuana and other illicit drugs. His clinical intake diagnoses were Dysthymia; Alcohol Dependence, in partial remission; Cannabis Abuse; Nicotine Dependence. His diagnoses based on the Structured Clinical Interview for DSM-III-R (SCID: Spitzer et al., 1988) was Major Depression.

The therapist was a young, married female. She was a third-year graduate student in clinical psychology participating in a practicum experience. Her therapeutic orientation was psychodynamic with an

FIGURE 4.7

Longer-Term Success

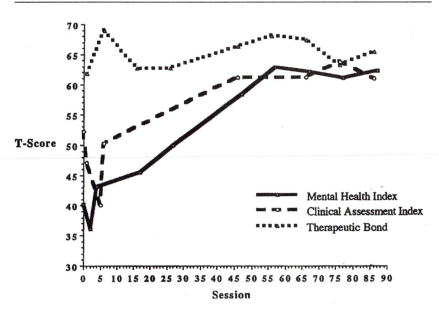

emphasis on the "here-and-now" interaction and the utilization of transference interpretations. She had only seen 6 to 10 patients in individual psychotherapy.

Figure 4.7 shows the course of therapy for this patient. As can be seen, the therapeutic bond was reasonably stable and was maintained at a very high level. From the perspective of both the therapist (Clinical Assessment Index) and the patient (Mental Health Index), the patient initially responded to treatment with a decrease in functioning. Following this initial decrease, the patient made steady progress and was seen as functioning in the normal range (a T-score of above 60) by session 60.

This course of therapy at the clinic was terminated after 135 sessions because the therapist was leaving to begin a predoctoral internship. At discharge, the therapist rated the patient as "moderately improved," "slightly distressed," and getting along "quite well; has no important complaints." However, the patient continued in treatment with the same therapist at the new location.

A Longer-Term Failure

This patient was a single female in her late twenties and employed in a managerial position. She had a history of unsatisfying relationships with peers, both male and female, and, she had never had an intimate relationship with anyone. She was reasonably successful in her vocation. However, the patient reported that she never developed avenues for enjoyment—no hobbies or recreational activities.

She grew up in a home with alcoholic parents. During her childhood, the patient was sexually abused by her father for several years. As an adult, the patient continued to be hypervigilant for abuse in interpersonal relationships in a way that rendered her unable to approach others to help satisfy emotional needs. She experienced high levels of interpersonal tension and, consequently, extreme distress—anxiety, sadness, anger, and frustration.

The patient had recently suffered a life-threatening injury. She was simultaneously mourning the recent death of her father, which followed a prolonged illness, and working through her anger at him for his abuse of her. The patient was engaged in multiple heterosexual relationships that were conflictual in nature. She was drinking alcohol to an abusive extent and had a tendency to overeat in a pattern of bingeing. Though she viewed her alcohol consumption as problematic, she drank to excess every day.

The patient reported crying easily, experienced mood swings, and generally felt "stressed out." She was consistently unhappy and had a tendency to act out in self-destructive ways (i.e., with alcohol, in relationships, and with binge eating). Her intake diagnoses were Borderline Personality Disorder; Posttraumatic Stress Disorder; Adjustment Disorder with atypical features; Alcohol Dependency; Nicotine Dependency; Asthma and Allergies. She did not meet criteria for any Axis I SCID diagnosis, but the clinical interviewer rated her very high on Borderline Personality Disorder (Axis II) characteristics.

The therapist was a young, single female. She was an advanced graduate student in clinical psychology participating in a clinical practicum experience. Her therapeutic orientation was psychodynamic with an emphasis on object relations. She had previously seen 11 to 20 patients in individual psychotherapy.

FIGURE 4.8

Longer-Term Failure

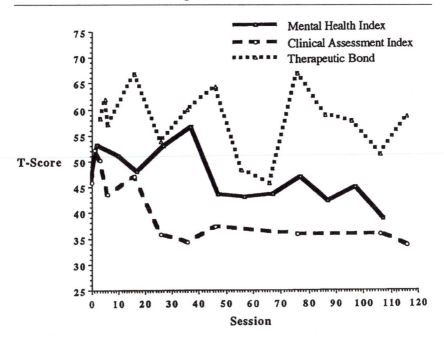

Figure 4.8 shows the course of therapy for this patient. As can be seen, the therapeutic bond was very unstable, illustrating a border-line relational style. From the perspective of both the therapist (Clinical Assessment Index) and the patient (Mental Health Index), the patient showed a steady decline in functioning over the course of this treatment.

The therapist characterized the first year of treatment (one session a week) as ". . . supportive with some interpretive work accomplished" and the second year (two sessions a week) as ". . . marked by much progress and movement toward insight." During this treatment episode, the patient missed 31 scheduled appointments and made considerable use of the clinic's crisis hotline. This course of therapy at the clinic was terminated after 121 sessions because the therapist was leaving to begin a predoctoral internship. At discharge, the therapist rated the patient as "moderately improved," "extremely distressed," and getting along "quite poorly; can barely manage to deal with things." The patient continued in treatment with the same therapist at the new location.

USEFUL INFORMATION TO THE PROVIDER OR UTILIZATION REVIEWER

The tracking information could have been useful to the therapists and utilization reviewers in the cases just described in several ways. Answers to the following questions would have provided some guidance.

Has an effective therapeutic alliance been established? Both of the successful therapies involved a stable therapeutic bond that was maintained at a slightly higher than average level. Conversely, the two treatment failures involved therapeutic bonds that were erratic or lower than average. The level and stability of the therapeutic bond within the first half-dozen sessions appear to be predictive of later development, given the same conditions of therapist, patient, and therapeutic approach. Objective information about the quality of the therapeutic alliance lends evidence that the therapy process is on the right track, or that the therapist–patient match is not yet working and is in need of adjustment, or that the therapist is incapable of establishing an effective working relationship with this particular patient at this particular time. At any rate, continuation of an erratic or poor therapeutic relationship bodes ill for the outcome of the treatment.

Has the patient shown a stable pattern of remoralization in the early course of treatment? Improvement in subjective well-being reflects a recovery of the capacity to mobilize one's coping strategies and to potentiate an alleviation of symptoms. Psychotherapy is an interactive process requiring energy, focus, and commitment from the patient and a workable frame (reframe) of the key therapeutic issues of change on the part of the therapist. Among the three components of the phase model, subjective well-being is the most immediate response to an effective therapy and thus may have the strongest causal linkage to the treatment.

Following remoralization, has the patient shown alleviation in symptoms? Treatment outcomes studies of specific disorders, for example, depression, frequently use an improvement criteria of consistent absence of key symptoms for a specific period of time. Our research has shown that the symptoms of specific diagnostic categories are not uniform in their response to treatment (e.g., Kopta, Howard, Lowry, & Beutler, 1994). The effective dose for depression symptoms ranged from 3 sessions for "cries too easily" to 25 sessions for "sleep disturbances." Therapists are likely to mark improvement of specific symptoms both generally and specifically: "Is the patient improving in symptomatic distress?" and "Is the patient better able to concentrate at work"? According to the phase model, general symptomatic improvement is a prerequisite for subsequent improvement in life functioning.

Are the patient's dysfunctional areas being addressed? Conversely, are the patient's functional areas respected? The short-term failure case is an excellent example of misreading the functional status of a patient. The therapist linked the patient's work and intimacy functioning as a common failure to make commitments that had origins in earlier family experiences. The patient showed little distress before therapy began, but lost confidence in her self-appraisal as the therapist hammered out his (the therapist's) noncommitment theme. The patient of the longer-term success case presented with work, family, and friends intact. His main dysfunction was not being the kind of person he wished to be. The short-term success case patient was dysfunctional in acts of appropriate assertiveness at intake. This dysfunction responded positively in a relatively short therapy. The long-term failure case presented with some functional and some dysfunctional areas. Although employed as a manager, she was dissatisfied with her friendships, had not established effective intimate relationships, and had few satisfying leisure activities. This dysfunction was deeply rooted in traumatic childhood experiences that had not been mediated by more healthy subsequent experiences. In all of these cases, tracking would have confirmed progress or indicated the need for some change in treatment.

MEDICAL NECESSITY

Our more recent work, based on samples collected from managed care case loads, has focused on sharpening the usefulness of the tracking system. The approach we have taken to medical necessity (i.e., whether treatment is indicated) is to determine whether a patient's score is more likely to belong to the distribution of patient or nonpatient scores. When such score distributions of patients and non-patients are available, Jacobson and Truax (1991; modified by Speer, 1992) have provided a system for assessing whether a score is more likely to represent a patient or a "normal" person—that is, whether the score is in the normal range. Assuming homogeneity of variance and normal distributions, they state this criterion as follows: "(c) The level of functioning subsequent to therapy places that client closer to the mean of the functional population than it does to the mean of the dysfunctional population" (p.13). In the event that variances of functional and dysfunctional populations are unequal, Jacobson & Truax present an alternative method for calculating (c). Whether variances are equal or not, Jacobson & Truax's method is functionally the same as fitting two normal frequency functions to patient and nonpatient data, respectively, and estimating that point at which a score is more likely to have been sampled from the nonpatient population than from the patient population. Using this system, we have determined that an MHI T-score below 60 represents a need for treatment—represents "medical necessity."

PATIENT PROFILING
AND THE DETERMINATION OF PROGRESS

As we have emphasized, the success of psychotherapy with the individual patient is of paramount interest to consumers, therapists, and purchasers. Likewise, the designation of "success" or "failure" after the therapy has ended is useful for audits of system effectiveness or therapist efficacy. But the most useful information concerns the progress of the individual patient assessed during the course of treatment. Is the patient "on track" for a successful outcome? Has the therapy yet achieved success in the outcomes area most important to the patient? to the therapist? to the purchaser? to the significant other?

Given a measure (the Mental Health Index: MHI) and a criterion for initiating or terminating treatment (e.g., exceeding the medical necessity criterion: a T-score of 60), it is relatively straightforward to plot the course of treatment for a patient. This simply entails periodic assessments during treatment (as in the preceding cases). But every patient does not have the same expected outcome or expected course of treatment. In order to accommodate this individuality, it is necessary to estimate an expected course of recovery for patients based on their initial clinical characteristics.

We use 18 such characteristics taken from the COMPASS™ outpatient form (Howard, Brill, Lueger, & O'Mahoney, 1995):

1. Importance of receiving psychotherapy;
2. Confidence in psychotherapy;
3. Amount of previous psychotherapy;
4. Chronicity of problem;
5. How well the patient was getting along emotionally and psychologically at time of making an appointment;
6. How upset or distressed patient was at time of making appointment;
7. Therapist rating of patient well-being;
8. Therapist rating—Global Assessment Scale;
9. Therapist rating of six Level of Functioning scales;
10. Patient Subjective well-being initial score;
11. Patient Current Symptoms initial total score;
12. Patient Current Life Functioning initial total score;
13. Patient Presenting Problem: Family functioning;
14. Patient Presenting Problem: Health and grooming;
15 Patient Presenting Problem: Intimate relationships;
16. Patient Presenting Problem: Self-management;
17. Patient Presenting Problem: Social relationships;
18. Patient Presenting Problem: Work, school, or household.

In accordance with the dosage model, each patient's Mental Health Index is modeled as a log-linear function of session number. For each patient, two parameters are estimated: intercept and slope. The intercept represents each patient's expected MHI at the first session. The slope represents the expected change in MHI per log of the session number. After obtaining estimates of intercept and slope at this first level, it is possible to search for predictors of these parameters by constructing second- level models (level 2) in which level 1 estimates of intercepts or slopes are dependent variables. Hierarchical linear modeling (HLM) is particularly appropriate for this task. After obtaining intercept and slope estimates at this first level, two second level models were constructed in which level 1 intercepts or slopes were dependent variables. Variation in level 1 intercepts and slopes was modeled as a linear function of the 18 initial status measures. For any patient, this fixed effect model was used to generate an expected MHI status at any session.

The random effect estimates are used to describe residual deviations away from predicted values based on intake characteristics. These residual deviations are a function of session number. Since residual deviations were plausibly normally distributed, this variance–covariance matrix may be used to generate a failure found below the expected values for any session for any patient.

Expected T-score values are converted to percentile ranks based on session 1 norms. For evaluating treatment progress in terms of the deviation between observed and expected MHI scores (e.g., 25th percentile failure bound), any observed T-score after session 1 also is converted into a percentile scale.

All of this allows us to draw a graph of the expected response of a patient (based on clinical characteristics at the initiation of treatment) that depicts the expected course of response for that patient during treatment. We can then plot actual assessments for a patient on the same graph in order to evaluate the extent to which the patient is making adequate progress.

SOME CASE EXAMPLES

Figure 4.9 depicts the course of therapy for a patient (A) who was a 39-year-old, employed, married, woman. Her clinical diagnosis was Adjustment Disorder. She sought treatment because the stress of a physically abusive relationship was causing sleeping and eating problems that resulted in missing work. Although this patient began therapy with relatively severe problems, her clinical profile generated the prediction that therapy would be effective over the long run. The therapist assisted the patient in obtaining safer housing and legal protection and provided encouragement and support that resulted in the patient progressing very much better than expected.

Figure 4.10 depicts a patient (B) who began therapy in the average patient range (56th percentile). This patient was a 36-year-old, employed, married man diagnosed with an Adjustment Disorder. He

FIGURE 4.9

Patient A

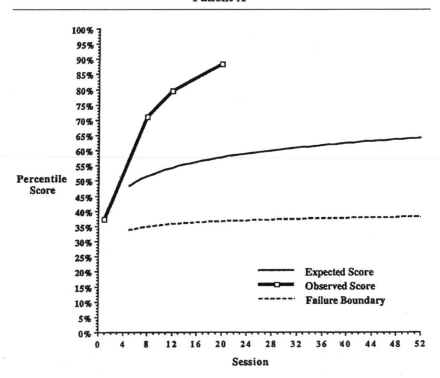

sought treatment for a "marital relationship problem" with attendant job problems. His wife also had significant psychological disorders. His clinical characteristics indicated that therapy would be at best moderately effective. But even these modest goals were not achieved and the patient spent almost a year in an unproductive treatment. Throughout treatment, he refused to follow recommendations that he be evaluated for a trial of psychoactive medication.

The patient (C) shown in Figure 4.11 was a 52-year-old, employed, married woman. She presented with significant family problems and was diagnosed with an Adjustment Disorder. This patient began therapy in the moderate range of severity, but profited nicely (and as expected) from a year of treatment. The dip in her mental health status around session 20 was due to the stress of the sudden death of her mother.

FIGURE 4.10
Patient B

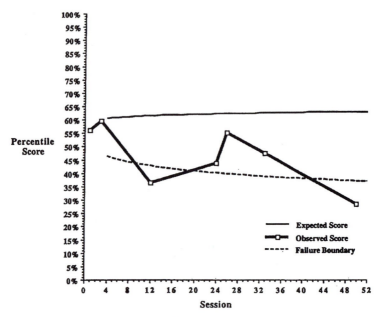

FIGURE 4.11
Patient C

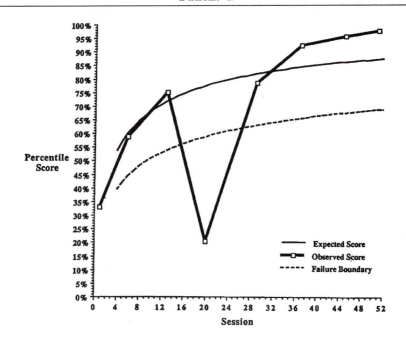

100

PROVIDER PROFILING AND TREATMENT SYSTEM OUTCOME ASSESSMENT

The MHI provides important capabilities for managing individual patient outcomes, profiling of provider performance, and assessing outcomes for treatment. In the previous section we presented a system for managing individual patient outcomes. Briefly, this is achieved by comparing a patient's progress as measured by the MHI against benchmarks concurrently with treatment. It is possible to identify those who no longer have a medical necessity for treatment—i.e., those whose MHI scores have reached the normal range. It is also possible to identify cases that are failing to respond to treatment (e.g., declining MHI scores) and change the treatment strategy to deflect a deteriorating course.

Provider Profiling

The ability to objectively evaluate ("profile") the performance of therapists is a powerful tool for outcomes management. Knowledge of each provider's level of effectiveness for different kinds of patients makes possible better treatment at lower cost. Differential referral of patients to therapists who have achieved unusually favorable outcomes with similar types of patients can result in substantial improvement in the cost-effectiveness of treatment.

Table 4.3 shows the difference in cost associated with treating patients of varying initial severity (i.e., initial MHI scores) by therapists whose patients improve at different rates. The costs assume a per session fee of $80. Table 4.3 indicates that a patient who enters treatment with an MHI of 50 (a typical level of severity) and experiences a rate of improvement of .5 MHI units per session will reach the normal range after 66 sessions at a cost of $5,280. In contrast, if the same patient were referred to a therapist who could help him or her improve at a rate of 4 MHI units per session, the patient would accomplish the same result after 8 sessions at a cost of only $640. The effect is seen most clearly by contrasting the cost-effectiveness of providers who vary widely in terms of their patients' rate of improvement for patients presenting with a low MHI score. For a patient with an initial MHI of 10, the cost savings achieved by referral to a provider whose patients improve at a rate of 6 MHI units per session versus a provider who achieves only .5 MHI units per ses-

TABLE 4.3

Cost of Reaching a Normal MHI Range

MHI CHANGE PER SESSION

INITIAL MHI	0.50	2.00	4.00	6.00
70	$2,080	$520	$260	$173
50	$5,280	$1,320	$660	$440
30	$8,480	$2,120	$1,060	$707
10	$11,680	$2,920	$1,460	$973

Note: Based on normal MHI=83 and cost per session=$80.
Calculation: (Normal MHI – Initial MHI) / MHI Change Per Session × $80

sion is $10,707 ($11,680 – $973). The ability to match patients to efficient therapists is critical to cost-effective treatment and outcomes management.

This type of cost analysis highlights the need for "case mix adjustment" in evaluating provider performance. However, it may be that a provider's patients improve at a rapid (slow) rate because they are "easier" (more difficult) to treat than most other patients. Since there are differences among patients, and since some of these differences are related to outcomes, unadjusted comparison of outcomes data is inappropriate and may yield very misleading results. If patients in a particular program show little improvement, it may be because the program is ineffective, or the lack of improvement may be due to characteristics (e.g., severity of disorders, lack of motivation) that make the patients in that program unusually difficult to treat relative to patients in other programs.

This problem can be easily illustrated by comparing the effectiveness of two hypothetical programs. A direct comparison of outcomes data indicates that more improvement is achieved by patients in program A than by those in program B. However, analysis of patient characteristics reveals that, relative to program B, patients in program A are more likely to be highly motivated, diagnosed for minor depression or adjustment disorder, married; employed; and function well in their jobs. Some of these differences suggest that the greater success of program A may be due in part, and perhaps entirely, to the fact that program A has "easier" patients. That is, patients in program A often have characteristics that would promote rapid improvement independently of program quality.

A meaningful comparison between these two programs requires that the differences in outcomes be adjusted to take into consideration ("control for") differences in their patient populations, or "case mix." Some of the differences may be unrelated to outcomes and can safely be ignored. Others are highly likely to effect outcomes and must be addressed.

What are the requirements for case mix adjustment, and how can data be analyzed so that comparisons are valid and meaningful? First, since it is not possible to adjust for a characteristic that is not measured, effective case mix adjustment requires that the assessment system include any patient variables that have an important effect upon outcomes. For example, a system that does not assess a patient's treatment motivation will be limited by its inability to take this important factor into account. Second, it is essential that the measurement system include a robust outcomes variable that accurately reflects patient change during treatment. Third, since it would be very risky to make a priori assumptions about which patient characteristics may effect outcomes, all reasonably plausible patient variables (characteristics) should be tested for their statistical relationship to the outcomes variable; this allows for the identification of a broad range of characteristics that may impact outcomes.

These are the characteristics that "make a difference," that should be "controlled for" by the case mix adjustment procedure. However, this pool of variables may include characteristics that, in combination with others, make little or no independent contribution to outcomes and can be safely excluded from the analysis. A fourth step is necessary to derive the optimal weighting and combination of the patient variable that is most strongly associated with outcomes; this can be achieved by a statistical procedure known as multiple regression.

The COMPASS system includes a very broad range of patient characteristics believed by researchers and clinicians to be associated with outcomes: motivation, expectations, symptom severity, level of functioning, and many others. Availability of these data for thousands of cases enable us to take all of these factors into consideration when comparing outcomes involving different patient populations. The COMPASS Mental Health Index is exceptionally well suited to serve as a unitary measure of patients' mental health status. "Outcomes" is operationally defined as the change in the patient's MHI score over the course of treatment. As suggested above, COMPASS data have been analyzed to identify all characteristics that are statistically associated with outcomes. Then, through multiple regression, a "weighted" formula has been derived that provides the best possible prediction of a patient's outcomes that can be made based on the patient's characteristics and the treatment experience (outcomes) of thousands of patients. These calculations adjusted for case mix indicate, for every case, the degree of patient improvement that would be expected after adjustment for dosage of treatment (log of the number of sessions), initial severity (MHI score at intake), and the patient characteristics that have been shown to affect outcomes. Outcomes data for programs (or providers) can then be adjusted by computing, for each patient, the difference between the expected and actual outcomes and aggregating these difference scores across all patients treated by the program (provider). Mean difference scores can be usefully and validly compared to reach conclusions about program (provider) performance that equate any differences in patient characteristics across programs.

The COMPASS system of provider profiling and program outcomes comparisons represents a significant advance in mental health systems research. The availability of a psychometrically strong, unitary outcomes measure and the patient data necessary to effective case mix adjustment, has created the "level field" necessary for valid profiling and performance assessment. These profiling systems represent a major advance for continuous quality improvement at the provider, program, and treatment system levels; for differential referral of patients to programs and providers who are most likely to be helpful; and for valid cost-effectiveness analyses that control for case difficulty.

Tables 4.4 and 4.5 illustrate the usefulness of case mix adjustment to provider profiling. Each table presents hypothetical performance data for a provider over a six-month period. Shown are the diagnostic groupings; number of patients treated in each grouping; average improvement per session (in MHI units); the expected average improvement based upon case mix adjustment analyses; the corrected average improvement and its associated percentile score.

The corrected score includes an adjustment of the rate actually achieved (average improvement per session) to correct for patient characteristics; it provides for valid comparison among therapists.

For example, consider the performance of providers Jones and Smith, presented in Tables 4.4 and 4.5 respectively. Patients of each provider improved at an average rate of 2.7 MHI units per session. Based upon these uncorrected data, it would appear that the two providers are equally effective. However, review of the improvement rates corrected for case mix leads to a very different conclusion. Provider Jones, whose patients were unusually difficult, achieved a higher average improvement per session than expected in every diagnostic group (e.g., 2.9 versus 2.5 for Mood Disorders). Table 4.4 shows that Jones' corrected improvement per session is 3.0 for all cases combined, placing Jones in the 73rd percentile of all therapists in the network. In contrast, Smith's patients improved at a rate slightly below expectation in each grouping. Smith's corrected average improvement per session across all cases was 2.5 MHI units per session, placing Smith in the 42nd percentile. Case mix adjustment reveals a significant difference in the performance of Jones and Smith not apparent in the raw (unadjusted) data.

The importance of case mix adjustment is seen even more clearly in comparing the effectiveness of Smith and Jones in treating anxiety disorders. Smith's patients achieve 2.8 units of improvement per session, while Jones' patients achieve only 2.5. The unadjusted data suggest that Smith is the more effective provider. However, case mix adjustment indicates that the expected rates of improvement for the two sets of patients were 3.0 and 1.9 respectively. Jones' "corrected" performance for patients with anxiety disorders was 3.0 versus 2.2 for Smith; placing Jones in the 91st percentile of all providers, with Smith far below (39th percentile).

TABLE 4.4

Severity Adjustment

COMPASS
INFORMATION
SERVICES, INC

Provider Profile Report

January 1996 through June 1996

Provider: Jones

Diagnostic Group	Number of Cases	Avg. Imp. Per Session (Unadjusted)	Expected Avg. Imp. (Case-Mix Adjusted)	Corrected Avg. Imp. Per Session	Performance Percentile
Mood	35	2.9	2.5	3.2	86%
Anxiety	20	2.5	1.9	3.0	91%
Adjustment	46	3.1	2.9	3.3	62%
Other	18	1.7	1.6	2.0	54%
All Cases	119	2.7	2.4	3.0	73%

TABLE 4.5

Severity Adjustment

COMPASS
INFORMATION
SERVICES, INC

Provider Profile Report

January 1996 through June 1996

Provider: Smith

Diagnostic Group	Number of Cases	Avg. Imp. Per Session (Unadjusted)	Expected Avg. Imp. (Case-Mix Adjusted)	Corrected Avg. Imp. Per Session	Performance Percentile
Mood	20	2.7	2.9	2.6	41%
Anxiety	10	2.8	3.0	2.2	39%
Adjustment	30	3.0	3.1	3.0	47%
Other	13	2.0	2.3	1.6	37%
All Cases	73	2.7	2.9	2.5	42%

TABLE 4.6

MHI Trend Analysis Report

**COMPASS
INFORMATION
SERVICES, INC**

SYSTEM-WIDE VIEW
October 1, 1995 through December 31, 1995

Percentages.

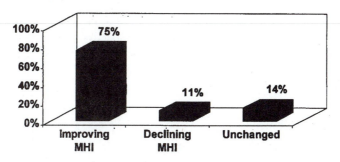

Treatment Systems Outcomes Assessment

Treatment systems often wish to compare outcomes across sites, and providers within each site. Tables 4.6, 4.7, and 4.8 illustrate the use of MHI trend data for such purposes.

When data are collected on two or more occasions within the same treatment episode, it becomes possible to compare the most recent MHI score with the initial score to assess improvement. A recent MHI that is higher than the initial score indicates improvement; alternatively, the trend may be declining (i.e., initial MHI is the higher of the two) or unchanged.

Table 4.6 presents "MHI Trend" data for all sites of a treatment system combined. It shows that, of patients treated in the final quarter of 1995 for whom data were collected at intake and at least one subsequent session, 75% had improved, 11% had declined, and 14% had experienced no change in their MHI scores. Table 4.7 provides a breakdown of these data across seven sites within the treatment system. It indicates that sites #10003 and #10007 achieved relatively

TABLE 4.7

MHI Trend Analysis Report

COMPASS INFORMATION SERVICES, INC

SITE VIEW					
October 1, 1995 through December 31, 1995					

Site	Total Patients	% of Multiple Admin. with Improving MHI Trend	% of Multiple Admin. with Declining MHI Trend	% of Multiple Admin. with Unchanged MHI Trend	System-Wide Norms
SITE #10001	80	75%	13%	12%	**Improved** 75%
SITE #10002	97	85%	10%	5%	
SITE #10003	55	57%	29%	14%	**Declined** 11%
SITE #10004	63	79%	11%	10%	
SITE #10005	90	70%	15%	15%	
SITE #10006	45	89%	5%	6%	**Unchanged** 14%
SITE #10007	60	57%	14%	29%	

TABLE 4.8

MHI Trend Analysis Report

COMPASS INFORMATION SERVICES, INC

PROVIDER VIEW						
SITE #10001						
October 1, 1995 through December 31, 1995						

Provider ID	(Last)	(First)	Total Patients	% of Multiple Admin. With Improving MHI Trend	% of Multiple Admin. With Declining MHI Trend	% of Multiple Admin. With Unchanged MHI Trend
666-00-1234	Light	Douglas	16	70	10	20
666-00-5678	Brill	Chester	17	82	12	6
666-00-1259	Adams	Nancy	15	75	13	12
666-00-3456	Clemens	Jane	19	91	0	9
666-00-9876	Black	Harold	13	76	7	17

Total Patients: 80

Site #10001 Norms	Improved 75%	Declined 13%	Unchanged 12%

poor patient improvement (57%), while #10002 and #10006 were top performers.

Table 4.8 provides a further breakdown by provider, for the 80 patients treated at site #10001. It indicates that Jane Clemens (91% of whose patients experienced improvement) was a star performer within a site that, as a whole, yielded average results (75% improvement).

Similar System/Site/Provider-level reports can be developed for a variety of indices, including the "case mix adjusted improvement per session" data presented above for provider profiling. These reports suggest the value and utility of rigorous outcomes assessment for continuous quality improvement, establishment of performance standards and benchmarks, documentation of program quality, identification of top performers whose expertise can be tapped for system-wide training and improvement, and targeting of weaker performers who may be in need of additional training or supervision.

In short, such data make possible, for the first time, a valid and practical approach to continuous quality improvement of mental health treatment. Other predictive factors that are currently being investigated should add even more predictive power to the treatment process.

CONCLUDING NOTE

Using clinical information, we have developed a method for modeling the expected course of progress for an individual patient. This information can be used to determine the need for further treatment and the appropriateness (i.e., effectiveness) of the current treatment. This determination, in turn, can be used to review cases that have achieved their therapeutic goals in order to evaluate the possibility of discontinuing treatment. It can also be used to identify patients who are not likely to benefit from outpatient psychotherapy and to prompt a clinical consultation for patients who are continuing to suffer in an unproductive treatment. Finally, we have a method for providing systematic feedback about the status of a patient in treatment, feedback that can guide treatment decisions.

5

Level of Care and Inpatient Treatment Outcomes

Among the major changes in mental health treatment in recent years, one of the most far-reaching in its impact is the development of multiple levels of care intermediary between inpatient hospitalization and traditional outpatient treatment. Partial hospital programs, 23-hour beds, in-home services, assertive community treatment, and intensive outpatient programs are some of the options, featuring varying degrees of treatment intensity, that have filled this gap.

This range of alternatives presents new challenges for clinicians and program administrators. Particularly vexing are level-of-care decisions and the problem of patient monitoring. If the goal is to provide safe, effective treatment at the least intensive and costly appropriate level of care, how should decisions regarding admission or discharge be made? What standardized, relevant information is available to support such decisions?

The need to monitor patients across settings and programs of varying intensity suggests the desirability of an index, or score, that can be consistently interpreted across all levels of care. Such an index

The author is pleased to acknowledge the assistance of Laura Dietzen and Heather Duncan, members of the COMPASS INT development team, for their assistance in preparing this chapter.

would provide "seamless" measurement—the ability to monitor patient progress within and across all levels of care.

This chapter describes the development of an instrument, COMPASS INT (INT = intensive), designed by the authors to provide level-of-care decision support and seamless measurement across the entire continuum of behavioral health care.

THE IMPACT OF MANAGED CARE UPON MEASUREMENT IN INTENSIVE TREATMENT SETTINGS

The radical change of the past decade in the field of mental health treatment is nowhere more evident than in U.S. psychiatric hospitals. Inpatient treatment, the most expensive component of mental health services, was an early target of managed care cost containment efforts. Reduction in the length of hospital stays and increased use of intermediate levels of care were major contributors to the early success of managed care in obtaining dramatic savings for insurers and other third-party payers.

The oversight of managed care companies has led to pronounced changes in intensive psychiatric treatment. Relative to the 1980s, there are now fewer inpatient psychiatric admissions as well as sharp reductions in the average length of stay. Treatment is less oriented toward psychotherapy and more goal directed. The treating psychiatrist's role in decision making has been supplanted in part by that of the psychiatric team acting in conjunction with a reviewing agency. Loading dose medication strategies are used to produce rapid change. Psychodynamic treatments intended to remove symptoms or produce character change have given way to therapy designed for crisis resolution and medication compliance, intended to reduce risk and prepare patients for less intensive treatment environments. A continuum of new types of care intermediate between traditional inpatient and outpatient treatment have been developed to ensure that care is provided in the least costly, safest environment. These changes have been accompanied by an escalation of financial pressures familiar to every staff member of an inpatient unit. Virtually every facility in the nation has been affected, many have sharply reduced or altered their services—or closed.

The dimension of this trend most relevant to the measurement/ management of outcomes is its strong emphasis upon accountability. A central focus of managed care at all levels of treatment, the requirement to document treatment effectiveness and justify requests for continued care, is most strict for inpatient and partial hospital services. Both the clinical and economic consequences are most significant in these settings.

For example, inpatient providers must now be prepared to respond convincingly to questions that were rarely asked as recently as 5 or 10 years ago: How cost effective are your services? Why do you believe this patient should be admitted to the hospital? What are the specific goals of treatment? How will you determine whether the goals have been achieved? How long do you expect that inpatient care will be necessary? (The preferred answer is in days, not weeks.) Why do you believe that this patient should not be discharged?

It is not only the nature of the questions that has changed. Increasingly, case managers are unwilling to accept "clinical judgment" as the sole basis for the response. There is an expectation that similar types of patients having similar clinical problems will also require approximately the same length of hospitalization. In short, normative data will become increasingly vital.

Diagnostic Related Group (DRG) standards now familiar to general medical practitioners play a lesser role in mental health decision making only because clinical psychiatric diagnoses (unlike those achieved in research settings using structured interview techniques) are less reliable and have fewer treatment implications. But the basic principle is the same: There is a normative length of stay determined by patient characteristics and conditions. Deviations from a case manager's experience with similar patients must be clearly justified if a provider requests approval for unusually lengthy or expensive care. In some form, the question, "What are the data?" quickly becomes central.

To summarize: Standardized measurement in support of clinical decision making was minimal or unknown to intensive psychiatric care until quite recently. Its role is evolving rapidly. Sophisticated measurement systems will be developed to support clinical decision making and document the cost-effectiveness of treatment services. We turn now to a consideration of the requirements for effective measurement systems in intensive mental health treatment settings, and the purposes such systems will serve.

REQUIREMENTS FOR EFFECTIVE MEASUREMENT SYSTEMS: A CULTURE OF MEASUREMENT

There are two important requirements for effective measurement of inpatient treatment. A clinically appropriate, administratively efficient, and scientifically sound process for the collection, storage, analysis, and reporting of outcomes data is the first, and most obvious, requirement. The second requirement is the establishment of a "culture of measurement" within the facility. Staff must value measurement as an important factor in the organization's success, as well as a powerful clinical tool that, properly used, can substantially improve patient care. It is the responsibility of management to communicate its full support for the establishment of sound measurement systems, educate staff as to the role and importance of measurement to success in a managed care environment, and help personnel at all levels to authentically embrace measurement as contributing to improvement in the performance of both the facility and of individual clinicians.

When measurement is seen as important to personal and organizational success, a well-designed system can meaningfully contribute to (1) "marketing" initiatives, (2) continuous quality improvement in clinical care, (3) greater effectiveness of individual staff, and (4) substantial improvement in the cost-effectiveness of operations. Where measurement is seen as a burdensome requirement unrelated to legitimate personal or organizational goals, the best designed system will produce expense and employee grumbling, but little else.

MEASUREMENT OBJECTIVES

It is probable that measurement technology, as it advances, will come to serve three major goals: documentation of the quality/cost-effectiveness of care; improvement of clinical system performance; and decision support for treatment planning at the individual patient level.

System-Level Objectives

Documentation and improvement of treatment system performance involve similar measurement techniques. These objectives are distinct primarily in that the purposes of the former is to support marketing efforts, while enhanced cost-effectiveness of care is the objective of the latter.

Currently, competition among hospitals is fierce in many areas of the nation. Marketing has taken on a new urgency as psychiatric systems, hospitals, and units struggle to survive. Patient testimonials and documentation of the qualifications of clinical staff may carry some weight with individuals seeking treatment, but it is the major third-party payers to whom a convincing appeal must be made if treatment facilities are to weather the managed care storm. And they're all from Missouri, you have to show them. Thus, most systems want to derive marketing value from outcomes data. For many, objective documentation of the quality and cost-effectiveness of care is the primary (or sole) measurement objective.

Many facilities have extended their measurement goals to the enhancement of overall system performance. Standardized measurement provides for the possibility of meaningful comparisons and establishment of norms. System performance can be improved by determining which treatment methods are most efficacious for different types of patients; by identifying treatment units and staff who are unusually effective and learning from them; by identifying and addressing staff weaknesses. Quality and cost-effectiveness of care improve when:

- Better treatment strategies are devised;
- Strengths of exemplary treatment units or individual staff are made available system-wide;
- Staff weaknesses are addressed through training or—in the case of incompetent or unmotivated individuals—dismissal;
- Staff performance replaces longevity/"connections"/ credentials as the primary basis for advancement.

Most of the measurement strategies embraced by mental health treatment systems in recent years support system-level objectives: Utilization review, continuous quality improvement (CQI), and outcomes management systems all aim at the documentation and improvement of system performance.

Utilization review. Refers to the monitoring of utilization (e.g., admission) decisions for clinical appropriateness, for the purpose of improving the cost-effectiveness of system resource allocation. The focus is normally upon the "medical necessity" guidelines for the use of the most costly system resources: Which types of patients require hospitalization for a mental health diagnosis? What are the patient characteristics that should lead to referral to a residential freestanding substance abuse treatment facility? The goal of utilization review is to ensure that these decisions are consistent with established policies, and to suggest whether these policies may require modification.

Continuous quality improvement. Refers to the systematic analysis of service quality indicators for the purpose of optimizing service delivery programs and procedures. It involves an organizational philosophy and commitment to incremental improvement through objective, ongoing evaluation. Successful efforts often feature a staff norm of responsibility to identify programmatic weaknesses and actively participate in brainstorming, focused studies, experimentation with innovative techniques, and other activities designed to improve service. The monitoring of quality indicators (e.g. clinical outcomes, patient satisfaction) is a central CQI focus, as well as the regular review of data related to cost-effectiveness (e.g., length of stay, number and type of treatment services provided to various types of patients). These reviews are intended to suggest areas where further study to improve cost-effectiveness of care might be warranted.

The term *outcomes management* refers to the broadest class of activities designed to improve clinical performance. It suggests a proactive management approach to the use of outcomes information to improve treatment system performance, in contrast with "outcomes measurement," which refers to the documentation of outcomes for public relations or marketing purposes. Outcomes management requires collection of clinical data for a representative example of patients at both admission and discharge, and possibly at some point post-discharge. In addition, meaningful use of the clinical data requires collection and analysis of patient characteristics that may be predictive of clinical outcomes so as to allow for case mix adjusting and meaningful comparisons of clinical outcomes among providers and sites.

Measurement systems to achieve marketing objectives and systems enhancement will become increasingly sophisticated and effective during the next few years. The major technical challenge is the development of case mix adjustment ("severity adjustment") methodologies.

Patient-Level Objectives: Clinical Decision Support

The role that standardized measurement will play in support of clinical decision making for individual patients is less certain, but potentially of major significance. The trend toward briefer periods of hospitalization and modest clinical goals will not likely be reversed in the foreseeable future. Inpatient treatment consists largely of preparing the patient to function outside the hospital and participate effectively in outpatient care. Nonetheless, measurement will almost certainly come to play an important role with respect to admission, discharge, and discharge placement decisions; it will become the sine qua non for payment approval by managed care companies. It is likely that the monitoring of patient progress will become less subjective as measurement systems mature and appropriate normative data become available. Finally, it is possible that key treatment planning decisions (What type of medication, at what dosage, is optimal for this patient? Which combination of treatment services is most cost-effective for this individual at this point in his/her recovery?) will one day be informed by timely, relevant, and reliable standardized measures in combination with validated practice guidelines.

The major obstacles to the use of measurement for decision support—development of appropriate measures, efficient administration systems, timely scoring and reporting of data in a clinically meaningful context—have been overcome in the outpatient arena. Though inpatient settings present unique challenges, there are good reasons to expect that those obstacles will be overcome there as well.

These advances required careful attention to a wide range of measurement issues. They suggest a radical change to the way inpatient treatment is delivered and evaluated. These issues are addressed in the following section, and illustrated by the development of the COMPASS INT measurement system.

MEASUREMENT SYSTEM DESIGN ISSUES

The rate of advancement of any field depends as much upon "asking the right questions" as it does upon creative problem solving.

Most nonresearchers exploring outcomes assessment soon discover that asking the "right" questions about the development of a measuring system is less straightforward than they supposed.

There are two mind sets common among the practitioners and administrators who find themselves on their organization's version of an Outcomes System Development Task Force. The first is the view that, once an appropriate scale is selected, outcomes assessment requires little more than common sense. The problem is seen entirely in terms of instrument selection or development, a task considered difficult because it involves unfamiliar disciplines such as psychometrics.

Other individuals feel overwhelmed by measurement questions that seem foreign to them. In this view, outcomes assessment is an arcane practice whose methods are accessible only to a small, elite group of specialists.

Neither of these mindsets is accurate. Outcomes assessment systems that are administratively useful, clinically relevant, and operationally feasible can be established without recourse to an army of statisticians. However, it is necessary to be conscious of pitfalls that can undermine the usefulness of system data. Key measurement issues that must be addressed include:

- What to measure;

- Who (e.g., patients, staff) will provide the data;

- Psychometric properties (e.g., reliability, validity) of the measurement scales;

- Administrative procedures for data collection and their integration into clinical practice;

- Data handling and quality assurance;

- How data will be analyzed and interpreted;

- Clinical actionability—the conversion of data to information and information to knowledge.

It should be emphasized that these issues are secondary to the question of the measurement objectives. An assessment system appropriate to the documentation of outcomes will differ fundamentally from o..e that is intended to serve system enhancement or CQI objectives. And a system designed to provide clinical decision support will require even more rigor. The measurement issues listed above should be addressed only after decisions are made concerning system objectives—the types of questions the measurement system is intended to address.

Documentation of system outcomes is the most readily achievable objective. This is because documentation does not require that data be collected for all patients; it can be achieved through sampling. Therefore, since this type of outcomes assessment is often done on a "one shot" basis and not integrated into ongoing clinical practice, issues such as the length of the measures, time required for completion, and the efficiency of data collection procedures are less critical. It is feasible to obtain more data per patient, since only a subset of patients are involved and only for a limited period of time. The primary challenge is to design a sampling strategy that will yield a representative sample, and to employ a data analysis strategy that adjusts for sample attrition. The latter is never perfect (and will require the involvement of a statistician), but if done properly can yield a useful estimate of overall outcomes.

At the other end of the measurement spectrum is an outcomes system designed to support clinical decision making. This is at once the most powerful and demanding of the measurement options. Powerful, because a system appropriate to this purpose will also provide outcomes data for CQI and documentation purposes. Demanding, because clinical decision support normally requires that data be collected at multiple points, concurrent with treatment, for all patients. That is, outcomes assessment is made integral to the treatment process. Questions of patient and clinician acceptance, the length of the measures, ease of administration, and impact upon the treatment process are critical to system design.

While many of the measurement issues discussed below are common across treatment settings, the inpatient environment poses unique challenges. Some patients are unable to complete questionnaires, making self-report impossible. Overburdened staff are resistant to "filling out paperwork" not directly related to patient care. As lengths of stay are reduced, the types and amount of clinical change that can be expected also become more limited, requiring measures that are highly focused and sensitive to such limited change.

The remainder of this section discusses measurement issues in relation to the design of an inpatient outcomes assessment system for clinical decision support. The following section illustrates how each issue was addressed in the development of the COMPASS inpatient treatment assessment system.

What to Measure

The fundamental trade-off in decisions regarding the domain of measurement is between the length of the instrument versus its breadth and depth. This problem can appear unresolvable. A very common response by clinicians and administrators to a proposed assessment system is, "What's here is good, but it's far too long, and it fails to address the following important assessment factors. . . ." In other words, add more scales, but make the instrument shorter.

There are two approaches to achieving these seemingly incompatible goals; both require careful attention to the criteria for scale/item inclusion. In the first, theory-driven approach, decisions are made with reference to an espoused theory of mental health status change during treatment. In the second, scales/items are included on the basis of their relevance to the specific decisions that the assessment system must support. In both approaches, utility for decision support requires that items expected to show a substantial independent relationship to clinical outcomes be included as well. Decisions regarding "what to measure" may also reflect the characteristics of the treatment population. For example, a depression treatment clinic might adopt an outcomes system with a more extensive and nuanced depression scale than would be appropriate for a general treatment population.

The COMPASS INT scales discussed below are an example of a measurement tool constructed largely on the basis of the relevances of scales and items to specific treatment system decisions. As will be seen, this instrument retains the three core Mental Health Index scales, allowing for seamless monitoring of patient progress across inpatient and outpatient settings. However, decisions as to the specific items that were added to each scale, as well as to the inclusion of inpatient-specific scales, were made with reference not to a theory of mental health change but to the decisions required of clinicians and administrators working in a managed care treatment environment.

Who Will Provide the Data?

The answer to this question has major implications for the type of information the system will provide and the administrative burden imposed by data collection. Various stakeholders may have markedly different perceptions of treatment progress and outcome. At a minimum, the patient and clinician perspectives seem pertinent, and are often quite distinct. For specific populations, additional perspectives might be valuable. For example, parents' or teachers' ratings of a child's condition or of progress in treatment could be important components of an outcomes assessment for treatment of a socialization or school behavior problem. Here again, the system objective is the most critical factor in design decisions. Since documentation of outcomes can be achieved using sampling methodologies and time-limited data collection, it may well be feasible to include ratings by multiple stakeholders. As a practical matter, it is rarely administratively feasible to incorporate ratings by persons other than the patient and clinician in a decision support system that must be integrated into clinical operations.

The acceptance of an outcomes assessment system is directly related to the burden of data collection upon clinicians and administrators. This places a limit on the amount of data that can be obtained through clinician ratings in decision-support systems. However, the clinician may find the comparison of patients' self-report to their own assessment to be one of the most clinically useful features of the system. The ratio of clinical value to data collection burden is an important determinant of system acceptance.

Psychometric Properties

Psychometric strength—the reliability, validity, and sensitivity to change of scales—is necessary to useful measurement. Construction of psychometrically strong scales, or evaluation of the psychometric properties of existing scales, requires technical expertise. The following overview outlines key issues.

A reliable scale yields essentially identical results when the same set of objects/subjects are measured under similar conditions. Reliability refers to the stability, dependability, and consistency of measurement. Since all measurement involves error, no scale is

100% reliable. Such an "ideal" scale would yield precisely identical results when the same measure is repeated under identical conditions.

Two major types of reliability indices are internal consistency and test–retest. Internal consistency reflects the correlation among scale items, and indicates the degree to which the items "measure the same thing." The most common measure of a scale's internal consistency is a statistic known as Alpha. Since the computation of Alpha takes into account both the inter-item correlations and the number of items, it is nearly always the case that a scale's reliability can be improved simply by adding more items. The trade-off between the length of the scale and its reliability is an important design consideration.

Test–retest reliability indicates the reproducibility of the scale scores, i.e., the extent to which two separate administrations of the scale to the same subject on two occasions yield the same score. It is a measure of the stability of the scale scores over time. Due to changes in the subject with respect to the construct being measured (anxiety, depression, etc.), the scores would not be expected to be identical. But a reliable scale would normally be expected to produce very similar results if the construct is fairly stable and little time has elapsed between the two scale administrations.

What is "good" reliability? Reliability coefficients take on values between 0 and 1; the closer to 1 the better the reliability. Generally, coefficients above .7 are considered acceptable for most purposes; values of at least .85 are desirable if the scores are to be used in relation to individuals (as opposed to groups). Thus, scale reliability should be higher for a decision support system than is necessary for outcomes documentation.

"Validity" is a general term applied to a variety of dimensions of the "extent to which a scale measures what it is supposed to measure" or "does the job it's supposed to do." There is no such thing as a "valid test," there are only tests that are valid for specific combinations of respondents and purposes. Major types of validity include: face, content, criterion, and construct validity.

Face validity is the extent to which the scale items or questions are considered appropriate by the person completing the scale. Content validity is the extent to which a scale's content (e.g., items, questions) reflect the construct being measured. These types of validity are normally not quantified.

Criterion validity refers to the effectiveness of a scale in predicting some independent measure (criterion) of the construct the scale is intended to measure. Subtypes are concurrent validity, predictive validity, and discriminant validity. Concurrent validity involves demonstration of a statistically significant relationship between the scale and a criterion measure collected at approximately the same time. Predictive validity involves demonstration of a statistically significant relationship between the scale and some future criterion measure (e.g., relapse, hospitalization, suicide, etc.). Discriminant validity involves demonstration of a statistically significant difference between average scale scores for groups known to differ on the construct being measured. Criterion validity is measured quantitatively, usually via correlation coefficients or tests of differences in group means.

A scale's construct validity is the extent to which it can be said to measure a specific construct or trait. Construct validity requires that the scale yields results that are consistent with theoretical expectations. Demonstration of construct validity involves the accumulation of evidence from a variety of sources, such as the scale's positive correlation with other variables to which it should theoretically be related ("convergent" validity) and the absence of a statistically significant relationship between the scale scores and variables with which it would not be expected to be related. There is no single measure of a scale's construct validity; various analyses are usually presented as "evidence of a scale's construct validity."

Finally, sensitivity to change is of paramount importance to outcomes measurement. The usefulness of a scale is directly related to its ability to detect clinically meaningful change in the patient's condition.

Administrative Procedures

Successful outcomes assessment requires efficient data collection by well trained and supervised staff. A decision support system, which requires that data collection become an integral part of the clinical process, unavoidably makes demands upon patients, clinicians, and administrators. The needs of each of these groups must be taken into consideration. Clinicians and administrators should be directly involved in establishing data collection procedures. Preservation of patient confidentiality and incorporation of the patient's values and points of view into the outcomes assessment are of utmost importance. The role and organizational importance of the outcomes system must be made clear to administrative staff. The unambiguous commitment of top management is essential. It must be evidenced not only by their pronouncements, but by a willingness to provide necessary resources to support the measurement system. Managers should explicitly discuss the importance of outcomes data to the strategic future of the organization. Clinicians must be assured that system data are intended to support, not replace, clinical judgment in case management; the clinical value of the data must be demonstrated.

In short, the outcomes system will make significant demands upon staff and patients. Procedures must be designed to minimize the administrative burden and ensure that data collection have no adverse effect upon the treatment process. The commitment of the organization, the importance of the data, and its clinical value must be made evident to staff and patients.

Proper attention to administrative issues is the least technical, but most often neglected, step in the development of an outcomes system. When systems fail, lack of attention to this area is often the major contributing factor.

Patient Self-Report Completion Rates

Outcomes assessment for mental health treatment requires patient cooperation in providing self-report data, since the patient is the target of treatment and (as noted above) clinician assessment supplements, but cannot be substituted for self-report. Cooperation is usually obtained if the measures are introduced in a positive manner. The key message is that the information requested will be used to design the best possible treatment for the patient. This message is most convincingly delivered by a clinician, or a specially trained assistant. While it is true that some inpatients are incapable of reliable self-report (particularly at admission), it is realistic to expect admission completion rates of 65% or higher if the questionnaire and administrative process are well designed. Lower completion rates may suggest staff resistance, or an unusually impaired patient population.

Data Handling and Quality Assurance

Data quality must be regularly monitored and "dirty" data—invalid or incomplete records—must be cleaned or discarded to ensure the integrity of the outcomes system. Errors can be due to inaccurate recording of responses, so data should be reviewed before forms are forwarded for processing. Data entry is a second step in which errors can be introduced, whether the data are entered manually (e.g., keying errors) or scanned (e.g., mark sense errors). Also, flaws in data handling/analysis software can contaminate otherwise clean data files.

Data quality assurance plans must be designed to detect invalid data at each collection/processing step. Staff should be trained to check the forms for completeness. Reliability of the data entry process can be established through "double keying" (entry of forms twice) or, in the case of scanners, comparing the scan results against manual entry for a random subset of forms. A standardized (test) set of forms can be developed to include all possible responses to all items, with the set scanned periodically and the data file checked against the expected (known) results. Computations can be independently coded to allow for dual processing of a random subset of forms, with the end result (e.g., scale scores) compared to detect flaws in the data analysis code. Improbable or infrequent combinations of responses (e.g., patient reports chronic severe depression combined with high life satisfaction and no work impairment) can be flagged as potential indicators of unauthentic responding.

Even in the best of inpatient systems, data problems are unavoidable and likely to affect 15% or more of the records. Careful data handling and appropriate quality assurance procedures can minimize data loss and/or the contamination of data files with inaccurate records.

Data Analysis and Interpretation

As noted in Chapter 1, there is an important difference between data and information. Data are numbers (codes, ratings, scores, etc.).

Data are not meaningful—they provide no information until they are placed in a context, such as relevant norms, that allows for interpretation. The analysis plan and norms that are relevant depend on the questions to be asked of the data. In an inpatient setting these might include: Should this patient be admitted? Discharged? Is he/she making progress in treatment? Do clinicians at our hospital achieve unusually good (poor) results with certain patient subgroups? What patient characteristics are related to positive response to medication? How does the effectiveness of our Mood Disorders Treatment Unit compare with that of the other hospital in town? Has it declined since the 25% staffing reduction? Framing these questions is an important step in system design and in the establishment of measurement objectives; they determine which data are collected and how they are analyzed.

Clinical Actionability

Information is transformed into knowledge when it suggests a course of action. Suppose a patient's score on a discharge index is more positive than the average score of discharged patients. This may suggest action—that is, discharge. However, the action can be taken with more confidence if it is known that patients having the same score as the individual in question are successful postdischarge 75% of the time. Still more confidence is warranted if it is known that 90% of patients with this score and similar in significant ways to the patient in question (e.g., treatment history, age, socioeconomic status) are successful postdischarge.

In short, systematic collection and analysis of data relating to key clinical decisions can markedly enhance the clinical value of outcomes information. Clinical actionability, the value of outcomes information to clinical decision making, is the final test of an inpatient psychiatric decision support system.

DEVELOPMENT OF AN INPATIENT TREATMENT OUTCOMES ASSESSMENT SYSTEM

The development of the intensive treatment module of the COMPASS system (COMPASS INT) illustrates the steps referenced above. COMPASS INT was developed to supplement the assessment capabilities of COMPASS OP, providing for seamless measurement across the full spectrum of treatment settings and severity of patient disorders.

Design Specifications for COMPASS INT

The primary development goal for COMPASS INT was decision support for psychiatric inpatient settings. Specific objectives were established through consultation with inpatient experts in both clinical and research fields, and with representatives of more than 50 hospital systems who responded to an invitation for consideration as a development site. Through this process, organizational and clinical needs were identified that became the focus of instrument design.

Organizational Needs

- Documentation of treatment effectiveness (e.g., for marketing)
- Objective, standardized patient data for use in negotiations with payers/managed care case managers
- Outcomes data to support continuous quality improvement initiatives
- Outcomes data to support performance evaluation
- Information to evaluate appropriateness of admission and discharge policies and decisions

Clinical Needs: Patient Data and Norms to Support . . .

- Admission decision making
- Level of care decision making (inpatient, residential, partial hospital, 23-hour beds, in-home services, assertive community treatment)
- Discharge decision making
- Monitoring of patient improvement
- Postdischarge placement decisions
- Screening for patient symptoms/functional deficits
- Determination of treatment plans

The specifics of the treatment systems varied, but the underlying themes were quite similar: Hospitals had already reduced staff and patient length of stay as much as possible. Survival in the managed care environment would depend upon "working smarter," not harder. Timely, relevant, objective, and reliable information is essential to working smarter: information for individual patients relating to the appropriateness of admission and discharge decisions and the effectiveness of treatment plans; information required to "profile" units and individuals to evaluate performance and establish appropriate quality improvement systems and goals.

The new operating environment included far greater demand by payers/case managers, and the need to justify treatment plans. Documentation of the quality and cost-effectiveness of care were primary "marketing" concerns. Increasingly, it is necessary to fully justify additional patient days to case managers. Relevant objective data are an essential supplement to clinical information and judgment.

It should be stressed that most of the measurement objectives identified above are of recent vintage. Managed care has created a need for measurement and accountability unheard of as recently as five years ago. Our review quickly confirmed that, while some existing measures were well developed and psychometrically respectable, all were outdated in terms of current measurement needs.

Among the most widely used of the existing scales is the BASIS-32, developed by a respected team of clinicians and researchers at McLean Hospital. Its development was a significant landmark for inpatient measurement. Its psychometric properties have been well documented (Eisen et al., 1994). However, the inpatient treatment environment has changed markedly since the BASIS-32 became available; it is instructive to consider its limitations in relation to those needs previously identified.

The BASIS-32 was designed in the mid-1980s by asking patients why they came to the hospital and transforming their statements into questionnaire items. Thus, the source of the target symptoms was patients, many of whom may have limited insight and judgment regarding their illnesses, rather than the information requirements of the hospital systems. Furthermore, these target symptoms were identified prior to the managed care era limitation of hospital care to critically ill persons. The instrument, therefore, contains items that no managed care company in 1996 would consider to be justification of inpatient hospitalization, e.g., lack of goals and direction in life, isolation, or feelings of loneliness.

A second weakness of the BASIS-32 as a measure of patient improvement is its insensitivity to patient change in critical areas. Currently, a patient's level of care is determined primarily on the basis of five factors: suicidality, assaultiveness, overall symptom severity, capability of self-care (activities of daily living), and residential instability. Thus, a decision support tool appropriate to current hospital needs regarding admission and discharge decisions must assess these factors. The BASIS-32 contains only one item regarding suicidality (suicidal feelings and behavior), which would not differentiate between a patient with mild, passive suicidal ideation and one with a recent attempt and a serious plan. Similarly, it contains only one item regarding assaultiveness (controlling temper, outbursts or anger, violence), which does not provide sufficient measurement differentiation between a patient with moderate subjective feelings of anger, for example, and a patient with serious homicidal intent. There are no items relating to activities of daily living or residential instability.

Thus, of the dimensions that have been found to empirically predict level of care placement, only one (overall severity of symptoms) might be addressed adequately by the BASIS-32. However, the adequacy with which the BASIS-32 measures the severity of the target symptoms of inpatient or partial hospital treatment is also questionable, since (1) the symptoms of the major DSM-IV disorders are not adequately covered and (2) the internal consistency reliability of the psychosis scale is below the minimum acceptable for use with individuals, and psychosis is a key target symptom for inpatient/partial hospital treatment.

Probably because it does not measure the relevant variables, the BASIS-32 has very limited capability for decision support in that the difference in score between current inpatients and current outpatients is only 0.56 of a standard deviation (Eisen et. al., 1994). In order to achieve reasonable accuracy in the classification of patients presenting in ER or triage settings as needing inpatient treatment, the differences between inpatients and outpatients would need to be much larger. For the same reason, it is doubtful that the BASIS-32 would have utility for monitoring improvement of inpatients.

Finally, a serious problem with the BASIS-32 as the major measure in an outcomes measurement and decision support tool is that it is 100% self-report. Thirty to 40% of inpatients cannot complete the instrument, and data collected solely from patients who can complete a questionnaire will not accurately reflect their condition because poor insight and judgment regarding the illness is a cardinal symptom of some disorders (e.g., manic episodes, schizophrenia). For both of these reasons, using an instrument that consists only of self-report will not produce an accurate, representative estimate of the effectiveness of treatment, and will not enable accurate classification regarding level of care. Indeed, a report on the 60% of patients who are most well at admission and 100% of patients at discharge would show much less benefit from treatment than had occurred, because the assessment seriously underestimates how ill patients (as a group) were at admission. BASIS-32 data, therefore, may not accurately reflect the performance of a treatment program, and may have little utility for program evaluation.

In conclusion, the design goals for COMPASS INT were established to meet the measurement needs of providers of intensive mental health treatment services in the era of managed care, overcoming the deficiencies of existing instruments. The core dimensions of well-being, symptoms, and functioning were retained to provide for continuity and "seamless" measurement between the COMPASS INT and outpatient scales. The instrument includes both staff rating and self-report components, ensuring that relevant data would be available for even those patients incapable of self-report. Scales and items were developed to assess the constructs (suicidality, assaultiveness, etc.) most pertinent to intensive treatment settings. Most importantly, the plan for testing COMPASS INT would provide for the establishment of norms and indices useful for both clinical and organizational decision support.

Development of a Pilot Version of COMPASS INT

The initial challenge was to achieve these objectives without creating a measurement system so cumbersome or lengthy as to be impractical for routine inpatient use. Two resources were critical: the large COMPASS OP database and the prior research and consultation of several scientists, most notably John Lyons Ph.D., of Northwestern University Medical School.

To construct appropriate scales for the self-report component, relevant items from the COMPASS OP were supplemented with new items necessary for reliable measurement of the five core dimensions. For example, COMPASS OP items with high item–scale correlations became candidates for COMPASS INT. Their use would help to provide the seamless measurement considered to be particularly valuable for vertically integrated treatment systems wishing to track patients across levels of care. To these were added new items to provide for robust measurement of suicidality, assaultiveness, etc. In all, COMPASS INT includes 58 self-report items. Twenty-eight of these are identical to COMPASS OP items that contribute to the MHI. An MHI score estimated from these 28 items is correlated above .95 with the full MHI. The MHI thus provides seamless measurement across all levels of care, an important and unique capability for long-term monitoring and follow-up of severely disordered patients.

The development of the staff rating component was greatly facilitated by the consultation and prior research of Dr. Lyons. This earlier research involved development of a staff-rated, decision support tool, the Severity of Psychiatric Illness (SPI) scale, that has achieved significant improvement over base rate probabilities in predicting admission decisions (Lyons, 1991).

The SPI was not optimal for use as the staff rating component of COMPASS INT. It assesses 10 dimensions of clinical characteristics, several of which make little or no contribution to improved decision support once the primary dimensions of suicidality, dangerousness, and symptom severity are taken into account. However, experience with the SPI strongly suggested that a briefer staff rating scale (covering suicidality, dangerousness, symptom severity, residential stability, and self-care) could be developed that would prove very effective for decision support.

The staff ratings are an important adjunct to patient self-report since (1) both perspectives are relevant and often differ, (2) a significant minority of inpatients are incapable of self-report, and (3) they provide a "validity check" for the responses of patients who may deliberately or unintentionally misrepresent their status (e.g., to gain admission to the hospital, or due to dementia).

Finally, implementation success would require that COMPASS INT be appropriate to a broad range of inpatient settings and patients. Thus, the final COMPASS INT design criteria, included seven characteristics/objectives; the pilot version of the instrument was tested and evaluated against these criteria.

1. Support clinical decision making
2. Preserve the core dimensions of COMPASS OP
3. Include staff and self-report components
4. Brevity
5. Ease of integration into clinical practice
6. Appropriate to a broad range of hospital and intensive treatment settings
7. Psychometric strength

Testing. During the test phase, a variety of studies was designed to establish the psychometric properties of COMPASS INT to derive level of care indices for use in decision support, and to establish norms appropriate to the evaluation of individual patient progress and program level evaluation. The test phase also involved weekly communication with hospital staff over a three-month period to identify and resolve administrative problems. The measurement literature is replete with psychometrically strong and scientifically respectable scales that were never successfully integrated into clinical settings. Minimization of respondent (patient, clinical, and administrative staff) burden is a critical goal; efficient administrative systems are as necessary as scientific rigor to the success of a measurement system.

Announcement that the pilot instrument was available for testing drew responses from over 50 hospitals and treatment systems that expressed interest in serving as test sites. Each was evaluated in relation to three selection criteria: (1) the likelihood that they could successfully implement the test program, (2) admission rates and patient characteristics, and (3) the availability of multiple levels of care (e.g., inpatient, partial hospitalization, intensive outpatient).

The single most important consideration was whether the site had established a culture of measurement, or seemed capable of doing so within an acceptable time frame. As noted previously, the role and significance of measurement has changed dramatically in recent years and, systems such as COMPASS are foreign to many settings. Staff cutbacks and other budgeting stressors, combined with the lack of experience with measurement systems, make many treatment systems poor candidates for development sites. Sites were accepted for further consideration only if they could provide evidence of an existing culture of measurement (e.g., several had a long-standing history of research activity and existing mechanisms for data collection) or strong top management commitment to the project.

Since the test phase included multiple studies of psychometric properties of the COMPASS INT, prospective sites were also evaluated on their ability and willingness to collect data relating to one or more substudies. These involved:

- Collection of admission and discharge data for a sample of inpatients (necessary for decision support);

- Collection of admission and discharge data for partial hospital patients (necessary to establish level-of-care decision support capability);

- Frequent administration over the treatment period (to establish norms for the evaluation of patient progress);

- One month postdischarge follow-up (predictive validity);

- Administration to emergency room patients (to derive a Probability of Admission Index and document discriminant validity between patients who are admitted versus those who are not admitted as inpatients or partial hospital patients);

- Co-administration of COMPASS INT and the BASIS-32, and/or the Brief Symptom Inventory (to document criterion validity);

- Multiple staff ratings for the same patient (to document interrater reliability);

- Repeated assessment (same day) of patients (to document test–retest reliability).

Four sites that appeared to have the capability and willingness to conduct the necessary data collection were selected as test sites. The final selection decisions ensured that the sites would include a heterogeneous patient population from teaching hospitals, community hospital settings, and vertically integrated treatment systems providing the full spectrum of care from acute inpatient through partial hospital, intensive outpatient, and outpatient services.

Testing of the instrument is in progress as this text goes to print. COMPASS INT has been administered more than 2,000 times, to hundreds of patients in the four hospital systems. Results are promising in relation to the design goals. All four sites have successfully implemented the system; staff have found COMPASS INT to be well designed in terms of its face validity, length, and ease of integration into clinical operations. Approximately two-thirds of inpatients are able to complete the instrument within a day of admission; the COMPASS INT staff ratings provide assessment data for these and for patients incapable of self-report.

Initial findings also are very promising in relation to the use of the instrument for decision support. For example, comparison of scale scores based on admission data with scores for the same patients at a subsequent point of their hospitalization indicates substantial change (.5 to .9 standard deviations) on every scale. This suggests that COMPASS INT will be effective in support of level-of-care decisions, providing clinically meaningful discrimination among patients regarding their readiness for discharge.

Initial psychometric data indicate excellent reliability. The (internal consistency) reliability of the Symptom and Functioning scales are .94 and .92 respectively. Construct validity is excellent; many of the symptom items are extracted from the DSM-IV.

THE FUTURE ROLE OF MEASUREMENT FOR INPATIENT SETTINGS

COMPASS INT development, while incomplete, has demonstrated the feasibility of instrumentation useful for organizational and clinical decision making. The potential of measurement systems to alter treatment is quite significant. Specific applications might include the following.

Admission/Discharge Decision Making

A Patient Admission Index, (PAI) reflecting both staff and self-report standardized data, has been developed to assist with admission decisions for individual patients and evaluation of overall hospital performance. The initial version of the PAI has achieved a classification accuracy of over 70%. Comparison of an individual's PAI score and/or subscale scores (e.g., for suicidality, assaultiveness) with hospital norms will provide for the establishment of guidelines. Scores above an established threshold would suggest admission, scores below a (second) threshold would suggest no admission, and scores in an intermediate range (between the two thresholds) might trigger review by a clinical team. Dr. Lyon's work (Lyons et. al., 1996) indicates that, using staff ratings alone, it is possible to create an index that predicts actual admission decisions with good accuracy. The addition of patient self-report data will very likely improve upon Dr. Lyon's results.

PAI scores can also provide meaningful documentation of "diverted" admissions. A managed care system's success in providing effective treatment short of hospitalization for select patients with high PAI scores (who typically would be hospitalized in other systems) can provide credible evidence of cost-effective care.

The PAI score of COMPASS INT, in effect, reproduces current decision processes—that is, the PAI score indicates the likelihood that the patient *would have been* admitted using traditional admissions procedures. Eventually, it will be possible to enhance the PAI to indicate whether the patient *should* be admitted. That is, analysis of the success of hospitalization for patients having various levels of PAI scores will enable the measurement system to predict whether hospitalization is necessary or likely to benefit the patient.

The PAI will become an important focus of the dialogue between hospital staff and case managers asked to approve payment for treatment. Increasingly, managed care companies will insist upon objective, standardization measures to support such requests. The PAI will meet this need.

Similarly, a Discharge Readiness Index (DRI) will inform discharge decisions for individual patients. For the PAI, DRI and other decision support measures, the key term is "inform." Such data cannot replace clinical judgment because of the complexity of such decisions and the inability of a measurement system to take into consideration all of the myriad variables that may be relevant in an individual case. But such systems will play an important role by indicating the proper course of action in the absence of unusual circumstances.

Measures such as the PAI and DRI will also be useful in assessing treatment system performance and as a quality improvement tool. For example, a hospital might compare the average PAI scores of patients who have been admitted against regional or national norms for similar patients. Such an analysis could suggest whether admissions policies are too stringent or lenient.

Monitoring Patient Improvement

The daily norms provided by COMPASS INT illustrate the potential of measurement systems to assess whether a patient's progress is satisfactory. A patient admitted for agitation, paranoia, and assaultiveness and given antipsychotic medication might be assessed after four days, with his/her progress (e.g., as reflected in assaultiveness and DRI scale scores) compared against Day Four norms for similar patients. To be effective, such a system must be based on individual patient profiles (as presented in Chapter 4) so that the comparison takes into consideration not only the patient's clinical status currently and at the time of admission, but other factors that might be relevant to their expected rate of improvement (age, chronicity, etc.). The outpatient version of COMPASS has successfully employed severity adjustment; a similar capability is under development for COMPASS INT.

Patient profiling also allows for the severity adjustment of performance. The ability to take into consideration patient characteristics relating to clinical outcomes will allow behavioral health care organizations to evaluate the performance of treatment units and individual clinicians, by comparing measured clinical improvement against "case mix adjusted" normative expectations for similar patients. This will, in turn, allow hospitals to reward top performing units/individuals and learn from their successes, while targeting less effective units for problem solving, training, or other remedial activities to bring them up to standard. In short, severity adjustment will provide for the establishment of the meaningful benchmarks for clinical progress that are the cornerstone of CQI systems.

In summary, measurement systems will play a far more prominent role in the psychiatric hospital of the future. Data will inform virtually every decision affecting the individual patient: Should this person be admitted? What level of care is most appropriate? What is the optimal treatment plan? Is his/her condition responding satisfactorily? Can the patient safely be discharged to a less intensive level of care, with a high probability of successful postdischarge adjustment? Furthermore, measurement systems will provide for storage and analysis of data relating to the outcome of clinical decisions, thereby providing for "learning" and continual improvement in the ability of hospitals to transform data into information and information into knowledge of "what works."

Measurement systems will also play a greatly expanded role at the organizational level. Hospitals have already begun to use standardized measures for marketing (e.g., documentation of outcomes) and operational purposes (e.g., to justify requests for treatment approval within managed care systems). The measurement-driven evaluation and CQI systems familiar to many organizations will become commonplace in hospitals. Hospital performance will improve as their measurement systems enable them: (1) to "learn" from past decisions, continually improving their capacity to determine "what works" for specific types of patients and conditions; (2) to identify, reward, and learn from unusually effective treatment units or clinicians; and (3) to target poorer units for remedial training.

Individual and System-Level Reports

COMPASS INT data can be used to evaluate the progress of individual patients or the performance of large treatment facilities/systems.

The following figures, similar to those in the standard COMPASS INT Treatment Progress Report, illustrate the value of COMPASS INT for monitoring patient progress. Figure 5.1 shows how ready an inpatient named Mary J. is for discharge from an inpatient setting. It shows her status and progress in relation to other patients studied using COMPASS INT. A horizontal line shows the range of av-

FIGURE 5.1

Readiness for Discharge

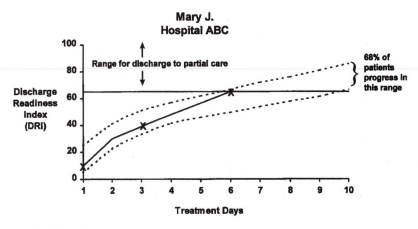

X = DRI for Mary J.

erage scores for inpatients at the point of discharge to partial hospital care. The curving dotted lines show the average score for inpatients who are not yet ready for discharge on each day of hospitalization. The Xs and the solid line connecting them show Mary J.'s scores.

Figure 5.2 presents key discharge indicators. Specifically, it provides various self-report and staff-related scale scores (symptom severity, social functioning, etc.) and their relationship to average discharge scores for the treatment facility or system. Patient scores shown in Figure 5.3 are favorable (i.e., similar to patients ready for discharge) on suicidality, ADL, and substance abuse scales; other scores suggest the need for more improvement prior to discharge. Review of this information alerts staff to areas where further improvement is necessary.

Treatment Outcomes

FIGURE 5.2

Significant Discharge Indicators

COMPASS
INFORMATION
SERVICES, INC

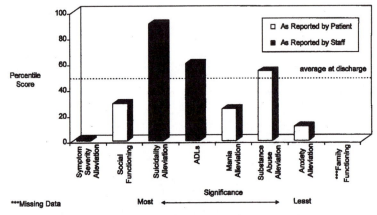

***Missing Data

FIGURE 5.3

Most Significant Discharge Indicators Change Since Intake

COMPASS
INFORMATION
SERVICES, INC

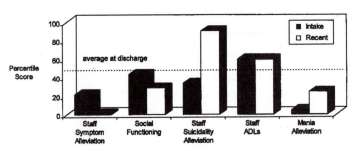

FIGURE 5.4

Patient and Staff Comparison

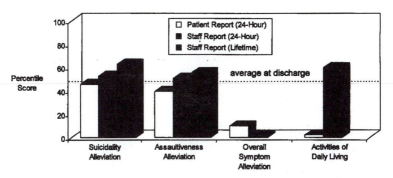

Figure 5.3 indicates the degree of change that has occurred since admission on the five dimensions most critical to discharge readiness. These data alert staff to areas where gains have been made, and where progress has been slow. As for Figure 5.2, these data also are provided in the context of an "average discharge" score.

Finally, Figure 5.4 shows the relationship between staff ratings and patient self-report on four scales. These data are useful in alerting staff to areas where the two perspectives are dissimilar, suggesting the need to review the basis for the ratings to ensure that staff are accurately evaluating patient status.

Figures 5.5 through 5.8 illustrate COMPASS system-level reports. The difference between admission and discharge represents the effect of treatment.

Figure 5.5 shows the average scores on the Discharge Readiness Index (DRI) for patients of ABC Hospital at admission and discharge.

Figure 5.6 shows the amount of improvement per day on the Discharge Readiness Index for patients at ABC Hospital compared to the average hospital. This figure shows that treatment at ABC Hospital is more effective than treatment at the average hospital.

FIGURE 5.5

Facility Profile

ABC Hospital

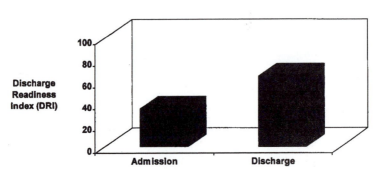

FIGURE 5.6

Facility Profile

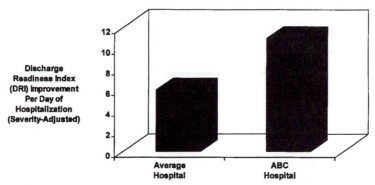

FIGURE 5.7

DRI Improvement Per Day for ABC Hospital

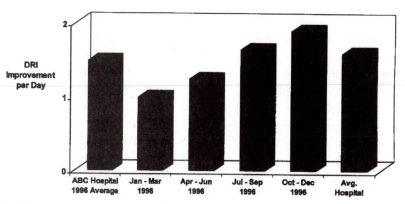

FIGURE 5.8

Unit Profile

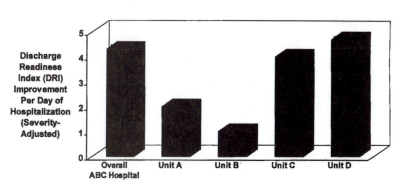

Figure 5.7 provides similar information, broken down by quarter (i.e., a trend over time) and shows the average amount of improvement per day produced in the Discharge Readiness Index at ABC Hospital for each quarter of 1996, and in 1996 overall, compared to the database norm ("Avg. Hospital"). Trend data may be useful, for example, in judging the impact of staffing and policy changes on outcomes at ABC Hospital.

Figure 5.8 provides a unit breakdown for these data. It shows the average amount of improvement in the Discharge Readiness Index produced per day of hospitalization. This figure can be useful in judging the impact on outcomes of differences between units in staffing, policy, and treatment approach. This figure can also incorporate cost information, and is useful for a variety of internal management purposes.

In summary, COMPASS INT data have both clinical and administrative utility. Data and trends showing a variety of breakdowns are readily developed to improve assessment, treatment planning, and systems refinement, converting outcomes data to outcomes information and, over time, to actionable knowledge.

In conclusion: Measurement systems will fundamentally alter the nature of intensive psychiatric treatment. By providing meaningful information in support of clinical decision making, and timely feedback about patient progress, it will provide a powerful tool for the clinician. Since it involves a strong focus upon accountability and results, the culture of measurement may initially be perceived as threatening. But strong measurement systems hold the potential to sharply improve the cost-effectiveness of treatment, an outcome which can be enthusiastically embraced not only by payers, but by clinicians, administrators, clients, patients, and their family members as well.

6

Substance Abuse Treatment Outcomes

Outcomes research has been a conspicuous feature in the field of substance abuse treatment longer than in other areas of mental health. Meaningful outcomes studies have been undertaken to evaluate the effectiveness of treatment models and individual programs for over a quarter century. More recently, outcomes methodologies have been adapted for the study of patient–treatment matching, and to inform the development of level of care and treatment guidelines. As in all other areas of mental health treatment, the enhanced role of measurement in substance abuse treatment is due to the impact of managed care, with its focus on accountability and cost-effectiveness.

THE USES OF SUBSTANCE ABUSE OUTCOMES RESEARCH: AN OVERVIEW

Outcomes research has been invoked to justify the most significant change in substance abuse treatment of the past decade—the shift from inpatient/freestanding residential settings to outpatient treatment programs for alcoholism and drug abuse. Just as the effect of managed care has been to reduce both the admission rates and average length of stay for inpatient mental health treatment, so has managed care caused a sharp decline in the use of residential programs to treat substance abuse. This has resulted in a major reduction in the cost of an episode of treatment.

The author is pleased to acknowledge the assistance of Meghan Byrne of Compass Information Systems in the preparation of this chapter.

To date there is no compelling evidence from outcomes studies to suggest that the effectiveness of treatment has been reduced by the shift away from residential care. Indeed, advocates of managed care believe that the reduction in cost will be accompanied by improved outcomes, due to the inherent advantages of outpatient care for many patients. Residential treatment, in this view, is inevitably less effective in helping patients to cope with life stresses that are associated with chemical dependency, and in responding constructively to the "triggers" (e.g., social situations, peer pressures, family dysfunction) of substance use in their usual living environment. Consequently, outpatient treatment may, for most substance abusers, be both less expensive and more effective than residential/inpatient treatment. If this proves to be the case, the managed care emphasis upon cost containment coupled with outcomes research will have led to a major improvement of both the quality and cost-effectiveness of treatment.

Research comparing inpatient versus outpatient treatment illustrates the role outcomes measurement can play in major system change. Three studies conducted by the Substance Abuse Treatment and Research Unit at the Philadelphia Veterans Affairs Medical Center compared inpatient to outpatient and day-hospital programs for alcohol detoxification, cocaine dependence, and alcohol dependence. In each case, larger percentages of the inpatient groups completed the program. However, follow-ups at seven months post-treatment indicated that outcomes for the detoxification and cocaine subjects treated in inpatient settings were not more favorable than those of outpatients, despite far higher treatment costs for the inpatient group. Among those treated for alcohol dependence, 73% of day-hospital patients reported abstinence at seven months post-treatment, compared to 40% of inpatients. In summary, these studies found no support for inpatient treatment for alcohol or cocaine dependence, or for alcohol detoxification.

It is important to note that these findings do not suggest that inpatient treatment is unnecessary, but merely that for the types of patients that were the subjects of these three studies, the inpatient services at the Philadelphia VA Medical Center were not more effective than much less expensive outpatient treatment. It is possible that for other types of patients or other facilities, findings may be more favorable to inpatient care. But it was the failure of studies such as these to document superior outcomes for any large class of substance abusers (except those who required hospitalization for other reasons, such as a serious mental health diagnosis or medical problems) that made possible the shift away from inpatient treatment.

The inpatient–outpatient controversy suggests one dimension of the role outcomes research will play in shaping the field of substance abuse treatment. To be sure, the radical shift toward outpatient treatment was driven by cost containment pressures, not by outcomes data. But it is unlikely that the change would have occurred had outcomes research yielded significant evidence of the superior effectiveness of residential treatment.

System-Level Applications

Outcomes data at the treatment system level will also be used to evaluate the performance of individual programs and staff. Comparison of treatment outcomes for various types of patients against relevant norms can suggest specific areas of strength or weakness, an essential step in continuous quality improvement (CQI) programs. Outcomes data can improve the cost-effectiveness of a treatment system by suggesting the "mix" of services that are optimal for a given patient population. If group treatment or education sessions were shown to be as effective as more expensive modalities (e.g., individual counseling) for some types of substance abuse, very substantial cost savings could be achieved by programs featuring individual counseling without any reduction in quality of care. Benchmarking, standardized measurement, and case mix adjustment are measurement issues relevant to these uses of outcomes data.

Benchmarking and Standardized Measurement. Benchmarking refers to the establishment of reference points that can be used to interpret data. Scores on measurement scales, patient responses to questions, and other outcomes data do not become useful information until they are placed in a meaningful context. Most often, such data are analyzed in relation to trends or norms.

Trend analysis involves comparison of data with similar measures collected over time. For example, a program may monitor its dropout rate on a quarterly basis to determine the effectiveness of an intervention to improve completion rates. Trend data could be examined to help determine whether an observed reduction in dropouts was due to the intervention or to other factors. To illustrate, suppose that the intervention occurred in the fourth quarter of 1995, and the dropout rate declined to 20% for that quarter as compared to 30% or higher earlier in the year. Was the reduction due to the intervention? If the trend data for a year or two prior to 1995 were stable at 30% [Figure 6.1(a)], this would suggest that the intervention had been effective (although the trend data alone do not rule out other possibilities). However, trend lines shown in Figures 6.1(b) and 6.1(c) lead to very different conclusions.

The trend shown in Figure 6.1(b) suggests that the dropout rate is cyclical; it drops during the fourth quarter every year. In the previous two years, the rate returned to 30% during the first quarter of the new year. Thus, the fourth quarter decline during 1995 cannot be attributed to the intervention; there is evidence that it would have occurred anyway. The evidence for the effectiveness of the intervention would be considerably strengthened if the rate were to remain at 20% for the first quarter of 1996, while a return to 30% for that quarter would suggest that the intervention had had no effect (i.e., it had not changed the pattern in dropout rates from that of previous years).

The trend shown in Figure 6.1(c) also weakens the argument in favor of the intervention, since it suggests that the reduction in the dropout rate began during the third quarter (prior to the intervention) and continued into the fourth. Of course, it remains possible that the intervention was indeed effective, that the reduction in dropouts that began in the third quarter would have "bottomed out" at 30% in the absence of the intervention. Within-program trend data alone may not be sufficient to confirm or to rule out this possibility; normative data from other programs would be helpful to further analysis.

The establishment of benchmarks, or norms, across a group of programs requires standardization of measurement. This is a very important consideration in the selection or construction of outcomes measurement. Use of a widely available, standardized measure makes possible cross-program comparisons, which are often highly useful in establishing benchmarks or determining the effectiveness of a program or treatment model. Availability of extensive normative data is a powerful argument in favor of widely used scales (such as the Addiction Severity Index) for outcomes research.

FIGURE 6.1

Trend Lines

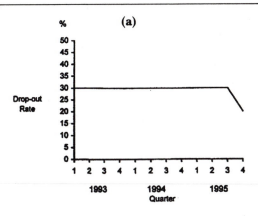

(a)

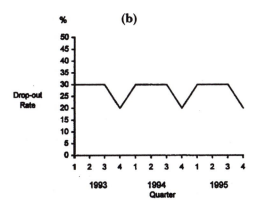

(b)

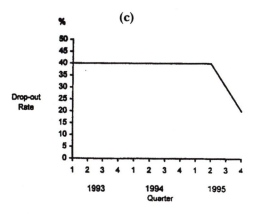

(c)

Suppose that dropout rates were monitored in the same way and at the same intervals for other substance abuse programs in the same geographical area. If their experience for the quarters in 1995 were similar to that shown in Figure 6.1(c), there would be little reason to conclude that this intervention to reduce dropouts in the target program had any effect. However, if the rate in other programs showed a corresponding decline for the third quarter but no further improvement during the fourth quarter of 1995, this would suggest that the intervention in the target program has extended the third-quarter, system-wide reduction in the dropout rate. These examples illustrate the importance of trend and/or benchmark data to CQI initiatives.

Case Mix Adjustment. Comparisons of outcomes across programs, or among clinicians within a program, are useful to the extent that the patients who receive the treatments are similar in terms of characteristics that are predictive of treatment success. Direct comparisons of outcomes for programs whose patients differ significantly in problem severity, relapse history, or treatment motivation would be inappropriate, while differences in characteristics such as height might safely be ignored. Since treatment populations are rarely similar on all relevant characteristics, statistical methods have been developed to adjust for them during analyses of outcomes data. This analytic process is known as *case mix adjustment.*

As discussed in earlier chapters, case mix adjustment provides for two of the most powerful strategies in outcomes management: prediction of course and differential referral. As has been shown, the prediction of course from initial severity and patient characteristics allows for review of actual progress against the most meaningful of all benchmarks. Differential referral is among the most powerful strategies for improving the cost-effectiveness of a treatment system.

Individual Level. At the individual case level, outcomes management will involve matching of patients to treatments and monitoring their progress to improve outcomes. It is likely that monitoring systems similar to the dose-response methods described in this text for mental health treatment will be developed for substance abuse treatment as well, though none currently exist. Research intended to improve treatment effectiveness by matching patients to programs has yielded disappointing results, still there is strong evidence that outcomes can be substantially improved through matching patients to services.

The following sections discuss the use of measurement to evaluate treatment programs, and to improve program effectiveness and individual patient outcomes. Finally, the potential for measurement systems to significantly improve the cost-effectiveness of treatment is illustrated by an innovative patient–treatment matching system.

OUTCOMES MEASUREMENT IN TREATMENT EVALUATION

The basic questions for substance abuse treatment evaluation are (1) What works? (2) At what cost? (3) For whom? These questions are far more complex than they appear.

What would it mean for a treatment to "work"? Most would agree that helping an individual overcome dependency on drugs or alcohol is a central goal, but closer examination reveals a far broader range of expectations of substance abuse treatment. Employers expect that treatment will help the patient to become a reliable and productive worker. Family members expect treatment to help the patient become a responsible parent/spouse/sibling who is emotionally available and no longer abusive. The taxpayer expects treatment to help the patient become self-supporting, get him/her off the welfare roles, reduce the likelihood of medical complications relating to substance use, and convert the patient into a law-abiding citizen who no longer steals to support addiction.

If the sole objective of treatment were to "help an addict stop using," substance abuse treatment would be among the most effective interventions in all of medicine or behavioral science. As suggested above, the actual goals are much broader. Furthermore, one crucial objective—relapse prevention—has proven especially difficult to achieve. As Mark Twain put it, "It's not so hard to stop smoking. I've done it dozens of times." Moreover, there is lack of agreement about whether total abstinence should be a treatment objective. It is seldom considered the sole treatment objective; most researchers and many clinicians consider improvements in employment status, family functioning, general mental health, medical condition, and legal status to be important outcomes. "Lapses"—renewed use for a brief period of time during recovery—are considered by many to be a learning opportunity, not a treatment failure. Some practitioners even consider nonproblematic use of a substance (e.g., "controlled drinking") to be an achievable and more realistic goal than total abstinence.

Like "What works?" the question "At what cost?" is also deceptively simple. The direct costs of treatment are relatively easy to identify and measure. But, from an evaluation standpoint, the more important issue is the cost–benefit of treatment, which requires quantification of the costs associated with treatment failure. These include medical, welfare, workplace, and legal system costs directly incurred by the addict, in addition to substantially increased costs of treatment and other services to the family members of the addict. For example, according to the National Institute of Drug Abuse (NIDA, 1992), the large majority (about 70%) of alcoholic and illicit drug abusers are employed, and these individuals on average are absent three weeks more per year, file twice as many workers compensation claims, use more than twice as many general medical services, and are fired for poor performance 47% more often than nonabusing employees.

When all factors are taken into consideration, the "cost" of substance abuse to the nation was estimated to be nearly $150 billion in 1988 (Rice et al., 1990); it is doubtless far greater today. This suggests that a relatively small improvement in treatment effectiveness might justify a far more expensive treatment program. However, the subject of cost is further complicated by the question, "Who pays?" The example of the self-insured corporation illustrates the significance of this issue. From the corporation's perspective, it may be considered more cost-effective to provide a minimal treatment benefit in combination with a "one chance and you're fired if you relapse" policy. While possibly misguided from an overall cost perspective, this approach in effect transfers the cost of treatment failure away from the corporation and onto society at large.

The "For whom?" question is also more complex than it appears. There is wide consensus that some patients are more difficult to treat than others; there is less agreement regarding the importance of specific factors. Depending upon the measurement goal, this problem may be negligible or crucial. For example, patient characteristics might be safely ignored if the objective is to monitor outcomes of treatment for a program whose patient population is fairly stable over time. But comparisons across programs are invalid to the extent that important patient characteristics—that is, those predictive of outcome—vary across programs and are not controlled through case mix adjustment.

Useful case mix adjustment requires measurement and analysis procedures that take into consideration patient characteristics related to success/failure in treatment. There is both research evidence and clinical consensus regarding some of these characteristics. Unemployment, comorbid psychiatric disorders, family dysfunction, a prior history of relapse, lack of any close friends who are nonabusers—each of these factors increases the likelihood of treatment failure or relapse. It is inappropriate to compare unadjusted outcomes for two programs whose patients differ significantly on these characteristics.

There is less consensus regarding the importance of other patient characteristics, some of which may prove to play a major role in treatment planning and effectiveness. For example, there is presently an open question regarding the role, if any, of genetic factors in addiction. If there is a gene or combination of genes that predispose toward addiction, this genetic factor would be important to case mix adjustment.

Doubtless there are, and for the foreseeable future will continue to be, unidentified patient characteristics that play a role in relapse. And even if this were not the case, the problem of "weighting" psychometrically adequate measures of these characteristics to provide a fully satisfactory case mix adjustment system would remain beyond the present capabilities of the field. Substantial advances in theory of both addictions and measurement are necessary before the question, "For whom is a program or treatment modality effective?" can be fully answered.

In the view of some researchers, evaluation of substance abuse treatment will be forever constrained by methodological problems that appear to be insolvable (Howard et al., 1986). Specifically, the problem of sample attrition has long plagued evaluation researchers. It may be that there are unavoidable weaknesses in all statistical approaches to control for attrition; substance abuse treatment evaluation will therefore remain an imperfect science.

THE USEFULNESS OF AN IMPERFECT SCIENCE.

It is possible to acknowledge both the limitations of outcomes measurement in substance abuse treatment and its utility. Advances in the
field suggest that, despite their limitations, current measures and
methodologies have considerable utility. There is much that has
been and remains to be accomplished before the theoretical limitations of evaluation methodologies become a practical concern.

Advances in instrumentation and methodologies are illustrated by
the development of sophisticated measures and the emergence of
firms specializing in treatment research.

Measures

The Addiction Severity Index (ASI), Substance Abuse Subtle Screening Inventory (SASSI), Alcohol Outcomes Module, and the
COMPASS system are leading examples of advances in substance
abuse measurement. The ASI represented a major advance in measurement when it was introduced by McLellan et al. (1980), for both
scientific and practical reasons. As an evaluation tool, it was a landmark instrument in that it provided reliable and valid (McLellan et
al., 1985) quantification in seven areas relating to addiction and relapse. Scores on its scales for alcohol use, drug use, employment,
medical, legal, psychiatric, and family/social problems indicate the
respondent's need for treatment in each of these areas. An abbreviated version, appropriate for posttreatment follow-up, yields scale
scores in the same seven areas and is therefore very useful for evaluating treatment outcomes. The ASI is commonly administered at the
start of treatment, at discharge, and at six months postdischarge to
evaluate treatment impact and the durability of gains. The developers of the ASI have provided norms for various populations (McLellan et al., 1992) as a further aide to evaluation research.

The ASI also has some practical advantages over most other substance abuse measures. An effective model and materials for training ASI interviewers have been developed, and a user "hotline" made
available, thanks to funding support from the National Institute on
Drug Abuse. The ASI is generic—that is, it is not reflective of any
particular theory of addictions or treatment model. It is available in
English and at least nine foreign languages. As will be seen, ASI data
are useful for treatment referral and planning, as well as for evalu-

ation. Finally, ASI interviews can be conducted reliably by a trained technician; data collection does not require involvement of clinical staff.

The major weakness of the ASI is its length; an ASI interview requires 45 to 60 minutes to complete. This makes it impractical for routine use in many clinical settings. Abbreviated versions have been developed to remedy this problem. Despite this limitation, the scientific and practical strengths of the ASI have made it the most widely used substance abuse evaluation instrument in the world.

The SASSI is a paper and pencil questionnaire (Miller, 1985). Its 88 items provide a brief (15 minutes to complete) and administratively simple measure easily integrated into clinical procedures. Like the ASI, it includes items in domains (emotional/interpersonal/cognitive/social/psychological) related to substance abuse, in addition to alcohol and drug use patterns.

The SASSI was designed with practitioners and individual case applications in mind. The SASSI Institute emphasizes the clinical value of the scales and provides guidelines relating to interpretation and feedback of scores to patients. While the ASI was designed as an outcomes research and treatment planning tool, the SASSI was developed as a screening and treatment planning instrument.

The SASSI has not attracted the attention of the scientific community to the extent that the ASI has and there are fewer publications documenting psychometric properties, norms, as so on. But according to the SASSI Institute, the instrument is the product of 20 years of research and clinical trials involving testing of over a thousand items. It includes scales claimed to discriminate substance abusers from nonabusers despite denial or minimization efforts by the former group. The developers assert that their validation research has documented over 90% classification accuracy.

The ASI and SASSI are important measures not only because they were responsibly developed by knowledgeable substance abuse and measurement experts, but also because they are widely used. These measures offer the substantial advantage of comparability across programs—that is, a user of either tool can compare the findings for his/her program or patients with norms based upon thousands of administrations nationwide.

The most recent noteworthy addition to the measurement armamentarium that holds promise for widespread use is the Substance

Abuse Outcomes Module (SAOM) (Smith et al., 1995) developed by Dr. G. Richard Smith and his colleagues in the Department of Psychiatry, University of Arkansas. SAOM is the most recent addition to a comprehensive outcomes management system, consisting of diagnosis-specific data collection protocols developed for a broad range of physical and mental health disorders.

As its name implies, SAOM was designed for the specific purpose of measuring treatment outcomes for substance abusers. When used (as recommended) in conjunction with the Personal Characteristics form and the Health Status questionnaire, the module provides for measurement of demographics, functional status, consumption, various alcohol-related physical, emotional, and social problems, and "case mix" variables (e.g., age at onset, parental alcoholism, social support, comorbid psychiatric conditions, and others) considered to have an effect upon outcomes.

The full set of alcohol outcomes instruments includes (1) a Patient Baseline Assessment form, (2) Clinician Baseline Assessment, (3) Patient Follow-up, and (4) Follow-up Assessment forms. The Patient Follow-up is recommended for completion every six months posttreatment for at least 18 months. Patient Baseline and Follow-up (exclusive of the comparison forms) each requires 15 to 20 minutes to complete; data provide for reliable, case mix adjusted assessment of treatment outcomes.

The COMPASS system, though its substance abuse scale is not finalized, illustrates the role of measurement in solving important problems in treatment planning, in this case, identification of substance abuse problems in patients who present for other mental health treatment. COMPASS (Compass Information Services, 1995) is the most widely used system for the concurrent management of individual patient care. It is quite likely that a substantial minority, perhaps 15% to 25%, of patients who complete COMPASS during general mental health treatment have unacknowledged substance abuse disorders seriously affecting their prognosis.

The addition to COMPASS of a scale to detect "hidden" substance abuse problems would alert therapists to the need to address their patient's addiction, substantially improving the likelihood of favorable treatment outcomes. A pilot version of the COMPASS substance abuse scale is being currently validated to determine its accuracy in detecting unacknowledged substance abuse, and its performance in relation to clinician evaluations.

Treatment Evaluation and Research Firms

Improvements in instrumentation have been accompanied by the establishment of large evaluation databases and of firms specializing in substance abuse outcomes research. Dr. A. Thomas McLellan, lead developer of the ASI, has established a highly regarded, ASI-based, evaluation service at the Treatment Research Institute (TRI) in Philadelphia. The TRI provides ASI training and user assistance, and conducts program evaluations and substance abuse research, using the ASI and a large ASI outcomes database. Typically, TRI provides ASI training to treatment program staff who administer the instrument to 50 to 100 patients at intake. TRI staff conduct ASI follow-up interviews via telephone six months after discharge. Comparison of the follow-up and intake ASI scale scores provides a measure of the change a patient experienced during and immediately following treatment. In addition to conducting the follow-up interviews, TRI staff analyze all data, access outcomes in relation to norms, and prepare reports of findings.

Less recent is the Chemical Abuse/Addiction Treatment Outcome Registry (CATOR) organization in St. Paul, Minnesota, which since 1980 has conducted more addiction treatment program evaluations than any other organization in the world. CATOR provides its clients with instrumentation and a database for program comparisons that includes data for over 25,000 adults.

Impact on the Field

Despite the limitations noted earlier, outcomes measurement by firms like TRI and CATOR, and by independent researchers, has played a positive role in the evolution of addictions treatment. For example, a landmark study on the effectiveness of substance abuse treatment (McLellan et al., 1982) provided compelling evidence that addictions treatment "works," documenting "significant and pervasive" improvement in a sample of 742 patients across six programs. Major positive changes were found six months posttreatment in alcohol use, drug use, employment, criminal behavior, and psychological functioning. Studies such as this have been critical to continued federal support for addictions treatment, and to the reimbursement for treatment costs under corporate benefit programs.

The finding that outcomes of nonresidential outpatient treatment were generally as favorable as those of inpatient/residential care was an important factor in the shift away from inpatient treatment in the early 1990s. Studies comparing the relative effectiveness of varying treatment modalities have yielded less clear-cut findings. Among the various treatment alternatives—drug-free modalities (i.e., therapeutic communities, self-help groups, psychotherapy, behavioral therapy for relapse prevention) and drug-assisted treatments involving methadone, naltrexone, and antabuse—there is ample evidence of global effectiveness, but little basis for differential referral.

Thus, the practical effect of much outcomes measurement has been to provide for the continued support of a variety of modalities, while referral decisions for specific patients are driven more by cost considerations and clinical judgments than by any empirically based matching process validated through outcomes research. The practice guidelines for treatment of substance use disorders published in 1995 by the American Psychiatric Association, and the patient placement criteria published in 1991 by the American Society of Addiction Medicine (ASAM) are very heavily influenced by clinical judgments. The predictive validity (Do patients treated in accordance with these guidelines/criteria have better outcomes?) of each remains to be determined.

Validation of guidelines is an important and, with some limitations, achievable goal of outcomes measurement. Outcomes measurement can provide useful information relating to a broad range of issues of interest to therapists, administrators, referral sources, and third-party payers.

- Are patients improved following treatment?
- Do treatment gains persist? For how long?
- Does treatment effectiveness vary by type of patient?
- Do some types of patients succeed more often in one treatment modality than another?

- What is the impact upon treatment effectiveness of a change in methods or staffing?

- What is the most cost-effective "mix" of services within a program?

- Which programs within a treatment modality are most effective?

- Which therapists within a program are most effective?

As program variations and costs increase, along with managed care pressures for accountability and cost-effectiveness, measurement systems providing even partial answers to these questions will become increasingly important. Ultimately, it may be possible to manage outcomes not only for treatment systems, but for individual patients, by monitoring progress in relation to risk-adjusted norms, as the COMPASS system has done for mental health patients.

Owing to the complexity of measurement issues and methodological weaknesses described above, measurement systems can be expected to provide useful, but not definitive, information relating to key issues. Beyond the overall effectiveness of a variety of treatment interventions, there is little that can be said to be "known," and practically no assertion goes unchallenged. Such basic questions as to the effectiveness of 12-step programs in achieving or maintaining sobriety, the existence of a genetic factor predisposing to addiction, the acceptability of controlled substance use as a treatment objective, and the characteristics of patients for whom residential or inpatient settings are optimal continue to be controversial.

In summary, outcomes measurement has played an important and expanding role in substance abuse treatment. The information it can provide is limited by weaknesses in instrumentation, methodologies, and theory. But information need not be perfect to be useful, and outcomes measurement can inform a broad range of decisions relating to both treatment systems and the placement and care of individual patients. Whatever the weaknesses of current measurement systems, the alternative—decisions driven by political and cost considerations—is unlikely to better serve the patient or to reduce the true "costs" of addictions.

This section described potential uses of measurement to improve treatment. The chapter concludes with a description of the use of measurement to produce substantial improvements in the referral, treatment planning, and outcomes for substance abusers in a managed mental health system.

MATCHING PATIENTS TO TREATMENT SERVICES

There is substantial variability among treatment modalities and the quantity and quality of services available from programs within each modality. Treatment options include weekly individual treatment provided by an addictions counselor or other mental health professional; various pharmacological treatments; drug-free programs that vary widely in intensity and may be offered in outpatient, freestanding residential, or hospital settings; and long-term residential care in a therapeutic community; all of which may (or may not) be offered in conjunction with a "12-step" program such as AA. Within each modality, a range of group, individual, or family treatment services may be offered. The staff providing these services brings a broad range of experience, training, and qualifications to their work. Modality, staff qualifications, and program differences in leadership, organization, and staffing patterns may affect outcomes (Ball & Ross, 1991).

There is also wide variability among patients demographically, clinically, and regarding their treatment history, expectations, and motivation. Program characteristics and patient characteristics may independently determine outcomes, but it is also reasonable to expect an interaction effect. Some types of programs may be more effective than others for a given patient, and some types of patients may experience more favorable outcomes than others in a given type of program. This hypothesis has prompted researchers to attempt to improve outcomes by matching patients to programs.

In 1989, researchers from the Center for Studies of Addictions at the University of Pennsylvania/Veterans Administration Medical Center, in collaboration with Integra, Inc. (a Philadelphia-based Employee Assistance Program/managed mental health care firm) initiated a five-year study of patient–program matching supported by funding from the National Institute on Drug Abuse.

The study design involved three phases. During the first phase, substance abusers seeking treatment within the Integra system would be referred to programs using a tripartite referral procedure common among EAPs:

1. An intake worker confirmed a presenting problem involving drug or alcohol abuse, recorded basic information about the case; and scheduled the patient for a full clinical evaluation by a substance abuse specialist.

2. The substance abuse specialist conducted the evaluation, attempted to motivate the patient for treatment, and tried to persuade him/her to accept a referral to one of four major treatment programs. Referral factors included HMO or insurance restrictions (when applicable); the level of care and type of program considered clinically appropriate; accessibility; patient preference; space availability in the program; and the evaluator's perception of the program quality.

3. If the patient accepted the referral and went to the treatment program, an evaluation was conducted by program staff for treatment planning.

The purpose of the initial study phase was to identify patient characteristics associated with favorable or unfavorable outcomes in various types of programs. The four programs were chosen to represent varying degrees of treatment settings, intensity (i.e., traditional outpatient, intensive outpatient, residential/inpatient) and philosophy of care (i.e., 12-step based, psychiatric). Importantly, all four were well established, respected, licensed, and accredited, with treatment sites conveniently located across the Philadelphia area.

To identify patient characteristics important to optimal referral, the project design called for an ASI interview to be conducted by the evaluator for all patients entering treatment. To measure the type and quantity of services provided to the patient, Treatment Service Review (TSR) data were collected for all patients during treatment. Finally, patient outcomes were assessed via ASI interviews conducted by research staff six months postdischarge.

Phase II of the research plan involved analysis of the Phase I data. The analysis goal was to examine the relationships among patient characteristics, program referrals, and outcomes to establish an empirically based matching strategy (referral guidelines) specifying which types of patients should be referred to each of the four programs. This strategy would then be evaluated during Phase III by determining whether patients referred to the "correct" (i.e., in relation to the guidelines) programs achieved more favorable outcomes than those who were mismatched.

Review of Phase I activities and analysis of Phase I data led to changes in both instrumentation and the research objective. The ASI proved too long to administer reliably when the clinician also had to establish rapport, make a referral, and motivate the patient for treatment—all within the same session. Consequently, an abbreviated version (the Index of Special Services) was developed that preserved the psychometric strengths of the full ASI while reducing its length by nearly half.

The modification to the research objectives proved necessary when it became apparent that the original objective—establishment of a procedure to match patients to programs based upon clinically relevant patient characteristics—was not achievable. Nearly two-thirds (62%) of the 186 Phase I patients could not be referred to the programs considered optimal by the evaluator. In order of importance, the reasons were that limitations in insurance or HMO plans precluded placement; the preferred program did not have a treatment slot or bed available; the patient insisted upon referral to the program most convenient to home or work; or the patient's beliefs about a program's quality (e.g., from prior experience or that of a friend/family member) were an important factor in referral. In short, even if patient–program matching were technically feasible, it is impractical since the referral decision is often driven, and always influenced, by nonclinical factors.

Though the Phase I results were discouraging in relation to the original research objectives, some of the findings suggested a hypothesis that ultimately proved fruitful and, for outcomes management, highly important. First, the TSR data showed quite unexpectedly that there were large differences among programs in the type and quantity of services they delivered, and those differences were not closely related to program structure or treatment philosophy. While the inpatient/residential programs provided more services overall, they were heavily concentrated in the alcohol/drug areas. However, there were no differences between inpatient and outpatient settings with regard to the quantity of employment, family, and psychiatric services offered.

Second, patient outcomes were generally very positive. On average, alcohol and drug use was reduced by 74% and 73% respectively from admission to follow-up. Six months after treatment, 77% were employed and only small percentages received welfare (11%) or required retreatment for substance abuse (12%). Most importantly, however, it appeared that the programs that provided the most services directed at a particular treatment problem achieved the most favorable outcomes. The quantity of services and the "fit" between patient problems areas and services delivered appeared more important predictors of outcome than setting (e.g., inpatient or outpatient) or treatment philosophy (e.g., 12-step or psychiatric).

In summary, the results of Phase II data analysis indicated that patient–program matching was not an effective strategy for managing outcomes since it was probably not technically possible, and it certainly was not practical. However, the data suggested that significant improvement in outcomes might be achieved through matching patients to services—that is, arranging for patients to receive the treatment services suggested by their ISS scale scores for employment, family, and psychiatric problem severity. The data analysis concluded with the establishment of threshold scores on these three scales that would be used, during the study's final phase, to trigger a request for special treatment services linked to these problem areas.

The Phase III research evaluated a radically altered referral process designed to efficiently match patients to services (rather than to programs). When a substance abuser contacts Integra seeking treatment (normally by phone), the Integra intake counselor conducts an ISS interview, entering the patient responses directly into a computer.

The computer immediately computes the severity scores for the medical, employment, family, and psychiatric scales, and alerts the intake counselor if any of these scores exceed the threshold indicating a need for treatment services focused on one or more of these areas. Extreme scores on the medical or psychiatric scales indicate referral to inpatient treatment. Less extreme scores that exceed a second, lower threshold on the psychiatric scale indicate a need for special, targeted services in an outpatient setting, as do elevated scores on the family and employment scales.

While the patient is still on the phone, a referral is made to an appropriate program, contingent upon that program's agreement to provide any special services that are indicated. Once the patient begins treatment, TSR interviews are conducted weekly to ensure that the needed services are, in fact, being delivered.

Phase III results illustrate the potential of measurement to improve outcomes and increase the cost-effectiveness of treatment—in short, to manage outcomes.

The Phase III matching process achieved substantially better outcomes while enabling Integra to reduce the costs of treatment referral. Substantial cost savings were achieved because the added expense of the extended phone interview by the intake counselor (who is expected to complete an ISS interview under the Phase III process) is more than offset by the elimination of the cost of the face-to-face evaluation by the substance abuse specialist, which is no longer normally required. In 82% of all cases, the intake counselor was able to make a direct referral.

The matching process achieved impressive results in relation to treatment outcomes. The "show rate," program completion rate, and six-month outcomes all improved. The "show rate" of patients who accepted the treatment referral and began treatment improved by 31%. Under the former referral process, a patient who was motivated for treatment would call Integra and speak to the intake counselor, who would schedule the patient for an evaluation by a substance abuse specialist (typically a day or two later). Several more days would often elapse following the evaluation before treatment could begin. It was not unusual for denial to set in during the period between the initial call and the scheduled start of treatment. The matching procedure, by sharply reducing this time, capitalizes on the patient motivation while at its peak to reduce "no shows".

Not only did "matched" patients present for treatment more often, but in comparison to other patients in the same programs those matched to services more often completed treatment (93% versus 81%). It is reasonable to expect that individuals who receive services directed toward their specific problems will more often feel they are being helped and will maintain their motivation for treatment; this appears to be the case.

Perhaps most importantly, matched patients demonstrated substantially better postdischarge outcomes as reported on the six-month follow-up ASI and confirmed (for a 25% subsample) via breathalyzer and urinalysis results. The recidivism rate (reentry into treatment) was 44% greater for patients not matched to services (35% versus 24% for matched patients). Matched patients also experienced statistically significantly better outcomes in relation to employment, family, and legal problems. Additional details of this research are available in both research (McLellan et al., 1993) and practitioner (Byrne et al., 1996) publications.

In summary, the CSA-Integra research illustrates how measurement can be used to manage outcomes in substance abuse treatment. In this example, a comprehensive, standardized instrument (ASI) was modified to produce a more administratively efficient scale (ISS) for the assessment of problem severity. The ISS scale scores for an individual patient are compared to research-based thresholds to identify service needs, and another standardized instrument (TSR) is employed to ensure that needed services are being delivered. These procedures are readily integrated into clinical practice, and produce substantial improvement in the cost-effectiveness of treatment.

Despite advances in both instrumentation and methodologies in recent years, the application of measurement to manage outcomes is still in its infancy. Further advances will surely be made, to the benefit of payers, providers, patients, their families, and the millions of Americans whose lives are touched by substance abuse.

7

Psychopharmacotherapy Treatment Outcomes

Psychotropic medications have changed, and will continue to change, the practice of psychiatry and behavioral health. It is common knowledge that antipsychotics, antidepressants, and antimanics have an efficacy of about 70%, meaning that approximately 70% of patients can expect moderate to total symptom remission. This percent is often compared to the rather dismal figure of 30 to 40% efficacy of other medical treatments. What is less well known and understood is that the actual efficacy of psychopharmacotherapy is in the same range as medical treatments. This is largely due to high rates of noncompliance and of relapse and recurrence, as well as biological factors such as receptor downregulation. Nevertheless, in the "treatment-receptive" patient, the use of medication alone or in combination with other treatment modalities can quickly and effectively ameliorate symptoms of most Axis I disorders.

The questions become: What is a "treatment-receptive" patient? and How can those who are less receptive become "treatment-receptive" so that psychopharmacological treatment can be maximized? This chapter addresses these two questions by describing five treatment strategies that have been shown to maximize treatment outcomes when psychotropic medications are indicated. These overlapping strategies are designed to assist the provider in planning and implementing tailored, focused treatment. These strategies are delineated for the anxiety disorders, major depression, bipolar disorder, and schizophrenia. In addition, the chapter previews a psychopharmacotherapeutic outcomes measure and management system.

FIVE STRATEGIES FOR MAXIMIZING
PSYCHOPHARMOCOTHERAPY

Optimal treatment outcomes presume that a patient is prescribed and utilizes the most efficacious treatment. This presumption is seldom met in clinical practice. Even if the most potent, focused, and tailored treatment is prescribed, it cannot be assumed that the patient will commit to and cooperate with the treatment over an extended period of time. The treatment-responsive patient is able to make and keep this commitment. The challenge for providers— both those who are prescribers and those who are therapists, if joint treatment is involved—is to expect and facilitate treatment-responsiveness in their patients. Five treatment strategies have been noted to optimize treatment response and outcome (Sperry, 1995b). The five strategies are (1) focused assessment, (2) combining treatment modalities, (3) enhancing medication compliance, (4) incorporating psychoeducational interventions, and (5) preventing relapse and recurrence.

Focused Assessment

Focused assessment should include two patient characteristics that are predictive of treatment-responsiveness and, hence, positive treatment outcomes: treatment readiness and explanatory model (Ward, 1991; Beitman, 1993). Treatment readiness refers to the patient's motivation and capacity to cooperate with treatment. Assessment of treatment readiness, as well as prompting and facilitating the highest level of readiness that the patient is capable of, is particularly important when psychotropic agents are the principal treatment modality. Chapter 3 describes the elements of treatment readiness.

The explanatory model is a patient's personal interpretation or explanation of disease and symptoms (Kleinman, 1988). This model can be fraught with misinformation or misattribution. Such "explanations" become the basis for patient education and negotiation. For instance, bipolar patients who believe that their illness was caused by insomnia and can be cured by a good night's sleep need to have their "explanation" corrected and polarized. Similarly, the patient who explains the experience of generalized anxiety in terms of a single early-life trauma should hear the provider describe a more complete model of the illness that also allows for these particular concerns about the early trauma.

Specific irrational beliefs about illness or treatment must also be elicited and addressed. The delusional belief that the medication to be prescribed is a poison is one obvious example. A less obvious irrational belief involves patients with low self-esteem. They may ascribe negative meaning to medication, viewing it as representative of their personal deficiency or worthlessness. This projected badness can then be externalized and dismissed by their refusing to accept the medication and thus protecting themselves from further loss of self-esteem (Docherty, 1988).

Helping patients understand their illness is best done in a biopsychosocial context, particularly for those patients seeking the magic pill (Ward, 1991). Negotiated explanations that are tailored to the patient's experience are particularly valuable. Such an explanation should be simple, integrate biological and psychosocial mechanisms, and incorporate some elements of the patient's explanation. For example, a schizophrenic male may accept that he has a biochemical imbalance that leaves him overly reactive to his environment and to other people—the perceptual filter model of psychosis—resulting in social withdrawal and simple phobia. Or, the patient insisting that hypoglycemia is the basis for his major depressive episode might be offered a treatment plan in which blood glucose would be checked immediately and reevaluated if a four-week trial of medication is not successful (Ward, 1991).

Finally, medication can be perceived as both a vehicle and an agent of control. It may be viewed as a chemical means by which the clinician exerts control over the patient's thoughts or actions, and, thereby, the patient's noncompliance is a means of controlling and defeating the clinician. Similarly, noncompliance may function as a projective identification, as when the patient's feeling of helplessness is projected onto and induced in the clinician.

Combining Treatment Modalities

Combined treatment refers to adding other modalities to the primary modality. In psychopharmacotherapy, this usually means that individual psychotherapy, group psychotherapy, couple, or family therapy is added to the medication management treatment so as to increase treatment response and outcomes. Chapter 3 offers a number of guidelines for combining various treatment modalities.

Enhancing Medication Compliance

A major challenge facing both prescribing and nonprescribing clinicians is that of enhancing medication compliance. Key factors that are known to affect compliance include patient factors, provider–patient interaction, the treatment regimen itself, and family factors. Guidelines germane to these factors are noted for each of the four classes of psychiatric disorders discussed in following sections.

Incorporating Psychoeducational Interventions

A powerful optimizing strategy in psychopharmacotherapy is the incorporation of psychoeducational interventions. Psychoeducation refers to much more than merely explaining the medication, dosing schedule, and side effect profile. Psychoeducation includes drug information sheets, patient education videos, medication groups, self-help organizations, support groups, social skills training, and more. Incorporating psychoeducational strategies and tactics in medication management is almost always essential in order to achieve symptom amelioration, particularly in the long term.

Preventing Relapse and Recurrence

A set of strategies for maintaining treatment gains once they have been achieved is termed prevention of relapse and recurrence. Technically, relapse refers to a continuation of the "original" episode, while recurrence is the instigation of a "new" episode. For this discussion, both terms will be used synonymously. In order to prevent relapse, the provider must assess the patient's risk factors and potential for relapse, and incorporate relapse prevention strategies into the treatment process.

For each of the following classes of psychiatric disorders, a number of suggestions for utilizing each of these five maximizing strategies for psychopharmacological treatment are described.

ANXIETY DISORDERS

The following strategies and guidelines reflect the current state of the art in the integrative, combined treatment of the anxiety disorders based largely on reported clinical trials. They are meant to assist the provider in thinking through treatment decisions, rather than as definitive treatment protocol. Definitive protocol will be available only after considerably more research results are reported. Guidelines and strategies are given for combined treatment of five anxiety disorders. (1) panic and agoraphobia, (2) obsessive-compulsive disorder, (3) generalized anxiety disorder, (4) social phobia, and (5) simple phobia.

A thorough diagnostic evaluation is essential. Before treatment can begin, stimulants (nicotine, caffeine, and other xanthenes) must be reduced or stopped. Alcohol and substance abuse or dependence must first be treated before any of the following guidelines are initiated.

Medication (antidepressant or benzodiazepene) is typically the initial treatment, unless the patient presents with any of the following: (a) refusal to take, failure to respond, or poor tolerance of the medication; (b) reappearance of symptoms after medication is stopped; or (c) residual symptoms remaining while the dosage is at therapeutic levels. If any one or all are present, add behavioral interventions and/or psychotherapy. A variety of pharmacologic strategies for those refractory to a single medication should be tried. If the initial antidepressant is a tricyclic or SSRI and is not effective, an adequate trial of an MAOI should be considered. Switching to another class of antidepressants or an augmentation strategy, such as adding valproic acid, lithium, or busprone may also be tried (Pollack & Otto, 1994).

The treatment of choice for most patients will be combined treatment: antidepressant plus exposure therapy. Add exposure therapy after medication is begun. When symptom relief is achieved, begin weaning and eventually discontinue medication while continuing exposure.

For individuals in combined treatment with poor medication tolerance, various options exist. They are: (1) identifying the cognitive and interpersonal roots of medication-triggered anxiety, (2) educating the patient and correcting misinformation about the meaning and consequences of panic episodes and medication, (3) delaying the start of medication while the patient convinces himself or herself of the acceptability of the medication trail, and (4) training in controlled breathing, which may be useful for patients experiencing a jitteriness response to tricyclics.

Benzodiazepenes and other drugs that affect state-dependent learning (barbiturates, antihistamines, hydroxyzine, meprobamate) tend to interfere with exposure training and should be avoided. Griest and Jefferson (1992) offer this as an explanation for loss of treatment effect and recurrence of symptoms.

For patients only partially responsive to combined treatment, the presence of a treatment-antagonistic personality factor or personality disorder must be identified. Patients with comorbid personality disorders, especially dependent, histrionic, and avoidant disorders, require focal psychotherapy in addition to medication and exposure training. This psychotherapy should be targeted at changing ingrained avoidance patterns of thinking and behavior.

First, patients who remain intensely fearful tend to balk when exposure training is prescribed. They primarily need medication alone with a graduated exposure schedule. Second, they may perceive treatment as ineffective or not credible. Exploring their treatment expectations and fantasies about their illness is necessary. Third, a lack of social support can minimize motivation as well as readiness to relinquish their pattern of avoidance. Fourth, concurrent depression can also reduce motivation for compliance with psychosocial interventions (Craske & Waikar, 1994).

Relapse prevention is a critical issue in the treatment of the anxiety disorders, especially when medication has been the sole treatment. For this reason, combined treatment involving both cognitive-behavioral and medication, along with a relapse prevention plan, is necessary. The patient should be helped to develop and write one. Booster sessions may also be helpful. When indicated, they can be scheduled at two-, four-, and eight-month intervals after treatment is terminated.

Panic and Agoraphobia

Exposure-based treatments are probably as effective as medication for both panic and agoraphobia. While relapse is common when medication is discontinued, the effects of exposure endure. It is recommended that when combined medication and psychotherapy is utilized, both be started simultaneously with medication weaned when symptoms remit. The use of benzodiazepines is not recommended since they appear to interfere with exposure and other behavioral interventions (Mavissakalian, 1993).

Group therapy can be particularly valuable in both the treatment of panic and agoraphobic symptoms and in enhancing compliance and adherence. Cognitve-behavioral groups have been shown to be effective with panic and agoraphobia, particularly with techniques such as group in vivo exposure and relearning (Brook, 1993). Barlow and Waddell (1985) describe a 10-session treatment protocol for couples therapy for agoraphobia.

Marital therapy or the addition of a significant other as a cotherapist for the behavioral component may be indicated. When the significant other is hostile, critical, and unsupportive or has some investment in maintaining the patient's symptoms, it may be necessary to involve the significant other in treatment. On the other hand, when these negative features are not present, the agoraphobic patient may be successfully treated individually with behavioral interventions (Glick, Clarkin, & Goldsmith, 1993).

Obsessive-Compulsive Disorder

Before treatment for obsessive-compulsive disorder is initiated, a complete diagnostic evaluation is essential. It is necessary because manic, psychotic, cognitively impaired, and severely personality-disordered patients require special treatment strategies and guidelines beyond those listed below. Alcohol and other substance abuse and dependence must be treated before the OCD treatment can be initiated.

If the patient is severely depressed, is purely obsessional, is taking CNS depressogenic medication, or refuses behavioral interventions, begin psychopharmacology with anafranil or a serotonergic uptake inhibitor. Medication is usually required for most OCD patients at some point in treatment, particularly when the aforementioned indications are present.

If rituals are present, the patient has a drug allergy, or is reluctant to begin a medication trial, begin with office-based behavior therapy. This would include instruction on behavioral exposure training and response prevention training, supplemented with between session homework assignments (initially three hrs per day). Providing the patient with a copy of *Obsessive Compulsive Disorder: A Guide* by Greist (1992b) is recommended.

For most patients, a combination of behavior therapy (exposure and response prevention) with a serotonergic uptake inhibitor is the treatment of choice, with both treatments starting simultaneously. Research consistently shows the value of this particular treatment combination (Mavissakalian et al., 1993).

For an Axis II disorder and/or to increase compliance treatability, provide focal psychotherapy. As previously indicated, personality pathology can negatively impact efforts to treat Axis I symptomatology.

If there is an unsatisfactory response, consider the following: (a) consultation with or referral to a behavior therapist with OCD expertise, and (b) reevaluation of dosage, duration, and medication compliance. Consider utilizing an augmentation strategy that further enhances serotonergic activity or decreases dopaminergic, particularly when a concomitant schizotypal personality disorder or tic disorder is present; or switch to another serotonergic agent.

If treatment fails, rediagnose and consider referral for psychosurgery for very severe, intractable conditions. Often, another diagnostic evaluation reveals unexpected conditions such as an undetected or untreated substance disorder, the presence of schizotypal personality disorder, or a space-occupying lesion. If no such diagnosis can be made, and all other medication trials, including augmentation, have failed, a neurosurgical consult can be made.

Relapse prevention is an important part of the treatment plan in OCD. The patient should be helped to develop and write a personalized relapse prevention plan. This plan should specify high-risk circumstance and triggers, as well as a plan for anticipating and dealing with them. Adverse life events and depression are often associated with the reemergence of OCD symptoms. Since exposure and response prevention are primary intervention strategies, the patient must be coached in applying them in times of relapse. Booster sessions may be necessary to reestablish symptom remission. The availability of these sessions should be made known and the patient should be encouraged to schedule them as needed.

Generalized Anxiety Disorder

A complete functional psychiatric evaluation is a prerequisite to tailoring treatment for a generalized anxiety disorder, based on the patient's perpetuants, pattern, and prognostic factors. Alcohol and/or substance abuse or dependence must be treated prior to treatment of GAD.

Treatment modality depends on the severity of the anxiety. For mild cases, psychotherapy may be sufficient. For moderate anxiety, medication or cognitive behavior therapy with exposure training is indicated.

Combined treatment is probably indicated for severe anxiety. In treatment-resistant cases, an undiagnosed or untreated substance or personality disorder is probably present. Appropriate focal psychotherapeutic interventions should be added to the combined treatment.

Strategies for preventing relapse and maintaining gains should be incorporated throughout treatment and emphasized as termination draws near. If the patient had been on medication, it usually will be weaned and discontinued by this time. The patient should be helped to write an individualized relapse prevention plan that includes high-risk circumstances and triggers, along with the specific preventive measures, including desensitization strategies. Toward the end of treatment, the patient's expectations of future worries about anxiety episodes should be frankly discussed. Role playing can be utilized to prepare for such newly encountered situations. One or two booster sessions can be scheduled at 4- and 8-week intervals to review progress as well as maintenance and relapse issues.

Social Phobia

Before initiating treatment of the phobia, a complete functional psychiatric evaluation is needed to diagnose concurrent alcohol and substance abuse or dependence. Detoxification is necessary to establish the patient's baseline functioning and to diagnose a treatable Axis I disorder.

Begin treatment with either medication or cognitive behavioral therapy, depending on patient preference and/or clinician's expertise. Assuming the symptom presentation is mild to moderate, either modality can be effective.

When treatment outcomes are limited, consider combined treatment. As with other anxiety disorders, combined treatment is particularly useful with moderately severe to severe presentations.

Relapse prevention is more an issue with the generalized rather than focal form of social phobia. Whereas brief targeted interventions may be sufficient for the focal form, the generalized form may require longer-term treatment, particularly for individuals with dependent or avoidant personality structures. Developing an individualized relapse prevention plan and booster sessions are necessary. Scheduling booster sessions at monthly intervals for four months and then spaced two months apart for a further eight months may be indicated (Mattick & Andrews, 1994).

Simple Phobia

When treating a simple phobia, a complete functional psychiatric evaluation is essential to determine that the phobic avoidance is not associated with schizophrenia, posttraumatic stress disorder, obsessive-compulsive disorder, or a medical condition.

Employ exposure therapy or refer the patient to a behavior therapist with expertise in simple phobias. Clark (1989) describes exposure protocol that most clinicians with little or no behavior therapy experience can easily master. Behavior therapists who specialize in simple phobia treatment can often effect a cure in a single session.

Medications are contraindicated in simple phobias. However, a limited course of benzodiazepine might be prescribed to enable the phobic patient to engage in an otherwise "unavoidable" situation.

Fear levels may increase some time after treatment. Thus, patients should be instructed to anticipate and prepare for this eventuality. They should also be instructed not to give in to the impulse to avoid or escape the fear, but to face it as they have learned. An individualized relapse plan should be developed prior to termination. Although there is less likelihood that patients with simple phobias will need booster sessions, that option should be made known to the patient.

MAJOR DEPRESSION

This section describes specific treatment guidelines for various combinations of medication and psychotherapy modalities. The combined modalities are individual, group, marital and family psychotherapy, and psychosocial interventions.

Individual Therapy Plus Medication

Individual intervention strategies that include medication should be offered to patients who meet specific indications. Joyce (1992) lists five predictors for positive responses to antidepressants alone: good premorbid personality; psychomotor retardation; an intermediate level of severity and endogeneity; no psychotic features; and the absence of "atypical" features such as panic attacks or reversed vegetative symptoms. In their exhaustive evaluation of the research studies summarized in their monograph, Manning and Frances (1990) found that there was a U-shaped relationship between the use of combined treatment and the severity of depression. They contend that combined treatment should be offered to those in the middle: from moderate to moderately severe depression. For those with mild depression, psychotherapy is the initial treatment of choice, while for very severe depression, medication and hospitalization are usually required as the initial treatment of choice. Only after some recompensation is achieved can combined treatment be considered. Thus, combined treatment for major depression is the first-line treatment for patients midway between the extreme of mild and very severe.

Cognitive Therapy Plus Medication

Manning and Francis (1990) also found, like much of the outcomes data from the NIMH Collaboration Depression Studies, that cognitive therapy plus medication had an additive effect with regard to preventing relapse (Rush & Hollon, 1991). Some specific contraindications for a time-limited course of cognitive therapy and medication were noted: organic brain syndrome, severe depression with hallucinations or delusions, and schizoaffective disorder. In addition, social systems factors such as negative attitudes of family members or hopelessness regarding the patient's depression can negatively impact the combined cognitive therapy–medication treatment. Finally, cognitive therapy and medication are so compatible that either can be added readily after the other has begun without adversely affecting the treatment process (Rush & Hollon, 1991).

Interpersonal Psychotherapy Plus Medication

Interpersonal psychotherapy (Weissman & Klerman, 1991) plus medication had an additive effect with regard to preventing relapse, and also decreased premature dropout from treatment. In addition, interpersonal therapy and medication increased acceptance of treatment, leading to more rapid and pervasive symptom improvement than placebo, medication alone, or cognitive therapy. Finally, interpersonal psychotherapy seemed to be more effective with more severe presentations of depression than was cognitive therapy.

Group Therapy and Medication

When indicated, consider combining group therapy with medication. Although Manning and Frances (1990) found only a marginal advantage to combining group therapy and medication as compared to each alone, Salvendy and Toffe (1991) found that combined treatment enabled 83% of patients to achieve positive treatment outcomes, as compared to 60% on medication only.

Salvendy and Toffe (1991) offer indications and contraindications for this form of combined treatment. Positive responders are individuals who most resemble this profile: (1) have had at least one good relationship prior to treatment, (2) have achieved a reasonable self-concept, (3) are capable of trusting others, (4) have few problems with control issues, (5) are capable of establishing rapport with the group therapist, (6) are willing to take risks, and (7) were capable of engaging and becoming integrated into the group at the time of referral. Nonresponders tended to include patients with prominent narcissistic and/or borderline features, or patients with hypochondrial or significant somatoform presentations.

Brook (1993) suggests that the type of group therapy offered should be consonant with the severity and chronicity of the depression. He favors homogeneous medication groups, supportive groups, or cognitive-behavior groups for more severe and chronic depressed patients, while interpersonal and psychodynamically oriented groups are considered more appropriate for less severe and less chronic patients.

Family Therapy and Medication

When indicated, combine family therapy with medication for depressed patients. When marital or family conflict appear to be the primary precipitant in episodes of clinical depression, marital or family therapy is probably indicated for treatment of interpersonal conflict. Such treatment would be directed at reducing the frequency of aversive communication, increasing more frequent positive experiences between family members, and modifying distorted cognitive and perceptual responses to the behavior of the identified patient. Typically, in major depression, medication is begun first. Then, after florid symptoms have diminished, conjoint couples or family sessions are started (Glick et al., 1993).

Compliance with Medication

It is essential to enhance compliance with medication and other aspects of treatment with depressed patients. Begin by evaluating those patients for risk factors of noncompliance. The literature on medication compliance is relatively sparse. As with other psychiatric disorders, noncompliance is relatively high—in the range of 40%. Rehm (1994) profiles the high-risk patient for noncompliance and treatment dropout. The profile indicates that patients with a lower level of formal education, lower income or socioeconomic status, and severe levels of depression are most likely to terminate therapy prematurely. However, similar patients with mild to moderate severity of depression are more likely to be noncompliant with medication.

It is important to incorporate strategies to maximize medication compliance in the treatment plan and process. The cognitive therapy of depression (Beck et al., 1979; Rush, 1988) typically incorporates strategies to enhance compliance with medication and adherence to treatment, particularly homework assignments and monitoring dysfunctional thoughts. The collaborative nature of treatment approaches like cognitive therapy naturally fosters compliance and adherence.

Research by Frank et al. (1992) showed that medication compliance is not related to age, sex, type of depression, or initial or baseline severity of depression. Rather, compliance was significantly associated with the adequacy of prophylaxis. In other words, when medication levels were subtherapeutic or intermittent, noncompliance was likely. Mann (1986) contends that the critical factor in compliance with antidepressants is sensitivity to the patient's subjective response to medication. The more side effects the patient experiences that are unheeded, the more likely the patient is to either stop medication entirely or titrate down the dosage without telling the prescribing clinician.

Psychoeducational Interventions

Psychoeducational interventions should also be employed. Fortunately, a large number of psychoeducational interventions regarding depression are available. As with the treatment of other psychiatric disorders, psychoeducational interventions can "supercharge" treatment process and outcomes. This section briefly describes three classes of psychoeducational intervention: bibliotherapy and patient educational materials, medication groups, and community support groups.

Patient education and bibliotherapy. Make patient education and bibliotherapy available to both depressed patients and their families. Bibliotherapy has proven to be surprisingly effective in the amelioration of symptoms and, some would say, in the cure of depression (Hoberman & Lewisohn, 1990). Lewisohn and his colleagues have developed an intervention called the "Coping with Depression" course, which consists of 12 two-hour sessions conducted over eight weeks in group sessions, or held twice a week during the first four weeks of treatment and once a week for the final four weeks. The course has a didactic format, which permits more group interaction. It emphasizes the attainment of knowledge and skills rather than an intensive relationship with a clinician. A basic premise of the course is that depression results from a decrease of pleasant experiences and an increase of unpleasant ones, and that treatment of depression requires that unpleasant experiences decrease, while pleasant experiences increase.

The content of the course has been adapted to a book format. The paperback, *Control Your Depression* (Lewisohn et al., 1978) essentially is a condensation of the course. Several studies cited by Hoberman and Lewisohn (1990) demonstrate that participation in either the course or the book produces improvement equivalent to other forms of individual or group therapy. By and large, persons with mild to moderate depression and who haven't been taking a prescribed antidepressant are candidates for this form of psycho-education.

Hoberman and Lewisohn list five predictors of positive treatment response: (1) higher expectation of improvement, (2) greater perceived control over symptoms, (3) lack of concurrent psychotherapy or medication, (4) higher levels of perceived family support, and (5) younger age. The two most powerful predictors are expectation of improvement and perceived control over symptoms. Furthermore, the value of the book as bibliotherapy for more severely depressed patients already in combined treatment has also been demonstrated.

Bisbee's (1991) *Educating Patients and Families About Mental Illness: A Practical Guide* has excellent modules on depression and its treatment. This material lends itself to individual or class use with patients and/or family members. Materials are camera-ready for making overhead transparencies and handouts.

Homogeneous medication groups. Refer patients with chronic, severe depression to homogeneous medication groups. Such groups where all patients carry the diagnosis of a depressive disorder have particular value for depressed patients who are lower functioning and/or have a chronic, recurring pattern of episodes. The emphasis in medication groups is on education, compliance, and socialization. The goals are to increase patients' knowledge about their illness and its treatment, to decrease their isolation, to increase social skills, to allow for the expression of feeling in a safe and nonjudgmental environment, and to provide group support (Brook, 1993). The methodology of such groups is supportive and educational. Concurrent individual sessions should be made available when necessary.

Community support groups. Encourage patient involvement in community support groups. The National Depressive and Manic Depressive Association (NDMA) has local chapters, educational resource materials and newsletters, and sponsors community support groups in many metropolitan areas of the United States and Canada. Typically, support groups meet weekly. In some communities, one or two meetings a month schedule professionals to address specific treatment issues or new medications, followed by questions and answers, while the other meetings are devoted to a self-help support-group format. Patients and their families have profited from involvement with NDMA activities, particularly with the support groups.

Prevention of Relapse and Recurrence

Prevention of relapse and recurrence is also important. Rates of relapse are very high among depressed patients. More than 50% experience relapse within three months after discontinuing maintenance or continuation treatment, and more than 80% experience recurrence within three years (Fava & Kaji, 1994). Not surprisingly, maintenance therapies have become increasingly important, particularly for patients at high risk for relapse.

It is important to evaluate depressed patients for high-risk factors for relapse and recurrence. Fava and Kaji (1994) profile the depressed patient at risk for relapse. Relapse predictors include: (1) chronicity of the illness, three or more previous episodes, (2) those with double depression (i.e., major depression superimposed over dysthymia), (3) those with a long duration of index or first depression prior to assessment and treatment, (4) the presence of persistent or residual symptoms, (5) single or unmarried status, (6) persistent with negative self-appraisal, (7) younger age, and (8) those with a greater degree of neuroticism and personality disorder traits. Hooley and Teasdale (1989) have studied relapse in married depressed patients. They found that several factors predict relapse, but the single best predictor is the patient's response to the question: "How critical is your spouse of you?" Patients who relapsed tended to have highly critical spouses.

Relapse prevention intervention should be incorporated for depressed patients, particularly those with risk factors for relapse. Cognitive therapy and other problem-focused treatment approaches tend to incorporate relapse prevention strategies as part of the treatment process. Rush and Hollon (1991) report that when cognitive therapy is combined with medication, cognitive therapy provides protection against relapse. This is the case even when medication has been stopped.

Serotonergic agents have recently gained considerable popularity in the long-term treatment of depression. This is largely due to the limited side effect profile of these agents. However, recent data suggest that long-term treatment with these agents may require higher rather than lower doses, as compared to those utilized during the acute phase of treatment. This, of course, is the opposite pattern of treatment with tricyclic agents.

BIPOLAR DISORDER

Combined treatment is nearly always necessary with this disorder. While antimanic agents free most patients from the severe disruptions of manic and depressive episodes, psychotherapy helps patients come to terms with the repercussions of past episodes and comprehend the practical and existential implications of having bipolar disorder. Although not all patients require psychotherapy, most can benefit from one of its modalities: individual, family, or group.

Combined Individual and Medication Treatment

Most bipolar patients should be offered combined individual and medication treatment. This combined treatment is the most common, whether in specialized "lithium clinics" or in general psychiatric practice (Schou, 1991). Patients who engage in a psychotherapeutic process are more likely to comply with medication regimens, are less likely to deny their illness, suffer less trauma from having bipolar disorder, and show improved social and occupational functioning. Furthermore, relapse and recurrence are considerably reduced with this form of combined treatment (Fuerst, 1994).

Nevertheless, prescribing clinicians seem to be rather ambivalent about the role of psychotherapy and their own psychotherapeutic role in the treatment of bipolar disorder. One study revealed that patients were twice as likely as clinicians to believe that psychotherapy aided medication compliance (Jamison, 1991). Limited clinical knowledge and experience with combined treatment, as well as countertransferences such as: "No one should feel this good, I'm glad the patient crashed," further reinforce the myth that lithium alone—or another antimanic—cures.

Psychotherapeutic support is essential when only medication monitoring sessions are possible. The clinician can establish an emotionally supportive atmosphere, be cognizant of and focus on general issues related to bipolar illness—specifically dependency, loss, and need for medication—and encourage patients to express their concerns. Providing such a therapeutic relationship increases the likelihood of medication compliance, and sets the stage for formal psychotherapy should it be indicated.

Formal individual psychotherapy is indicated in the following situations: those unwilling to take medication in the prescribed manner, those who are suicidal, those in whom an Axis II personality disorder is prominent, and those for whom issues of dependency and symbolic loss are particularly problematic (Jamison & Goodwin, 1983; Goodwin & Jamison, 1990; Jamison, 1991).

Issues of dependency and counterdependency, poor self-esteem, problems of intimacy, medication noncompliance, and denial of illness are major issues in psychotherapy of bipolar patients. There are different clinical formulations of the diagnosis of the bipolar disorder. While the analyst attributes the cause of the disorder and associated personality deficits to the early family environment, Jamison and Goodwin (1983) assert that the traumatic experience of the disorder itself and the nature of treatment result in the losses that dominate the patient's life. Accordingly, Jamison and Goodwin advocate focusing treatment on losses—realistic, symbolic, and unrealistic; fears of recurrence; and denial of illness.

Realistic losses include decreased energy level, loss of euphoric states, increased need for sleep, decreased sexuality, and possible decreases in productivity. Symbolic losses include loss of perceived omnipotence and independence. Unrealistic losses include circumstances where the antimanic agent and psychotherapy come to symbolize the patient's personal failure. That is, the antimanic becomes a psychological "whipping boy," representing other failure predating the onset of the bipolar illness. A major task of treatment is to help the patient understand and mourn these losses.

Kahn (1990) offers a synthesis of Jamison and Goodwin's problem-solving approach with the psychoanalytic approach. Kahn would focus individual psychotherapy on six areas: realistic losses; symbolic losses; concerns about genetic transmission; effects on family, spouse, and others; problems in learning to discriminate normal from abnormal moods; and interrupted developmental tasks, particularly if the disorder began during adolescence.

Family Therapy and Medication

When appropriate, incorporate family therapy with medication management. There are at least three indications for combined family and medication treatment: to increase medication compliance, to reduce relapse, and to increase social support, especially for high-risk patients. Family stress, particularly expressed emotion and a rejecting attitude, are predictors of relapse. High levels of family rejection together with previous hospitalizations and medication noncompliance have been shown to predict rehospitalization within 18 months (Glick et al., 1993). Miklowitz has developed a behavioral family management intervention for bipolar patients that is described under Guideline #3 (Fuerst, 1994). Davenport et al. (1977) describe the use of couples therapy in the long-term treatment of married bipolar patients on medication.

Group Therapy and Medication

Consider group therapy an adjunct to antimanic medication. Indications for combined group therapy include: medication noncompliance, relapse prevention, social support—in the absence of a supportive family, and to increase social skills and functioning. Most of the studies on combined group therapy and medication treatment involve homogeneous groups, with all patients diagnosed with bipolar disorder. Kanas (1993) has reviewed four such studies. Common goals in these groups were: sharing information about the illness, learning strategies for coping with it, and improving interpersonal relationships. To achieve these goals, treatment interventions included education, support, and facilitation of group discussions.

Multimodal Treatment and Medication

For the lithium-resistant bipolar patient, utilize a multimodal approach. The great majority of bipolar patients respond to some form of combined treatment. It has been estimated that only 5 to 10% of bipolars are truly treatment-resistant. According to Goodwin (Zoler, 1994), two factors account for lithium resistance: substance abuse and the increased use of tricyclic antidepressants with bipolar patients. About 60% of bipolar patients have a substance abuse history and must be detoxed before treatment for the bipolar illness is started. Because of the increased incidence of induced rapid cycling, tricyclics should not be routinely prescribed. Instead, an MAOI or serotonergic agent might be considered. Or, if a tricyclic must be used—as with severe depression—it should be tapered as soon as remission occurs.

The utilization of lithium-augmentation is recommended. Valproate, carbamezapine, an MAOI, thyroxin, or a calcium channel blocker like verapamil are suggested. Nonmedication modalities such as sleep deprivation and high-density light therapy are also recommended by Goodwin. Such a multimodal approach to supplement apparent lithium-resistance should be done in a sequential fashion, with each modality being added slowly and in a logical way (Zoler, 1994).

Enhancing Compliance

Enhancing compliance with medication and other aspects of treatment is advisable. Noncompliance with antimanic agents is costly not only to the patient and their families but to society as well. Patients who fail to comply with medication have a rather predictable profile, and they tend to cite medication side effects and numerous psychological factors as the reasons for their noncompliance. A number of strategies to enhance compliance are available.

Evaluate each patient for risk factors of noncompliance. Patients who are at high risk for medication noncompliance are likely to have some or many factors of this profile: They are likely to be in the first year of antimanic treatment; they tend to have a prior history of medication noncompliance; they tend to be younger; they are more likely to be male; they have a history of grandiose, euphoric manias rather than the bipolar type II presentation; they have elevated mood and fewer episodes; and they complain of "missing highs" when they are in remission of symptoms (Goodwin & Jamison, 1990).

Evaluate the patient's explanatory model as well as the provider's countertransference. Clinical experience suggests that "missing highs" is the most ominous risk factor. Accordingly, the clinician would do well to elicit the patient's explanatory model, including what bipolar illness and its symptoms represent for him or her. Since mania or hypomania associated with bipolar is, for all practical purposes, an endogenous stimulant that can be quite addicting, the "high" is preferred to the "blahs" associated with medications. Noncompliance is the patient's strategy to induce mania not just when depressed but when faced with problematic decisions and life events. Since the negative consequences accrue only later, the patient may not easily comprehend how the costs of noncompliance outweigh the benefits.

Similarly, for the patient who has already had a trial of an antimanic, the learned association between the use of the antimanic and the subsequent normothymic or dysphoric state may come to symbolize a loss of innocence from prepsychotic to postpsychotic consciousness. Thus, medication noncompliance can represent an attempt to recapture an earlier prepsychotic existence, one not yet despoiled by mania or depression (Jamison & Goodwin, 1983).

Transference and countertransference can complicate treatment and may trigger noncompliance. For this reason, the clinician must carefully monitor and deal with both. In the manic phase, patients attempt to impress and manipulate or reject the clinician in an effort to enhance self-esteem. Later, transference shifts to dependency in an effort to avoid further illness and suffering. This shift from manipulation or rejection to open dependency provides the clinician with considerable therapeutic leverage. The main countertransference issues in bipolar patients are excessive anger or excessive fear. Urges to punish the patient are evidenced in many ways, including under- or overmedicating patients, which could result in noncompliance. Kahn (1990) further discusses these and other transference and countertransference issues.

Incorporate strategies for maximizing medication compliance in the treatment plan and process. Goodwin and Jamison (1990) summarize six guidelines for maximizing compliance. They include: (1) monitoring compliance with regular inquiries about medication use, main effects and side effects, and regular serum levels, (2) monitoring side effects and treating them aggressively, (3) education, particularly about prodromal signs and persistent symptoms, (4) effecting a reasonable dosing schedule and providing written instructions, as well as involving family members in administering medications, if appropriate, (5) adjunctive psychotherapy, and (6) self-help groups.

Cochran (1984) describes an individual psychotherapeutic format for enhancing compliance that is noteworthy. A clinician meets for six sessions—one hour each—and follows a structured cognitive-behavioral outline. Topics include eliciting patients' beliefs about their illness and the medication, identifying and monitoring negative thoughts about medication, coping skills, and problem solving regarding medication issues. Not surprisingly, encouraging patients to express their beliefs and feelings about medication and then anticipating possible noncompliance issues not only increase commitment to treatment, but also will prevent noncompliance.

Psychoeducation and Treatment

Psychoeducation needs to be incorporated in the treatment process. There are probably more forms of psychoeducation that are readily available to bipolar patients than for most other psychiatric disorders, particularly in the area of patient education and bibliotherapy. Other forms of psychoeducation include family education and intervention, and support groups.

Make patient education and bibliotherapy available to bipolar patients. There are three booklets written by the staff of the nationwide Lithium Information Center that clinicians would do well to make available to bipolar patients and their families.* These booklets are informative and accurately represent the cutting edge of treatment for the bipolar disorder. The booklets include a form for recording serum levels (lithium, carbomezapine, valproate) and a

---

*Booklets available from the Lithium Information Center, Dean Foundation, 3000 Excelsior Drive, Suite 203, Madison, WI 53719-1914:
- *Lithium and Manic Depression: A Guide* (1992), by John Bohn, M.D., and James Jefferson, M.D. Madison, WI: Dean Foundation (30 pp).
- *Valproate and Manic Depression: A Guide* (1993) by James Jefferson, M.D., and John Greist, M.D. Madison, WI: Dean Foundation (30 pp).
- *Carbamezapine and Manic Depression: A Guide* (1990) by Janet Medenwald, M.D., John Greist, M.D., and James Jefferson, M.D., Madison, WI: Dean Foundation (30 pp).

list of suggested technical and nontechnical readings. Since bipolar patients and their families tend to have higher levels of educational attainment, they are often quite interested and willing to learn more about their illness and its treatment. In addition, there are a number of autobiographies of recovery by bipolar patients. The actress, Patty Duke Astin, is a spokesperson for the NIMH on bipolar disorder and her book *A Brilliant Madness: Living with Manic Depressive Illness* (1992) has been well received by bipolar patients and their families.

Family Education and Management

Incorporate family education and management when possible. Bisbee's *Educating Patients and Families About Mental Illness* (1991) has a teaching module on bipolar disorder and its treatment with copy-ready material for overhead transparencies and handouts. This material can easily be incorporated into clinical practice. Miklowitz (Fuerst, 1994) has designed a family behavioral management intervention for lower-functioning bipolar patients and their families. Used in conjunction with medication, this 21-session program is held in the patient's home over a period of nine months. After a functional assessment, the family is educated about bipolar disorders and their treatment. The families are then taught to improve family communication and problem solving. Results of the pilot study show increased compliance and reduced relapse.

Community Support Groups

Encourage patient involvement in community support groups. Perhaps the oldest and most widely known support group geared toward bipolar patients' needs are those sponsored by the National Depressive and Manic Depressive Association (NDMDA). The NDMDA has programs and materials directed to patients and their families. In addition to a network of local chapters throughout North America, the association sponsors an annual national convention, distributes audio and video programs, and publishes a national newsletter. The heart of NDMDA, however, is the scheduled community meetings, which consist of input from professionals in the community, in addition to a traditional support group function.

Preventing Relapse and Recurrence

Preventing relapse and recurrence is also important. Relapse rates in bipolar disorders are estimated to be approximately 40% and are usually attributed to medication noncompliance (Kahn, 1990). Schou (1991) indicates that the treatment context is correlated with relapse and treatment dropout. Schou contends that where treatment is provided in a lithium or mood disorders clinic, the dropout rate is 10% per year, while in other settings the dropout rate may be 50% within the first six months and increases to 90% in five years. The advantage of a specialty clinic is that clinicians have specialty training, can provide a consistent treatment environment, can select appropriate patients for treatment, and thus can more effectively motivate them to remain in treatment. The literature on relapse in bipolar disorder is rather sparse and focuses largely on medication use (Goodwin & Jamison, 1990). For example, Schou's article on relapse prevention lists 14 guidelines, of which 12 are directly focused on medication and side effects! Nevertheless, Post's "kindling model" (1986) suggests that relapse and recurrence can be attenuated.

Develop a relapse prevention plan for each bipolar patient. Post (1986) suggests that an important task of psychotherapy—or other psychosocial interventions—is to develop a relapse plan. This would include a hierarchy of external events and cognition that are particularly prone to trigger dysphoria or hypomanic feeling. Since Post posits that bipolar disorder involves behavioral hypersensitivity that primes electrophysiological kindling, he recommends the focus of treatment be on "working through and systematic desensitization" (Post, 1986, p.198).

SCHIZOPHRENIA

This section provides treatment guidelines involving three types of combined modalities, various means of incorporating psychoeducation and social skill training—including medication groups, and a number of recommendations for dealing with two major issues in the outpatient treatment of schizophrenia: compliance and relapse.

The first concern is *noncompliance*. According to the "rule of thirds," one-third of all individuals diagnosed and hospitalized with schizophrenia recover completely, one-third need ongoing treatment and occasional hospitalization, while one-third remain unimproved (Torrey, 1983). Even though recent changes in diagnostic criteria and the introduction of promising treatments may modify this "rule" somewhat, schizophrenia is often a devastating lifelong illness marked by exacerbations and remission. Research suggests that this illness is more likely to respond to multimodal rather than to single modality treatment. Considered here are guidelines for combining individual psychotherapy and medication management, family therapy and medication, group therapy and medication, and other combinations of these modalities.

Individual Psychotherapy and Medication

Schizophrenic patients can profit from focused individual psychotherapeutic intervention. Although most schizophrenics are unsuitable for traditional psychodynamic psychotherapy, the judicious use of tailored psychotherapeutic techniques is essential to engage resistant and medication noncompliant patients to accept medical intervention. Although brief sessions of 15 to 30 minutes may be scheduled, an outpatient program that is sufficiently flexible can effectively serve this patient population. This is especially true if occasional unscheduled brief contacts and phone calls are possible. The inability of many chronic patients to tolerate or benefit from the traditional 50-minute hour prompts this briefer, more flexible approach.

The course of treatment should be marked by the clinician's focus on the rational part of the patient's mind. Rather than exploring affects or delusional material, the clinician emphasizes the rational and healthy aspects of the patient's mind, and the measure of actual control that the patient has over his or her life. Thus, the clinician avoids direct challenges to the patient's psychotic belief system, utilizes reality testing and psychoeducation, and avoids emotional, stressful topics. Furthermore, a cautious optimism for the treatment of this disorder must be communicated by the clinician to the patient. The patient's refusal to take medication is viewed as resistance that needs to be explored. Does it originate from side effects, psychotic beliefs, or the patients's personality structure? Rather than allowing transference and countertransference to destroy treatment, the clinician must exhibit a willingness to compromise and negotiate, while sustaining the goal of the therapeutic alliance (Sarti & Courmos, 1990).

Group Therapy and Medication

There are some specific indications for combining medication and group therapy with schizophrenic patients. Group therapy has been shown to be quite effective with schizophrenic patients in increasing social relatedness, increasing medication compliance and treatment adherence, and learning social skills (Kanas, 1993). The type of group—homogeneous or heterogeneous—seems to influence the outcomes. The question of whether schizophrenic patients should be involved in groups consisting of diagnostically similar patients or in groups that also involve nonpsychotic members has yet to be definitively answered. Those advocating heterogeneous groups note that such groups permit psychotic patients to relate to firm reality-based nonpsychotic patients. Such groups also more closely reflect life outside the group. Kanas (1993) indicates that heterogeneous groups may be best utilized with schizophrenic patients who are sufficiently stable to tolerate anxiety-producing feedback from others, and who can tolerate and commit to involvement in a long-term outpatient group that meets weekly for 60 to 90 minutes. In short, heterogeneous groups are for the relatively higher functioning and stable schizophrenic patients and thus have limited applicability to this patient population. Heterogeneous groups tend to follow an interpersonal or psychodynamic model (Vinogradov & Yalom, 1989).

Homogeneous groups should involve patients with schizophrenic as well as those with schizoaffective disorders. These groups have less restrictive entrance requirements than heterogeneous groups, and so have greater applicability to this patient population. Perhaps the only contraindication for this type of group is the patient who is so disruptive or psychotic that he or she cannot follow the group's discussion.

Family Intervention and Medication

Combining medication and family intervention strategies is probably the most efficacious combined treatment for schizophrenic patients.

This combination of modalities is one of the earliest and most effective treatments. Sufficient research has been done to be able to specify the type of family intervention most helpful during different phases of the illness (Wynne, 1983). For example, during the crisis period when the patient is actively psychotic and may need hospitalization, the family should be involved to facilitate crisis resolution (i.e., getting the patient to take medication or be admitted to the hospital). The acute psychotic phase may last for several days, and although conjoint family sessions may be contraindicated as being too stimulating for the patient, family members should not be ruled out automatically. However, during the subsequent subacute phase as positive symptoms subside, conjoint sessions are most fitting.

In the subchronic phase when the negative symptoms of schizophrenia are prominent (i.e., lack of initiative, apathy, and perhaps medication noncompliance), family involvement takes the form of providing information, supporting, and establishing a compliance and relapse prevention plan. Psychoeducational approaches are best initiated at this point. These include family support groups and educational workshops, for example. Generally speaking, traditional forms or systems of psychodynamic family therapy are no longer considered useful for the majority of schizophrenic patients. Instead, psychoeducation family interventions are considered the treatment of choice (Glick, Clarkin, & Goldsmith, 1993).

Enhancing and Maintaining Medication Compliance

Since medication noncompliance is a major treatment issue, enhancing and maintaining compliance has to be a central part of the treatment plan. Noncompliance with medication regimens for schizophrenic outpatients shows a medium noncompliance rate of 41% with oral neuroleptics. Noncompliance with long-acting depot neuroleptics is also surprisingly high (Young, Zonana, & Shepler, 1986). Factors accounting for noncompliance range from psychotic ideation to rational responses and include thought disturbance, grandiosity, hostility, denial of illness, chronicity, paranoia, side effects, lack of drug efficacy, and a desire to be in control (Sarti & Courmos, 1990). The following specific guidelines are suggested.

1. Monitor the patient's subjective response to neuroleptics. Research consistently shows that patients who do not fare subjectively well on medications are less likely to accept them (Awad, 1993). Thus, it is recommended that the clinician pay close attention to patients' self-reports on how they feel taking the medication and whether or not their medication agrees with them. If patients report that they feel awful, or like zombies, or can't think straight, or that it makes them feel worse, especially dysphoric, they will either request a medication change, press for discontinuation of medication, or simply stop the medications unbeknownst to the clinician. Awad (1993) reports that noncompliance can be predicted if a schizophrenic patient has a dysphoric response to medication. At least two valid and reliable short self-rating instruments are available, one being the 10-item "Drug Attitude Inventory" (Awad, 1993). The value of such inventory is that a patient may be more willing to disclose negative subjective response in writing rather than verbally and face to face.

2. Identify and monitor the patient's use of alcohol and other substances. There is a startlingly high correlation between alcohol and substance use and medication noncompliance. Pristach and Smith (1990) found that 72% of substance-using schizophrenic patients were medication noncompliant prior to rehospitalization. Those patients with a history of alcohol abuse admitted to drinking alcohol in the month prior to admission, and 62% specifically reported being noncompliant when drinking alcohol.

Mason and Siris (1992) report that among schizophrenic patients with postpsychotic depression and/or negative symptoms, cocaine or cannabis abuse was highly correlated with medication noncompliance. Perhaps, such substance use and abuse may be related to untreated postpsychotic depression or to medication-induced dysphoria. Whatever the cause, the clinician would do well to monitor the patient's use of substances. Furthermore, because alcohol decreases serum levels of antipsychotic agents, patients may not have reached or maintained therapeutic effect. Thus, patients will discontinue medication, believing it is not effective when in fact they may need medication dosages considerably higher than normal maintenance doses.

3. Encourage family involvement in ensuring medication compliance. Family compliance counseling strategies can be quite useful with schizophrenic patients.

Psychoeducational Methods

Incorporating pychoeducational methods in the treatment of schizophrenia is another important treatment strategy. Four specific types of psychoeducation have proved effective with this patient population. They are: social skills training; family psychoeducational interventions; medication and symptom management groups; and community support groups.

Social skills training should be tailored and incorporated into the treatment plan based on the patient's skill deficits. Skill deficits range from personal self-care and self-management skills to interpersonal relationship skills. Examples of such interpersonal deficits include poor eye contact, inappropriate facial expressions, poor response timing, limited spontaneity in social interactions, poor interpersonal judgment, and the inability to recognize and respond to emotion in others (Marder et al., 1991).

When social skill training is combined with medication in schizophrenic patients, there is an additive effect over either treatment alone. Marder et al. (1991) report that a skill training group focused on both medication management and symptom management greatly increased the knowledge level and social skills of patients; these gains were sustained over at least six months. Eckman et al. (1990) also showed that medication compliance was significantly increased by this same intervention.

Psychoeducational family intervention efforts are effective treatment adjuncts. Perhaps one of the best known psychoeducational programs involving family members has been described and researched by Anderson et al. (1986). The outcome goals of this program are to reduce the patient's vulnerability to environmental stress through maintenance medication, and to stabilize the family environment by increasing knowledge, coping skills, and level of support of family members. These goals are achieved through a four-phase program that extends over a course of several years.

Phase I and II emphasize information and realistic attitudes toward the chronic illness, while Phase III focuses on family communication and problem-solving strategies. Phase IV involves either a maintenance modality or more extensive use of psychodynamic and family system strategies for restructuring family systems behavior. Research on this and other family psychosocial interventions has concluded that compliance is achieved and the patient and family functioning is improved. Not surprisingly, these interventions are time-intensive, costly, and difficult to implement (Glick et al., 1993).

Again, Brisbee's (1991) *Educating Patients and Families about Mental Illness* is an excellent practical resource that is less extensive and intensive than Anderson's program and probably is more suitable for most clinic programs.

Refer chronic schizophrenic patients to medication groups. Medication groups were initially established for patients beginning prescribed neuroleptic medication. Medication groups for chronic schizophrenic and schizoaffective disordered patients tend to be long-term, ongoing groups.

Encourage patient involvement in a community support group. Currently, schizophrenic patients in the U.S., many Canadian provinces, and some cities in Ireland and the United Kingdom can find support groups sponsored by Recovery, Inc. Recovery is probably the oldest patient-led support group for psychiatric patients. Recovery is a system of self-help aftercare techniques developed by the late Abraham Low, M.D., a Chicago psychiatrist. Meetings are based on Low's method of "will training." Recovery's stated purpose is to help prevent relapse and forestall chronicity in psychiatric patients. Patients are expected to comply with medication and other treatment prescriptions while practicing Recovery principles daily. Another community support group is Schizophrenics Anonymous which is based on the 12-step philosophy.

Preventing Relapse

Relapse prevention is another critical component in the treatment of schizophrenia. Preventing relapse and recurrence in schizophrenia is a challenge given that relapse rates are exceedingly high. Davis et al. (1993) report that *all* schizophrenic patients not treated with neuroleptics will relapse within three years. Goldstein (1991) reports that 30% of all patients on neuroleptics relapse during the first year, whereas about 70% of patients on placebo relapse during that same period. Hogarty (1984) reports that of those willing to take medication, approximately 40% relapse during the first year after hospital discharge, and 15% each year thereafter.

The goal of outpatient maintenance treatment with schizophrenic patients is to prevent relapse in order for the patient to function within the community. Three specific guidelines are offered: appropriate dosing, family involvement, and developing a personal relapse plan.

1. Achieve appropriate medication dosage. Strategies for long-term medication maintenance have been advocated to reduce relapse. The two most commonly practiced are "targeted," or "intermittent," dosing and "lower dosing." In the targeted strategy, the patient is placed on a drug-free regimen after becoming stabilized, and restarted on aggressive drug regimen only when prodromal signs appear. The lower dosing strategy involves continuous use of medication, but at substantially lower doses than the previous stabilization dose. If and when prodromal signs occurred, higher doses were utilized and thereafter the lower dose was reinstituted (Goldstein, 1991). There has been considerable research on these two strategies. Data now suggest that the "targeted" strategy results in very high levels of relapse and rehospitalization. Nevertheless, individuals on this dose strategy do experience fewer side effects. Not surprisingly, many patients prefer this maintenance schedule. The standard dose, i.e., the dose usage most commonly used in clinical practice, showed the lowest relapse rates. Furthermore, when patients are stabilized and on a moderate to low dose and have concurrent psychosocial treatment, there is very little difference in the side effects experienced (Schooler, 1994b). It may well be that the newer serotonin-dopamine antagonists such as clozapine and respiridone will decrease relapse rates to some degree, since these newer agents have limited side-effect profiles, particularly extrapyramidal symptoms.

2. Involve the family whenever possible. When the family members are available and committed to the patient's treatment plan, at a minimum the clinician should engage the family's assistance in recognizing prodromal signs. During the relatively symptom-free maintenance phase, the patient and family should be instructed about the relationship between neuroleptic dosage, the potential for relapse, and the appearance of side effects. And since most patients experience predictable mood and behavioral changes, which serve as warning symptoms, the family should be enlisted so that medication and psychosocial strategies can be quickly utilized to prevent the acute symptoms of psychosis.

The symptom management module developed by Liberman (1988) teaches patients and family members to distinguish between warning symptoms, acute symptoms, and persistent symptoms. While persistent symptoms, i.e., chronic, subclinical symptoms, are not likely to precipitate relapse, they can result in endless requests for medication changes and may account for noncompliance. Strategies for dealing with persistent symptoms such as distraction and activity are also part of the module by Liberman. Breier and Strauss (1983) describe various self-control strategies for persistent symptoms common in schizophrenic patients.

Schooler (1994a) reports that it does not really matter what psychosocial or psychoeducational interventions are utilized with patients and their families, or how intensive they are. All that seems to matter is that the family be engaged in the treatment process, as the family is such a key factor in treatment outcomes.

Finally, Goldstein (1991) recommends that patients and family engage in anticipatory planning to prepare the patient and family for taxing events that might trigger relapse. Anticipatory planning includes identifying potential disruptive upcoming events and devising prevention and coping strategies for managing them.

3. Help the patient develop a personal treatment strategy for preventing relapse. Hogarty (1993) suggests that each patient needs a personal plan tailored to his or her unique circumstances. Such a relapse prevention plan includes attention to the emotional environment at home and in the treatment setting, coping skills, everyday stressors, and a realistic treatment plan. First, the patient and family need to create a stimuli-controlled environment that is safe and predictable. The family and patient need to learn day-to-day survival skills to cope with unexpected stressors. Clinicians need to be aware of and control their "expressed emotion" behaviors. Specifically, Hogarty refers to the clinician's withholding of warmth or nurturance and expressing subtle dissatisfaction when the patient's performance does not meet treatment expectation. He also believes that treatment must be based on patient and family goals that can be implemented in small steps. Finally, Hogarty assumes that the patient will take one step backward for each two steps forward.

A PSYCHOPHARMACOTHERAPEUTIC OUTCOME
MEASURES AND MANAGEMENT SYSTEM

This chapter has emphasized the importance of utilizing the strategies of focused assessment, combining treatment modalities, medication compliance, psychoeducation, and relapse prevention when psychopharmacotherapy is the central treatment modality. Of these, the strategies of focused assessment and enhancing treatment compliance are, perhaps, the most critical in maximizing treatment outcomes.

The treatment that involves medication as well as the prediction of treatment outcomes can be conceptualized as a psychopharmacotherapeutic system. The inputs to such a system would include the patient's biological and psychological capacity, and the prescribed medication. The process variables would include the direction and support of the provider(s).

The output of such a system would include treatment response and efficacy. Table 7.1 portrays these variables. In this systems model, the focused assessment strategy is emphasized with regard to the

TABLE 7.1
Psychopharmacotherapy Treatment System

Input	*Process*	*Output*
PATIENT— Biological substrate: **PATIENT—** Psychological dimensions: **explanatory model** **beliefs about Rx** **readiness for change** **specific treatment expectations** + **MEDICATION**	**PRESCRIBER/ PROVIDER SUPPORT** beliefs about Rx expectations re: positive treatment response availability to patient for Rx-related problems + **FAMILY/SUPPORT NETWORK** expectations/support re: Rx compliance/positive Tx outcomes	**MEDICATION TREATMENT OUTCOMES**

patient—psychological factors of explanatory model of the disorder or presenting problem, beliefs about medication, and readiness for change. Table 7.2 provides items from a self-report inventory that can be used to assess a patient's explanatory model of illness (Cf. "My problem is most likely caused by:"); beliefs about medication and medication effects (Cf. "It seems that:"); and treatment readiness (Cf. "With regard to my problem:"). The items can be used in conjunction with COMPASS instruments to predict and monitor treatment response.

TABLE 7.2

Treatment Need and Expectations

---

1. **How much medication treatment have you had in the past?**
   ☐ None
   ☐ Three to six months
   ☐ Less than one month
   ☐ One to three months
   ☐ Six months to one year
   ☐ More than one year
2. **How long has the problem for which you are presently seeking treatment been a concern to you?**

☐ Less than one month	☐ Six months to one year
☐ One to three months	☐ One to two years
☐ Three to six months	☐ More than two years

3. **When you finish this treatment, how well do you feel that you will be getting along emotionally and psychologically?**
   I WILL BE GETTING ALONG:
   ☐ Quite poorly; I will be barely able to deal with things.
   ☐ Fairly poorly; life will be pretty tough for me at times.
   ☐ So-so; I will be able to keep going with some effort.
   ☐ Fairly well; I will have my ups and downs.
   ☐ Quite well; I will have no important complaints.
   ☐ Very well; much the way I would like to.
4. **Please think back to when you decided to call for an appointment. At that time, how well did you feel that you were getting along emotionally and psychologically?**
   I WAS GETTING ALONG:
   ☐ Quite poorly; I was barely able to deal with things.
   ☐ Fairly poorly; life was pretty tough for me at times.

(continued on next page)

☐ So-so; I was able to keep going with some effort.
☐ Fairly well; I had my ups and downs.
☐ Quite well; I had no important complaints.
☐ Very well; much the way I wanted.

5. **When you decided to call for an appointment, how upset or distressed had you been feeling? I HAD BEEN FEELING:**

☐ Extremely distressed   ☐ Slightly distressed
☐ Very distressed   ☐ Not at all distressed
☐ Pretty distressed

My problem is most likely caused by: (1–5 scaling)

1. Early childhood experiences or trauma
2. A chemical imbalance in my brain
3. Too much stress or demands at work or school
4. Difficulties or stresses in a close relationship
5. Stress and chemical imbalance in my brain

It seems that: (1–5 scaling)

1. Psychotherapy is the only treatment of emotional problems that offers any hope of success.
2. I feel weird, like a "zombie," on medications.
3. Psychotherapy is more likely to be detrimental than beneficial.
4. Medications make me feel tired and sluggish.
5. I feel more normal on medications.
6. My thoughts are clear on medications.
7. It is unnatural for me to be controlled by medications.
8. By staying on medications, I can prevent getting sick.
9. The good things about medications outweigh the bad.
10. Psychotherapy is the treatment of choice in all psychiatric disorders.

With regard to my problem: (1–5 scaling)

1. Being here is pretty much of a waste of time for me because the problem doesn't have to do with me.
2. I have a problem and I really think I should work on it.
3. I am doing something about the problems that had been bothering me.
4. It is frustrating, but I feel I might be having a recurrence of a problem I thought I had resolved.

8

Primary Care and Behavioral Medicine Treatment Outcomes

Many individuals with psychosocial symptoms and concerns do not present for psychotherapy or psychiatry providers, but rather to primary care or behavioral medicine providers. While primary care providers are typically physicians, they may also be physicians' assistants or nurse practitioners who provide a full range of health care services. On the other hand, behavioral medicine specialists are usually psychologists or other nonphysicians who provide a more limited range of health care services, such as biofeedback and pain management, weight loss management, smoking cessation, and treatment of sleep disorders.

Providing cost-effective and efficacious diagnosis and treatment of psychiatric presentations such as anxiety, depression, and other psychiatric illnesses in primary care patients is an enormous challenge for MCOs. This is particularly the case when mental health care is considered a "carve out." The chapter discusses the phenomenon of psychiatric illness in primary care and other medical settings, the role of the primary care provider with regard to psychiatric presentations, and the value of treatment outcomes data in primary care and behavioral medicine settings. It also overviews the conflicting medical cost-offset literature and its implications for managed care. Finally, it illustrates a system for measuring and monitoring such treatment outcomes involving a common primary care and behavioral medicine presentation.

COMMON PSYCHIATRIC DISORDERS IN PRIMARY CARE

The NIMH-sponsored Epidemiological Catchment Area (ECA) Study found that most people with common psychiatric disorders seek care from general medical care providers rather than from mental health professionals (Regier, 1993). Anxiety, addictive, and depressive disorders are common in primary care (Von Korff, 1987; Sato, 1993). Among patients with certain functional somatic syndromes such as irritable bowel syndrome, atypical chest pain, and headaches, both anxiety and depressive disorders are highly prevalent (Lydiard, 1993). Substance use disorders and somatoform disorders are also highly prevalent in primary care patients (Skinner, 1990).

Of those who receive treatment for psychiatric illness, equally as many individuals receive care from their primary medical doctor as from mental health professionals (Regier, 1993; Narrow, 1993). Nearly half of all persons who have psychiatric disorders never see a mental health professional and seek care for their psychiatric illness only in the general medical sector. In short, about 6 to 16% of primary care patients have major depressive disorder, 10% have an anxiety disorder, and overall 10 to 30% of medical patients have some psychiatric disorder (Perez-Stable, 1990).

Although psychiatric disorders are common in medical patients of all ages, they are particularly unlikely to be detected and effectively treated in the elderly. Yet this is an especially important group of patients in which the quality of health care delivered and the outcomes of care could be improved while costs are decreased by better detection and treatment of psychiatric illness. Anxiety disorders are quite prevalent in the elderly. Of the elderly in the community, 4 to 10% have an anxiety disorder, more than double the number who have major depression (Regier, 1988). Panic disorder, agoraphobia, generalized anxiety disorder, obsessive-compulsive disorder, simple social phobias, and post-traumatic stress disorder most typically begin in adolescence or early adulthood, but often are chronic and persist into old age, and can begin for the first time in old age.

Because effective treatments for any anxiety disorders have become available or widely used only in recent years, many older patients with chronic, lifelong anxiety disorders have never received effective treatment. Several authors have argued that the low rates of detection and treatment of treatable, disabling psychiatric disorders in the elderly may be partly attributable to age-related prejudice (Larkin, 1992). That is, young and middle-aged professionals may consider restriction of activities and travel, social withdrawal, or preoccupation with physical illness to be appropriate, expectable consequences of advanced age, rather than recognizing them as symptoms of treatable mood, anxiety, somatoform, or substance abuse disorders. Wider use of efficient, broad, psychiatric screening questionnaires in primary care would improve the rate of recognition and treatment of the diverse psychiatric disorders that unnecessarily diminish the social productivity and quality of life of many individuals.

UNDERTREATMENT OF PSYCHIATRIC DISORDERS IN PRIMARY CARE

Although depression and other psychiatric disorders are common in medical patients, they are often not detected, and thus not treated (Keller, 1990). The ECA Study findings (Regier et al., 1988, 1993) indicate that most individuals with depression do not receive treatment. Primary care physicians recognize fewer than half of the cases of psychiatric disorders in their practices (Wells, 1989). The diagnosis of psychiatric disorders and the institution of appropriate management are often substantially delayed, thus increasing the morbidity, mortality, and cost to society. As a result, pyschiatric illness is to medicine today what hypertension was 20 years ago: a major source of morbidity, disability, and mortality that could be prevented by earlier detection of disease, accomplished via mass screening by primary care physicians. Because of the underrecognition of depression in medical patients, the Agency for Health Care Policy and Research (AHCPR) Task Force on Depression in Primary Care has promulgated practice guidelines that stress the importance of improved case finding for depression in medical settings.

THE COST OF UNTREATED AND UNDERTREATED PSYCHIATRIC DISORDERS

Untreated and undertreated psychiatric disorders are costly to patients and society. Panic disorder is associated with suicide, disability, excessive health care use, and premature death (Stewart, 1992; Klerman, 1991; Allgulander, 1991). Depression, anxiety, substance abuse and somatoform disorders are associated with substantial psychosocial morbidity, disability, mortality, and excessive medical care utilization (Klerman, 1992). The Medical Outcomes Study (MOS) found that the impairment and disability associated with depression are equal to that attributable to cardiovascular disease and greater than that due to other chronic physical disorders such as hypertension, diabetes mellitus, and arthritis (Wells, 1989). The economic burden of depression in this country is greater than 40 billion dollars per year (Greenberg, 1993). Alcohol abuse is a major risk factor for suicide (Roy, 1990). Somatoform disorders are by definition associated with excessive use of medical care and resources (Smith, 1986; Noyes, 1993). Alcoholism is associated with a tremendous number of severe medical sequelae, including premature death (Miller, 1991).

One important source of cost for depression and other psychiatric disorders that will become particularly important in the coming era of managed care, involves excessive medical diagnostic work-ups performed for somatic symptoms of psychiatric illness (Shaw, 1991). Patients frequently have multiple, expensive, unproductive medical work-ups and ineffective treatment for functional somatic symptoms, failing to receive available effective treatments for the underlying psychiatric disorder. Poorer perceived health, which has been found to be associated with screening positive for psychiatric illness (Borgquist, 1993), is the foremost predictor of total medical costs. Anxiety disorders and depression are associated with excessive medical care utilization in adults of all ages (Klerman, 1991). Poor perceived health is the most powerful predictor of medical care utilization in the elderly, and it predicts mortality on long-term follow-up. A community study of persons with panic attacks, for instance, showed that 35% of patients seek care from the family doctor, whereas only 26% seek care in mental health settings (Katerndahl, 1994). There is some evidence that certain kinds of interventions can reduce the excess medical costs associated with psychiatric illnesses (Noyes, 1986; Kashner, 1992).

Perhaps the ultimate cost associated with untreated and undertreated psychiatric disorders in primary care setting is suicide. Suicide is the eighth leading cause of death in the United States, accounting for more than 30,000 deaths per year (U.S. Bureau of Census, 1993), with a consequent loss of lifetime earnings that exceeds eight billion dollars (Greenberg, 1993). More than 90% of patients who commit suicide have a mental illness, the most frequent of these being depression and alcoholism (Hawton, 1992). However, almost all forms of psychopathology have been linked to suicidal behavior, including anxiety disorders, schizophrenia, and personality disorders (Coryell, 1982; Cox, 1994). Not surprisingly, one of the strongest correlates of suidical behavior is suicidal ideation. Suicide attempts result in substantial medical morbidity, medical costs, and functional disability. The role of the medical care delivery system in preventing suicidal behavior and associated costs deserves serious attention in the current era of health care reform.

The majority of those who attempt or complete suicide present themselves for medical treatment prior to their act. Like other patients with psychiatric illness, substantial proportions of suicidal patients present only to nonpsychiatric physicians. Suicide attempters consult their primary care practitioners more often during the four months prior to the suicide attempt than during the previous four months (Gorman, 1990) and 82% of people who commit suicide visit their physician within six months, 53% within one month, and 40% within one week of their death (Van Casteren, 1993). However, the suicidal state of these patients is frequently not detected by nonpsychiatric physicians.

Education of primary care practitioners regarding the diagnosis and treatment of depression has been shown to reduce the rate of suicide in their patients by 30% (Rutz, 1989). Many authors have called upon nonpsychiatric physicians to more effectively detect and treat suicidality in their patients (Westreich, 1991). The risk of suicide and suicide attempts is increased by major depression, alcohol abuse, drug abuse, panic disorder, generalized anxiety disorder (GAD), phobias, posttraumatic stress disorder (PTSD), obsessive-compulsive disorder (OCD), somatoform disorder, dysthymia, and especially by comorbidity of two or more of these conditions.

ARE PSYCHIATRIC INTERVENTIONS WORTHWHILE IN PRIMARY CARE? THE MEDICAL AND MENTAL HEALTH COST-OFFSET PERSPECTIVE

Many providers and some third party payers have come to believe that when certain medical patients are given psychotherapy and/or other psychiatric treatments they utilize fewer services. This phenomenon has been described as medical or mental health cost offset. A review of more than 25 studies of mental health cost offset published from 1965 to 1995 indicates that research findings are often contradictory. Studies frequently reach contradictory conclusions, and are vulnerable to criticism based upon methodological weaknesses.

Many studies have claimed to find evidence of a positive cost-offset effect. For example, a study by the Group Health Association of Washington found that patients who were treated for mental health problems reduced by 30.7% their visits to physicians in specialties other than psychiatry and that their usage of laboratory tests and x-rays decreased by 29.8% (Grotcher & Redfield, 1988). These results are questionable due to the lack of a control group.

A second example is provided by the study conducted by Follette and Cummings (1967) over a five-year period that revealed significant savings attributed to receipt of mental health care. Medical patients, matched for psychiatric disorder, severity of illness, age, sex, overall health status, and socioeconomic status, were divided into groups consisting of those seeking mental health care and those who did not and were followed for five years. Those receiving mental health care reduced their total health care expenditures (including the cost of the psychotherapy) by 60%. However, the comparison group did not seek psychiatric treatment, which could result in the skewing of data, (e.g., due to motivational differences between the two groups).

Studies that found minimal or no evidence of a cost-offset effect have also been criticized for design flaws. Kogan et al. (1975) studied all individuals seen in the mental health service during a one-year period at the Group Health Cooperative of Puget Sound. Two comparison groups who were not seen in mental health services during that year were generated: one to compare with the prepaid subgroup receiving services and one to compare with the fee-for-service group that received mental health intervention. The data consisted of medical visits for a seven-year period between 1962 and 1969 and mental health visits from 1967 and 1979. Investigators concluded that there was insufficient support for the notion that mental health services would produce an overall savings of medical care. A clear peak in medical utilization prior to being seen in the mental health service was identified. Investigators concluded that a reduction in medical visits would have occurred with or without the provision of mental health services. Critics of this study note that Kogan and his colleagues did not match control groups and experimental groups for initial level of utilization, nor did they use random assignment. They also did not provide for a separate analysis of self- and physician-referred individuals.

More recent studies, such as Manning & Wells (1992), have added a new dimension to the conundrum of the cost-offset question. They found that subjects with worse mental health status, whether assessed by a global self- report measure or by its two component parts (psychological well-being and psychological distress), significantly increased the use of both inpatient and outpatient general medical services. There was nearly a doubling in total medical care expenditures for persons in the lower third of the distribution for mental health status, relative to those in the upper third. Thus, one would expect that effective treatment would lead to sharply reduced utilization of general medical services. Strum & Wells (1995), however did not find any effect of depression treatments on the use of non-mental health care visits or on inpatient utilization. They claim that if a cost-offset effect exists it is too small to detect, and any such effect would be overwhelmed by the increased costs of additional care. They also add that measurement error can result in positive cost-offset effects in data sets that cannot distinguish mental health and medical reasons for a visit.

The only conclusion to come from research on cost-offset due to mental health treatment is that there is no clear-cut indication of cost savings. Studies that claim such an effect are often methodologically flawed. The same design problems also cast doubt on the findings of studies that claim to find no cost-offset effect. Future research needs stronger methodology to be considered valid. Future studies should be prospective in design, and incorporate random assignment of patients with similar psychiatric diagnosis to different treatment groups. Also, direct efforts need to be made towards determining which disorders are likely to demonstrate cost-offset effects, as well as studying which specific cost-offset effects occur with particular disorders.

DETECTION OF PSYCHIATRIC ILLNESSES IN PRIMARY CARE PATIENTS

Self-Administered Questionnaires

Self-administered questionnaires are an inexpensive method of screening for psychiatric disorders. A comprehensive psychiatric history evaluating the major domains of psychopathology in every single patient is prohibitively time-consuming for the busy primary care physician. One approach to large-scale psychiatric screening of medical patients that may be cost-effective and appropriate for use in busy doctors' offices is the self-administered questionnaire.

The use of depression questionnaires for routine screening is recommended by the AHCPR guidelines. Several questionnaires have acceptable sensitivity and specificity for detecting major depression in medical patients (Burke, 1991; Zimmerman, 1986, 1987). Useful questionnaires also exist to detect a variety of other psychiatric illnesses in primary care, including alcoholism, bulimia, panic disorder (Apfeldorf, 1994), and somatization disorder. A serious limitation of all of these scales is their focus on only one type of pathology. Studies have demonstrated high comorbidity among psychiatric disorders, and this also suggests that a focus on any single disorder is inappropriately narrow. Screening programs for psychiatric disorders in primary care settings should be broad-based, and not limited to any single disorder.

Three self-report screening questionnaires have recently been developed to achieve the goal of increased detection of psychiatric disorders in primary care patients: the PRIME-MD PQ (Spitzer et al., 1994), SDDS-PC, (Broadhead et al., in press) and SCREENER. (Zimmerman et al., 1994). These questionnaires are all intended to select patients for further mental health evaluation and to focus the attention of the physician on a particular disorder. Table 8.1 summarizes these screening instruments. Table 8.2 illustrates the disorder coverage of these three instruments, as well as of COMPASS OP, which is described in a subsequent section.

TABLE 8.1

Brief Description of Screening Instruments

SCREENER	A 72-page questionnaire with a yes-no format. The SCREENER screens for 14 specific psychiatric disorders: major depression, dysthymic disorder, bulimia nervosa, generalized anxiety disorder, obsessive-compulsive disorder, panic disorder, posttraumatic stress disorder, phobic disorder (social, specific, and agoraphobia), alcohol abuse/dependence, drug abuse/dependence, and somatoform disorder (somatization disorder and hypochondriasis).
SDDS-PC	A 49-item questionnaire with a yes-no format. The SDDS-PC contains 14 items that screen for six specific psychiatric disorders: major depression, generalized anxiety disorder, panic disorder, obsessive-compulsive disorder, and alcohol abuse/ dependence. The 49 item SDDS-PC self-report questionnaire also includes an "other symptoms" section that contains additional items relevant to these disorders and also to drug abuse, and agoraphobia. We will assess the performance of these screening items as well.
PRIME-MD PQ	A 27 item questionnaire with a yes-no format. The PRIME-MD PQ screens for six psychiatric disorders: somatoform disorder, major depression, generalized anxiety disorder, panic disorder, alcohol abuse/dependence, and bulimia.
COMPASS OP	A 28-item primary care version of COMPASS OP has been proposed. It would screen for depressive, anxiety, and substance abuse disorder. The advantage of COMPASS OP is the availability of normative data on speed of treatment response.

DSM-IV Primary Care Version

The American Psychiatric Association has recently published *The Diagnostic and Statistical Manual of Mental Disorders: Primary Care Version* (DSM-IV-PC). The DSM-IV-PC (or PC) offers a step-by-step algorithm targeted to the primary care provider. It was developed jointly by a number of medical groups, including the American Academy of Family Physicians, the American Academy of Pediatrics, the American Board of Family Practice, The American College of Obstretricians and Gynecologists, and the American Psychiatric Association. The PC organizes symptoms that primary care providers see most into nine groups: depressed mood, anxiety, cognitive disturbances,

TABLE 8.2

Screening and Diagnostic Instrument Disorder Coverage

Disorder	PQ[1]	SDDS-PC[1]	SCREENER	COMPASS OP[1]
Somatoform Disorder	X	—	X[3]	—
Hypochondriasis	X	—	X[3]	—
Bulimia Nervosa	X	—	X[2]	—
Major Depression	X	X	X[2]	X
Generalized Anxiety Disorder	X	X	X[3]	X
Panic Disorder	X	X	X[2]	X
Alcohol Abuse/ Dependence	X	X	X[3]	X
Drug Abuse/Dependence	—	—	X[3]	X
Obsessive-Compulsive Disorder	—	X	X[2]	X
Agoraphobia	—	—	X[3]	X
Specific Phobia	—	—	X[3]	X
Social Phobia	—	—	X[3]	—
Posttraumatic Stress Disorder	—	—	X[2]	—
Dysthymic Disorder	X	—	X[4]	X

[1]Past month.
[2]Past two weeks.
[3]Past six months.
[4]Lifetime.

unexplained physical symptoms, problematic substance use, sleep disturbances, sexual dysfunction, psychotic symptoms, and weight change or abnormal eating. There is an algorithm for each group.

To illustrate its use, let us say that the patient complains of being tired all the time. The primary care provider would be alerted to start with the depressed mood algorithm. This algorithm includes conditions that might account for the symptoms, such as a general medical condition, substance use, or bereavement, that are not major psychiatric disorders. Or, the algorithm could be followed to a major disorder such as Major Depressive Disorder, Dysthymic Disorder, or Depressive Disorder Not Otherwise Specified (NOS). Once the presumptive diagnosis is made, the primary care clinician then decides whether or not to provide the necessary treatment or to make an appropriate referral. In short, the PC is a diagnostic screening device that may have some value in primary care settings. While it provides a set of algorithms and an overview of psychiatric disorders common in primary care settings, it is not a treatment manual. Its developers anticipate that it will become a standard text in primary care residency programs.

OUTCOME for Windows

OUTCOME for Windows is an outcomes management system specifically designed for medical treatment. This software program reportedly documents clinical outcomes, functional outcomes, financial outcomes, patient descriptors, quality of life, and patient satisfaction. It can also provide predictors for costs, length of stay/number of sessions, and patient improvement. OUTCOME was developed by Evaluation Systems International, Inc. (1993–94). The current software program is generic, with a common set of database variables that can be added to or changed to meet the needs of the user.

COMPASS OP in Primary Care Settings

The COMPASS Outpatient Treatment Assessment System (COMPASS OP, Compass Information Services, 1995) scales measure a patient's progress in outpatient mental health treatment based on the patient's perspective, as well as on the clinician's perspective. The scales are designed to be completed periodically throughout the course of treatment, so that a patient's progress can be monitored in relation to a database of similar patients. COMPASS OP is a measure of treatment outcomes as well an assessment of treatment quality.

Three patient self-report scales—Subjective Well-being, Current Symptoms, and Current Life Functioning—are combined into a Mental Health Index (MHI). Additional patient scales include assessments of presenting problems and the patient's perceptions of the therapeutic relationship. Clinicians' ratings on the Global Assessment Scale and the Life Functioning Scales are combined to form the Clinical Assessment Index (CAI). Higher scores represent more healthy status and there are cutoff scores for the MHI and the CAI that indicate when the patient has returned to normal functioning. Chapter 4 provides a more detailed description of the instrument, its psychometric properties, and its utilization in outpatient psychiatric treatment settings.

Does COMPASS OP have a place in primary care and behavioral medicine settings? While no data on clinical trials of COMPASS OP in primary care settings have yet been published, such clinical trials are currently underway. Anecdotal evidence from primary care practictioners using the instruments with their patients suggests that COMPASS OP has value in three areas: (1) as a means of screening for psychopathology and psychological distress, (2) as a measure of treatment outcome, and (3) as a means of monitoring treatment efficacy and quality of care.

With slight modification, COMPASS OP can be used the same way in a primary care or behavioral medicine setting as it is utilized in a psychiatric setting. The instrument could be incorporated into the intake process, such that every new patient would complete the instrument as a general screening device. Or, it could be reserved for situations when psychiatric symptoms are reported or observed, at which time the patient and practitioner would complete the instrument. An appropriate psychosocial or psychopharmacological treatment plan would then be formulated, based on the MHI and CAI. This plan might entail direct treatment by the primary care practitioner or referral to a mental health or behavioral medicine provider. Similarly, the instrument would be completed periodically throughout the course of treatment. Because primary care patients who present with psychiatric symptoms tend to be sicker than patients presenting in psychiatric settings, it might be that the MHI cut point between health and illness be set at the 70th percentile rather than at the 84th percentile.

The prospect for the use of treatment outcomes measures, monitoring, and management systems in primary care settings has considerable appeal. With such systems in place, a clinic or an entire health care system can continually monitor measures of the patients' level of well-being, symptoms, and life functioning, the outcomes of treatment and patient satisfaction, as well as providing an estimate of medical offset.

Obstacles to Detecting and Treating Psychiatric Disorders in Primary Care

There are several potential physician-related obstacles to the diagnosis and treatment of mental disorders in primary care and other medical settings. These include adequacy of training, perceived competency in diagnosis and treatment, economic pressures (i.e., inadequate reimbursement for the time necessary to diagnose and counsel patients), and clinician discomfort discussing patients' emotional problems. Also, some clinicians believe that their patients are uncomfortable discussing psychological problems with them. Primary care physicians' perception that their patients do not want them to investigate depression accounted for one-third of the variance in physician belief of whether depression is an important clinical problem, and it was strongly associated with the clinicians' discomfort about exploring depression (Main, 1993). In a national survey of family practitioners, two-thirds of the respondents reported that patient resistance to psychiatric diagnosis and treatment was an obstacle in providing service or making treatment referral (Orleans, 1985).

To avoid stigmatizing patients, some physicians substitute technical sounding euphemisms such as "limbic system dysfunction" or deliberately fail to diagnose psychiatric disorders that they know are present or even are treating (Reynolds, 1993). Others have noted that this serves to perpetuate stigmatization. In fact, there is little to no empirical support for the primary care physician's perceptions of patient reluctance. Frowick (1986) found that fewer than 10% of family practice patients would not want their physician's involvement with psychological problems (Clark, 1983). Other studies have also reported that the majority of primary care patients want their doctor to address their psychosocial problems. Views may become self-fulfilling prophecies causing physicians to avoid addressing mental health issues (Williamson, 1981). The data, on the other hand, suggest that patients are more satisfied with their care if their physician inquires about and addresses psychosocial matters, and that patients wish to discuss these concerns with their primary care doctor (Brody, 1989). In fact, one study found that nearly one-quarter of patients want stress counseling from their physician, and of those who desired this, those who felt they had received it were more satisfied with their care than those who did not (Brody, 1989).

Payment for psychiatric treament provided may be the major obstacle. In managed care systems where psychiatric and behavioral health care is a carve-out, there may be a disincentive to treat psychiatric symptoms and syndromes in the primary care setting, particularly when the plan is tightly capitated. In such circumstances, primary care providers are likely to refer many or all cases, or to be reticent in detecting symptoms and syndromes.

ILLUSTRATION OF AN OUTCOMES SYSTEM IN PRIMARY CARE/BEHAVIORAL MEDICINE

How is an outcomes system utilized in a primary care or behavioral medicine setting? Keatley, Lemmon, Miller, and Miller (1995) describe a rather common application. They describe the case of a young woman who presents with depression, abdominal pain, tension headaches, peptic ulcer disease, and insomnia. She meets criteria for a DSM-IV Adjustment Disorder with Mixed Anxiety and Depressed Mood (309.28). Her score on the Global Assessment of Function Scale (GAF) was 61, with her highest GAF during the past year being 90. After being medically evaluated, the patient was started on Zantac for her ulcers and a complete psychological evaluation was undertaken. Data from this evaluation were analyzed by a computerized outcome program called OUTCOME for Windows. OUTCOME is designed to compare how a treatment plan for a given patient compares with regard to the duration, cost, and outcomes of treatment for other patients with similar presentations who experienced successful treatment outcomes.

After the diagnostic code and pertinent patient characteristics are entered, the software draws all similar cases from the database and yields an Outcome Report with predictive information. It addresses several predictive issues, including the number of treatment sessions required to decrease symptoms and achieve functional improvement, the average cost of treatment for similar patients, and the most effective treatment protocol with this particular diagnosis, as well as GAF, quality of life rating, and pain rating after treatment as compared to similar patients. Furthermore, OUTCOME provides

TABLE 8.3

Outcome Report: Treatment Comparison

Outcome Domains	Outcome Information	Protocol I (N=250)	Protocol II (N=250)
Treatment (Average Number of Sessions)	Doctor Visits	8.1	6.0
	Psychotherapy Sessions	0	16.3
	Biofeedback Sessions	0	8.6
	Total Treatment Sessions	8.4	30.2
Clinical Outcomes	Average Quality of Life Rating (1-100)	71.2	87.1
	Average Pain Rating (0-10)	6.4	3.6
	Average Client Satisfaction Rating (0-100)	80.5	93.8
	% of Patients Able to Discontinue Medications	39%	78%
	GAF Rating (1-100)	70.0	81.0
	% of Patients Returning for Treatment within 12 months	27%	3%
Finances (Cost in Dollars)	Average Total Cost (all treatment)	$550	$2,585
	Average Physician Cost	$550	$425
	Average Psychotherapy Cost	0	$1,520
	Average Biofeedback Cost	0	$640

Protocol I	Protocol II
1. Physician Visits 2. Medication Management	1. Physician Visits 2. Medication Management 3. Psychological Consulting 4. Biofeedback

information on other factors such as decrease in medication use following treatment and patient satisfaction with treatment.

These data come from a comparison of the various treatment protocols used for those similar patients. For instance, two protocols can be compared. Protocol I included visits with a family physician and medication management. Protocol II used a combined physician, medication, psychological counseling, and biofeedback treatment approach. (Table 8.3)

TABLE 8.4

Outcome Report: Patient Comparison

Outcome Domains	Outcome Information	Patient M.G.	Normative Values for Patients Treated Using Protocol II (N=250)
Treatment (Average Number of Sessions)	Doctor Visits	4	6.0
	Psychotherapy Sessions	12	16.3
	Biofeedback Sessions	8	8.6
	Total Treatment Sessions	24	30.2
Clinical Outcomes	Average Quality of Life Rating (1-100)	88	87.1
	Average Pain Rating (0-10)	2	3.6
	Average Client Satisfaction Rating (0-100)	95	93.8
	% of Patients Able to Discontinue Medications	yes	78%
	GAF Rating (1-100)	83	81.0
Finances (Cost in Dollars)	Average Total Cost (all treatment)	$2,008	$2,585
	Average Physician Cost	$288	$425
	Average Psychotherapy Cost	$1,080	$1,520
	Average Biofeedback Cost	$640	$640

It appears that overall improvement is much greater with Protocol II, as noted by a higher quality of life rating, a lower pain rating, and cessation of medication use, as well as a higher GAF rating following treatment. The cost of Treatment II was $2,035 more than Treatment I, but the overall effects were greater for all variables measured. Furthermore, only 3% of the patients treated with Protocol II returned for treatment for the same symptoms within the following 12 months, compared to 27% with Protocol I.

Table 8.4 compares this patient's treatment to those who received Protocol II. It appears her outcome was excellent, with improvement across all areas, with the cost $577 less than the predicted amount for similar patients treated with Protocol II. She no longer needed medication and her physical symptoms and GAF ratings returned to premorbid levels.

By using outcomes data in this manner, the provider is able to plan treatment, and predict long-term outcomes, total costs, and the number of sessions needed to maximize treatment outcomes. These data are useful not only in planning treatment but in supporting treatment decisions to patients, case managers, other providers, and third-party payers.

References

Acierno, R., Hersen, M., & Ammerman, R. (1994), Overview of the issues in prescriptive treatment. In M. Hersen & R. Ammerman (Eds.), *Handbook of prescriptive treatments for adults*. New York: Plenum, 3–30.

Allgulander, C. & Lavori, P. (1991). Excess mortality among 3302 patients with "pure" anxiety neurosis. *Archives of General Psychiatry, 48*:599–601

American Psychiatric Association. (1987). *Diagnostic and statistical manual of mental disorders, 3rd. ed. rev.* Washington, DC: American Psychiatric Association.

American Psychiatric Association. (1994). *Diagnostic and statistical manual of mental disorders 4th ed.* Washington, DC: American Psychiatric Association.

American Psychiatric Association. (1993). Practice guideline for eating disorders. *American Journal of Psychiatry, 150: 2,* 212–227

Anderson, C., Reiss, D., & Hogarty, G. (1986). *Schizophrenia and the family.* New York: Guilford.

Apfeldorf, W.J., Shear, M.K., Leon, A.C., et al. (1994). A brief screen for panic disorder. *Journal of Anxiety Disorders. 8*:71–78.

Attkisson, C.C., & Zwick, R. (1982). The Client Satisfaction Questionaire. Psychometric properties and correlations with service utilization. *Evaluation and Program Planning, 5,* 233–237.

Awad, G. (1993). Subjective response to neuroleptics in schizophrenia. *Schizophrenia Bulletin, 19,* 609–618.

Ball, J.C. & Ross, A. (1991). The effectiveness of methadone maintenance treatment: Patients, programs, services, and outcome. New York: Springer-Verlag.

Barlow, D., & Waddell, M. (1985). Agoraphobia. In D. Barlow (Ed.), *Clinical handbook of psychological disorders: A step-by-step treatment manual.* New York: Guilford.

Beavers, R., Hampson, R. (1990). *Successful families: Assessment and intervention.* New York: Norton.

Beck, A., Rush, A., Shaw, B., & Emery, G. (1979). *Cognitive therapy of depression.* New York: Guilford.

Beck, A.T., Ward, C.H., Mendelson, M., Mock, J., & Erbaugh, J. (1961). An inventory for measuring depression. *Archives of General Psychiatry, 4,* 561–571.

Beitman, B. (1993). Combined treatments. In J. Oldham, M. Riba, & A. Tasman (Eds.), *American psychiatric press review of psychiatry, Volume 12.* Washington, DC: American Psychiatric Press, 517–519.

Beitman, B. (1991). Medication during psychotherapy: Case studies of the reciprocal relationship between psychotherapy process and medication use. In B. Beitman & G. Klerman (Eds.), *Integrating pharmacotherapy and psychotherapy.* Washington, DC: American Psychiatric Press, 21–44.

Beitman, B. (1984). Introducing medication during psychotherapy. In B. Beitman & G. Klerman. (Eds.). *Combining psychotherapy and drug treatment in clinical practice.* New York: SP Medical and Scientific Books.

Beutler, L. (1979). Toward specific psychological therapies for specific conditions. *Journal of Consulting and Clinical Psychology,* 59: 226–232.

Bisbee, C. (1991). *Educating patients and families about mental illness: A practical guide.* Gaithersburg, MD: Aspen Publishers.

Borgquist, L., Hansson, L., Nettelbladt, P., et al. (1993). Perceived health and high consumers of care: Study of mental health problems in a Swedish primary health care district. *Psychological Medicine,* 23:763–770.

Breier, A., & Strauss, J. (1983). Self-control in psychotic disorders. *Archives of General Psychiatry, 40,* 1141–1145.

Broadhead, W.E., Leon, A.S., Weissman, M.M., et al. (in press) Gilbert TT, Keller MB, Olfson M. Development and validation of the SDDS-PC Screen for multiple mental disorders in primary care. *Archives of Family Medicine.*

Brody, D.S., Miller, S.M., Lerman, D.E., et al. (1989). The relationship between patients' satisfaction with their physicians and perceptions about interventions they desired and received. *Medical Care,* 27:1027–1035.

Brook, D. (1993). Group psychotherapy with anxiety and mood disorders. In H. Kaplan & B. Sadock (Eds.), *Comprehensive group psychotherapy 3rd ed.* Baltimore: Williams & Wilkins, 374–393.

Budman, S.H. and Springer, T., (1987). Treatment delay, outcome, and satisfaction in time-limited group and individual psychotherapy. *Professional Psychology: Research and Practice, 18:*647–649.

Burke, W.J., Roccaforte, W.H., & Wengel, S. (1991). The short form of the Geriatric Depression Scale: A comparison with the 30-item form. *Journal of Geriatric Psychiatry and Neurology, 4:*173–178.

Byrne, M.E., Fox, S. and McLellan, A.T. (1996). A breakthrough in EAP handling of substance abuse. *EAP Digest.*

Clark, D. (1989). Anxiety states: Panic and generalized anxiety. In K. Hawton, P. Salkovskis, J. Kirk, & D. Clark (Eds.), *Cognitive behavior therapy for psychiatric problems: A practical guide.* Oxford: Oxford University Press, 52–96.

Clark, A., & Friedman, M.J. (1983). Nine standardized scales for evaluating treatment outcomes in a mental health clinic. *Journal of Clinical Psychology, 39*(6), 939–950.

Clark, C.H., Schwenk, T.L., & Plackis, C. (1983). Patients' perspectives of behavioral science care by family practice physicians. *Journal of Medical Education,* 58:954–961.

Cochran, S. (1984). Preventing medical noncompliance in the outpatient treatment of bipolar affective disorders. *Journal of Consulting and Clinical Psychology, 52 (5)* 873–878.

Compass Information Services (1995). Scientific foundation of the COMPASS® System. Philadelphia: Compass Information Services, Inc.

Coryell, W., Noyes, R., & Clancy, J. (1982). Excess mortality in panic disorder: A comparison with primary unipolar depression. *Archives of General Psychiatry*, 39:701–703.

Cowen, E.L. (1991). In pursuit of wellness. *American Psychologist*, 46, 404–408.

Cox, B.J., Direnfeld, D.M., Swinson, R.P., & Norton, G.R. (1994). Suicidal ideation and suicide attempts in panic disorder and social phobia. *American Journal of Psychiatry*, 151:882–887.

Craske, M., & Waikar, S. (1994). Panic disorder. In M. Hersen & R. Ammerman (Eds.), *Handbook of prescribing of prescriptive treatments for adults*. New York: Plenum, 135–156.

Davenport, Y., Ebert, M., Adland, M., & Goodwin, F. (1977). Couples group therapy as an adjunct to lithium maintenance of the manic patient. *American Journal of Orthopsychiatry*, 47, 495–502.

Davis, J., Kane, J., Marder, S., et al. (1993). Dose response of prophylactic antipsychotics. *Journal of Clinical Psychiatry*, 54, 2(suppl).

Derogatis, L., Lipman, R.S., Rickels, K., Uhlenhuth, E.H., & Covi, L. (1974a). The Hopkins Symptom Checklist (HSCL): A measure of primary symptom dimensions. In P. Pinchot (Ed.), *Psychological measurements in psychopharmacology*. Basel: Karger.

Derogatis, L., Lipman, R.S., Rickels, K., Uhlenhuth, E.H., & Covi, L. (1974b). The Hopkins Symptom Checklist (HSCL): A self-report symptom inventory. *Behavioral Science*, 19, 1–15.

Derogatis, L. (1977). *SCL-90: Administration and procedures manual-I for the revised version*. Baltimore: Clinical Psychometrics Research.

Diener, E. (1984). Subjective well-being. *Psychological Bulletin*, 95(3), 542–575.

Docherty, (1988). Managing compliance problems in psychopharmacology. In F. Flack (Ed.), *Psychobiological and psychopharmacology, Vol. 2*. New York: Norton, 12–31.

Dupuy, H.J. (1977). *A current validational study of the NCHS general well-being schedule* (DHEW Publication No. HRA 78-1347). Hyattsville, MD: National Center for Health Statistics, U.S. Department of Health, Education, and Welfare.

Dworkin, R.J., Friedman, L.C., Telschow, R.L., Grant, K.D., Moffic, H.S., & Sloan, V.J. (1990). The longitudinal use of the Global Assessment Scale in multiple-rater situations. *Community Mental Health Journal*, 26(4), 335–344.

Eckman, T., & Liberman, R. (1990a). Teaching medication management skills to schizophrenic patients. *Journal of Clinical Psychopharmacology*, 10, (3) 3–38.

Eisen, S.V., Dill, D.L., & Grob, M.C. (1991). Reliability and validity of a brief patient-report instrument for psychiatric outcome evaluation, *Hospital and Community Psychiatry*, 45,3.

Endicott, J., Spitzer, R.L., Fleiss, J.L., & Cohen, J. (1976). The Global Assessment Scale: A procedure for measuring overall severity of psychiatric disturbance. *Archives of General Psychiatry*, 33, 766–771.

Evaluation Systems International, Inc. (1993–94). Documentation for outcome for Windows. Boulder, CO: Evaluation Systems International, Inc.

Eysenck, H. J. (1952). The effects of psychotherapy: An evaluation. *Journal of Consulting Psychology*, 16, 319–324.

Fava, M., & Kaji, J. (1994). Continuation and maintenance treatments of major depressive disorder. *Psychiatric Annals*, 24, 281–290.

Feldman, L. (1992). *Integrating individual and family therapy*. New York: Brunner/Mazel.

Feldman, J. & Fitzpatrick, R. (Eds.), (1992). *Managed mental health care: Administrative and clinical issues.* Washington, DC: American Psychiatric Press.

Follette, W. & Cummings, N. (1967). Psychiatric services and medical utilization in a prepaid health plan setting. *Medical Care, 5,* 15–35.

Frowick, B., Shank, J.C., Doherty, W.J., & Powell, T.A. (1986). What do patients really want? Redefining a behavioral science curriculum for family physicians. *Journal of Family Practice, 23,* 141–146.

Frances, A., Clarkin, J., & Perry, S. (1984). *Differential therapeutics in psychiatry: The art and science of treatment selection,* New York: Brunner/Mazel.

Frank, J. D. (1973). *Persuasion and healing.* Baltimore: Johns Hopkins University Press.

Frank, J. D., & Frank, J. B. (1991). *Persuasion and healing: A comparative study of psychotherapy.* Baltimore: Johns Hopkins University Press.

Frank, E., Perel J., Mallinger, A., et al. (1992). Relationship of pharmacologic compliance to long-term prophylaxis in recurrent depression. *Psychopharmacological Bulletin, 28,* 231–235.

Fuerst, M. (1994). Psychotherapy's role in treatment of bipolar disorder praised. First International Conference. *Psychiatric Times,* I, 33, August.

Glick, I., Clarkin, J, & Goldsmith, S. (1993). Combining medication with family psychotherapy. In J. Oldham, M. Riba & A. Tasman, (Eds.), *American psychiatric review.* Washington, DC: American Psychiatric Press, 585–586.

Goldstein, M., (1991). Schizophrenia and family therapy. In B. Beitman & G. Klerman. (Eds.), *Integrating pharmacotherapy and psychotherapy.* Washington, DC: American Psychiatric Press, 291–310.

Goodwin, F., & Jamison, K. (1990). *Manic-depressive illness.* New York: Oxford University Press.

Gorman, D., & Masterton, G. (1990). General practice consultation patterns before and after intentional overdose: A matched control study. *British Journal of General Practice, 40,* 102–105

Gotcher, P., & Redfield, D., (1988). Integrated managed behavioral health care: Road to success, *EAP Digest,* July/August.

Greenberg, P.E., Stiglin, L.E., Finkelstein, S.N., & Berndt, E.R. (1993). The economic burden of depression in 1990. *Journal of Clinical Psychiatry, 54,* 405–418.

Greenberg, P.E., Stiglin, L.E., Finkelstein, S.N., & Berndt, E.R. (1993). Depression: A neglected major illness. *Journal of Clinical Psychiatry, 54,* 419–424.

Greist, J., & Jefferson, J. (1992a). *Panic disorder and agoraphobia: A guide.* Madison, WI: Information Systems, Dean Foundation.

Greist, J., & Jefferson, J. (1992b). *Obsessive-compulsive disorder: A guide.* Madison, WI: Information Systems, Dean Foundation.

Grotcher, P. & Redfield, D. (1988). Integrated managed behavioral health care: Road to success, *EAP Digest,* July/August, 26–29.

Hawton, K. (1992). Suicide and attempted suicide. In E. Paykel (Ed.), *Handbook of Affective Disorders, (2nd ed.),* New York: The Guilford Press.

Heard, H. & Linehan, M. (1994). Dialectical behavior therapy: An integrative approach to the treatment of the borderline personality disorder. *Journal of Psychotherapy Integration, 4,* 55–82.

Hersen, M., & Ammerman, R. (Eds.) (1994). *Handbook of prescriptive treatment for adults.* New York: Plenum.

Hoberman, H., & Lewisohn, P. (1990). Behavioral approaches to the treatment of unipolar depression. In T. Karasu. (Ed.), *Treatments of psychiatric disorders*. Washington, DC: American Psychiatric Press, 1846–1862.

Hogarty, G. (1984). Depot neuroleptics: The relevance of psychosocial factors. *Journal of Clinical Psychiatry, 45*, 36–42.

Hooley, J., & Teasdale, J. (1989). Predictors of relapse in unipolar depression: Expressed emotion, marital distress, and perceived criticism. *Journal of Abnormal Psychology, 98*, 229–235.

Horowitz, L.M., Rosenberg, S.E., Baer, B.A., Ureño, G., & Villasenor, V.S. (1988). Inventory of interpersonal problems: Psychometric properties and clinical applications. *Journal of Consulting and Clinical Psychology, 56*, 885–892.

Howard, K.I., Lueger, R., Maling, M., & Martinovich, Z. (1993). A phase model of psychotherapy: Causal mediation of outcome. *Journal of Consulting and Clinical Psychology, 61*, 678–685.

Howard, K.I., Orlinsky, D.E., Saunders, S.M., Bankoff, E.A., Davidson, C.V., & O'Mahoney, M.T. (1991). Northwestern University–University of Chicago Psychotherapy Research Program. In L. Beutler & M. Crago (Eds.), *Psychotherapy Research: An International Review of Programmatic Studies*. Washington, DC: American Psychological Association, 65–73.

Howard, K.I., Krause, M.S., & Vessey, J.T. (1994). Analysis of clinical trial data: The problem of outcome overlap. *Psychotherapy, 31*, 302–307.

Howard, K.I., Orlinsky, D.E., & Lueger, R.L. (1995).The design of clinically relevant outcome research: Some considerations and an example. In M. Aveline & D.A. Shapiro (Eds.), *Research foundations for psychotherapy practice*. Sussex: Wiley, 3–47.

Howard, K.I., Brill, P.L., Lueger, R.J., & O'Mahoney, M.T. (1995) *Integra outpatient tracking assessment*. Philadelphia: Compass Information Services, Inc.

Howard, K.I., Brill, P.L., Lueger, R.J., O'Mahoney, M.T., & Grissom, G.R. (1992). *Integra outpatient tracking assessment: Psychometric properties*. Radnor, PA: Integra, Inc.

Howard, K.I., Krause, M.S., & Lyons, J. (1993). When clinical trials fail: A guide for disaggregation. In L.S. Onken & J.D. Blaine (Eds.), *Behavioral treatments for drug abuse and dependence*. NIDA Research Monograph 137. Washington, DC: National Institute of Drug Abuse, 291–302.

Howard, K. I., Kopta, S. M., Krause, M. S., & Orlinsky, D. E. (1986). The dose-effect relationship in psychotherapy. *American Psychologist, 41*, 159–164.

Jacobson, N.S., & Truax, P. (1991). Clinical significance: A statistical approach to defining meaningful change in psychotherapy research. *Journal of Consulting and Clinical Psychology, 59*, 12–19.

Jamison, K. (1991). Manic-depressive illness: The overlooked need for psychotherapy. In B. Beitman & G. Klerman (Eds.), *Integrating pharmacotherapy and psychotherapy*. Washington, DC: American Psychiatric Press, 409–422.

Jamison, K. & Goodwin, F. (1983). Psychotherapeutic issues in bipolar illness. In L. Greenspoon (Ed.), *Psychiatric update: The American Psychiatric Association Annual Review, Vol. 2*. Washington, DC: American Psychiatric Press, 319–337.

Joyce, P. (1992). Prediction of treatment response. In E. Paykel (Ed.), *Handbook of affective disorders (2nd ed.)*. New York: Guilford, 453–462.

Kahn, D. (1990). The psychotherapy of mania. *Psychiatric Clinics of North America, 13*, 229–240.

Kanas, N. (1993). Group psychotherapy with schizophrenia. In H. Kaplan & B. Sadock (Eds.), *Comprehensive group psychotherapy (3rd ed.)*. New York: Williams & Wilkins. 407–418.

Karasu, T. (1982). Psychotherapy and pharmacotherapy: Toward an integrated model. *American Journal of Psychotherapy, 139*, 1102–1113.

Kashner, T.M., Rost, K., Smith, G.R., et al. (1992). An analysis of panel data: The impact of a psychiatric consultation letter on the expenditures and outcomes of care for patients with somatization disorder. *Medical Care, 30*, 811–821.

Katerndahl, D.A., Realini, J.P., & Talamantes, M. (1994). Where do panic attack sufferers seek care for their attacks? *NIMH International Conference on Mental Health Problems in the General Health Care Sector.* McLean, VA.

Keatley, M., Lemmon, J., Miller., T., & Miller, M. (1995). Using 'normative' data for outcomes comparisons. *Behavioral Health Management. 15* (3), 20–21.

Keller, M.B. (1990). Depression underrecognition and undertreatment by psychiatrists and other health care professionals. *Archives of Internal Medicine, 150:*946–948.

Kleinman, A. (1988). *The illness narrative.* New York: Basic Books.

Klerman, G.L., Weissman, M.M., Ouellette, R., et al. (1991). Panic attacks in the community: Social morbidity and health care utilization. *Journal of the American Medical Association, 265*, 742–746.

Kogan, W., Thompson, D. & Brown, J. (1975). Impact of integration of mental health service and comprehensive medical care. *Medical Care, 13*, 934–942.

Kopta, S.M., Howard, K.I., Lowry, J.L., & Beutler, L.E. (1994). Patterns of symptomatic recovery in time-unlimted psychotherapy. *Journal of Clinical and Consulting Psychology, 62*, 1009–1016.

Lambert, M. & Bergin, A. (1994). The effectiveness of psychotherapy. In A. Bergin & S. Garfield (Eds.), *Handbook of psychotherapy and behavior change* (4th ed.). New York: Wiley, 143–189.

Larkin, B.A., Copeland, J.R., Dewey, M.E., et al. (1992). The natural history of neurotic disorder in an elderly urban population. Findings from the Liverpool longitudinal study of continuing health in the community. *British Journal of Psychiatry, 160*, 681–686.

Leon, A.C., Klerman, G.L., Weissman, M.M., et al. (1992). Evaluating the diagnostic criteria for panic disorder measures of social morbidity as criteria. *Social Psychiatry and Psychiatric Epidemiology, 27*, 180–184.

Lewisohn, P., Munoz, R., Youngren, M., et al. (1978). *Control your depression.* Englewood Cliffs, NJ: Prentice Hall.

Liberman, R. (1988). *Social and independent living skills: Symptom management module trainer's manual.* Los Angeles: Rehabilitation Research and Training Center in Mental Illness.

Linehan, M. (1987). Dialectical behavior therapy: A cognitive behavioral approach to parasuicide. *Journal of Personality Disorders, 14*, 328–333.

Linehan, M., Heard, H., & Armstrong, H., (1993). Naturalistic follow-up of a behavioral treatment for chronically parasuicidal borderline patients. *Archives of General Psychiatry, 50*, 971–974.

Lipsey, M.W. & Wilson, D.B. (1993). The efficacy of psychological, educational, and behavioral treatment: Confirmation from meta-analysis. *American Psychologist, 48*, 1181–1209.

Lipsius, S. (1991). Combined individual and group psychotherapy: Guidelines at the interface. *International Journal of Group Psychotherapy, 41*, 313–327.

Lydiard, R.B., Fossey, M.D., March, W., et al. (1993). Prevalence of psychiatric disorders in patients with irritable bowel syndrome. *Psychosomatics, 34,* 229–234.

Lyons, J.S. (1991) *Severity of psychiatric illness,* Northwestern University Medical School, Chicago, IL.

Lyons, J.S., Colletta, J., Devens, M., & Finkel, S.(in press). The validity of the severity of psychiatric illness scale in a sample of inpatients on a psychogeriatric unit, *International Psychogeriatrics.*

Lyons, J.S. & Howard, K.I. (1991). Main effects analysis in clinical research: Statistical guidelines for disaggregating treatment groups. *Journal of Consulting and Clinical Psychology, 59,* 745–748.

Lyons, J.S., O'Mahoney, M.T., Doheny, K.M., Dworkin, L.N., and Miller, S.I.(in press). The prediction of short-stay psychiatric inpatients. *Administration and Policy in Mental Health.*

Main, D.S., Lutz, L.J., Barrett, J.E., Matthew, J., & Miller, R.S. (1993). The role of primary care clinician attitudes, beliefs, and training in the diagnosis and treatment of depression: A report from the Ambulatory Sentinel Practice Network, Inc. *Archives of Family Medicine, 2,* 1061–1066.

Maling, M.S., Gurtman, M.B., & Howard, K.I. (1995). The response of interpersonal problems to varying doses of psychotherapy. *Psychotherapy Research, 5,* 63–75.

Mann, J. (1986). How medication compliance affects outcomes. *Psychiatric Annals, 16,* 537–570.

Manning, D., & Frances, A. (1990). Afterword. In D. Manning & A. Frances (Eds.), *Combined pharmacotherapy and psychotherapy for depression.* Washington, DC: American Psychiatric Press, 183–186.

Manning, W., & Wells, K. (1992). The effects of psychological distress and psychological well-being on the use of medical services, *Medical Care, 30,* 541–553.

Marder, S., Johnson-Cronk, K., Wirshing, W., & Eckman, T. (1991). Schizophrenia and behavioral skill training. In B. Beitman & G. Klerman (Eds.), *Integrating pharmacotherapy and psychotherapy.* Washington, DC: American Psychiatric Press 311–328.

Mason, S., & Siris, S. (1992). Dual diagnosis: The case for care management. *America Journal on Addictions, 1,* 77–82.

Mattick, R., & Andrews, F. (1994). Social phobia. In M. Hersen & R. Ammerman (Eds.), *Handbook of prescriptive treatment for adults.* New York: Plenum, 157–178.

Mavissakalian, M. (1993). Combined behavioral and pharmacological treatment of anxiety disorders. In J. Oldham, M. Riba, & A. Tasman (Eds.), *American psychiatric press review of psychiatry, Vol. 12.* Washington, DC: American Psychiatric Press, 541–564.

McLellan, A.T., Luborsky, L., O'Brien, C.P., & Woody, G.E. (1980). An improved diagnostic instrument for substance abuse patients: The Addiction Severity Index. *Journal of Nervous and Mental Disorders 168,* 26–33.

McLellan, A.T., Luborsky, L., O'Brien, C.P., Woody, G.E., and Druly, K.A. (1982). Is treatment for substance abuse effective? *Journal of the American Medical Association, 246, No. 10:* 1423–1428

McLellan, A.T., Luborsky, L., Cacciola, J., Griffith, J.E. (1985). New Data from the ASI: Reliability and Validity in Three Centers. *Journal of Nervous and Mental Disorders,* 173: 412–423

McLellan, A.T., Cacciola, J., Kushner, H., Peters, F., Smith, I., and Pettinati, H. (1992). The fifth edition of the Addiction Severity Index. *Journal of Substance Abuse Treatment, 9,* 199–213.

McLellan, A.T., Grissom, G.R., Brill, Peter L., Durell, J., Metzger, D.S., O'Brien, C.P., (1993). Private substance abuse treatments: Are some programs more effective than others? *Journal of Substance Abuse Treatment,* Vol. 10: 243–254.

Miller, G. (1985). The substance abuse subtle screening inventory manual. Bloomington, IN: Addiction Research & Consultation, 5–3.

Miller, N.S., Belkin, B.M., & Gold, M.S. (1991). Alcohol and drug dependence among the elderly: Epidemiology, diagnosis and treatment. *Comprehensive Psychiatry, 32,* 153–165.

National Institute on Drug Abuse (1992). *How drug abuse takes profit out of business.* Rockville, MD: National Clearinghouse for Alcohol and Drug Information.

Noyes, R., Kathol, R.C., Fisher, M.M., et al. (1993). The validity of DSM-III-R hypochondriasis. *Archives of General Psychiatry, 50,* 961–970.

Orleans, C.T., George, L.K., Houpt, J.L., & Brodie, H. (1985). How primary care physicians treat psychiatric disorders: A national survey of family practitioners. *American Journal of Psychiatry, 142,* 52–57.

Orlinsky, D. E. & Howard, K. I. (1986). Process and outcome in psychotherapy. In S. L. Garfield & A. E. Bergin (Eds.), *Handbook of psychotherapy and behavior change, (3rd ed.)* New York: John Wiley.

Orlinsky, D. E. & Howard, K.I. (1987). A generic model of psychotherapy. *Journal of Integrative and Eclectic Psychotherapy, 6,* 6–27.

Orlinsky, D.E., Park, J., & Grawe, K. (1994). Process and outcome in psychotherapy. In A. E. Bergin & S. L. Garfield (Eds.), *Handbook of psychotherapy and behavior change, (3rd ed.)* New York: John Wiley.

Paul, G. (1967). Outcome research in psychotherapy. *Journal of Consulting and Clinical Psychology. 31,* 109–118.

Perez-Stable E., Miranda J., Munoz R., & Ying Y. (1990). Depression in medical outpatients: Underrecognition and misdiagnosis. *Archives of Internal Medicine, 150,* 1083–1088.

Perry, S., Frances, A. & Clarkin, J. (1990). *A DSM-III-R casebook of treatment selection.* New York: Brunner/Mazel.

Pollack, M., & Otto, M. (1994). Long-term pharmacologies treatment of panic disorder. *Psychiatric Annuals, 24,* 291–298.

Porter, K. (1993). Combined individual and group psychotherapy. In H. Kaplan & B. Sadock (Eds.), *Comprehensive group psychotherapy (3rd ed.).* Baltimore: Williams & Wilkins, 314–324.

Post, R., Rubinow, D., & Ballengerj (1986). Conditioning and sensitization in the longitudinal course of affective illness. *British Journal of Psychiatry, 149,* 191–201.

Pristach, C., & Smith, C. (1990). Medication compliance and substance abuse among schizophrenic patients. *Hospital and Community Psychiatry, 41,* 1345–1348.

Prochaska, J., & DiClemente, C. (1986). The transtheoretical approach. In J. Norcross *(Ed.), Handbook of eclectic psychotherapy.* New York: Brunner/Mazel.

Radloff, L.S. (1977). The CES-D scale: A self-report depression scale for research in the general population. *Applied Psychological Measurement, 1,* 358–401.

Regier, D.A., Boyd, J.H., & Rae, D.S. (1988). One month prevalence of mental disorders in the U.S.—based on the five Epidemiologic Catchment Area sites. *Archives of General Psychiatry, 45,* 977–986.

Regier, D.A., Narrow, N.E., Rae, D.S., et al. (1993). The de facto U.S. mental and addictive disorders service system: Epidemiologic Catchment Area prospective 1-year prevalence rates of disorders and services. *Archives of General Psychiatry, 50,* 85–94.

Rehm, L., LePage, J., & Bailey, S. (1994). Unipolar depression. In M. Hersen & R. Ammerman (Eds.), *Handbook of prescriptive treatments for adults.* New York: Plenum, 95–118.

Reynolds, R. (1993). Practice commentary. *Archives of Family Medicine, 2,* 84.

Rice, D.R., Kelman, S., Miller, L.S., and Dunmeyer, S.(1990). *The Economic Costs of Alcohol and Drug Abuse and Mental Illness: 1985.* Washington, DC: Public Health Service.

Rodenhauser, P., & Stone, W. (1993). Combining psychopharmacology and group psychotherapy: Problems and advantages. *International Journal of Group Psychotherapy, 43,* 11–28.

Roy, A., Lamparski, D., DeJong, J. et al. (1990). Characteristics of alcoholics who attempt suicide. *American Journal of Psychiatry, 147,* 761–765.

Rush, A. (1988). Cognitive approaches to adherence. In A. Frances & R. Hales (Eds.), *The American psychiatric press review of psychiatry, Vol. 7.* Washington, DC: American Psychiatric Press.

Rush, D., & Hollon, S. (1991). Depression. In B. Beitman & G. Klerman (Eds.), *Integrating pharmacotherapy and psychotherapy.* Washington, DC: American Psychiatric Press, 121–142.

Rutz, W., von Knorring, L., & Walinder, J. (1989). Frequency of suicide on Gotland after systematic post-graduate education of general practioners. *Acta Psychiatrica Scandanavia, 80,* 151–154

Salvendy, J., & Toffe, R. (1991). Antidepressants in group psychotherapy. *International Journal of Group Psychotherapy, 41,* 465–480. New York: Jason Aronson.

Sanders, F., & Feldman, L. (1993). Integrating individual, marital, and family therapy. In J. Oldham, M. Riba, & A. Tasman (Eds.), *American psychiatric press review of psychiatry, Vol. 12.* Washington, DC: American Psychiatric Press, 611–629.

Sarti, P., & Coumos, F. (1990). Medication and psychotherapy in the treatment of chronic schizophrenia. *Psychiatric Clinics of North America, 13,* 215–228.

Sato, T. & Takeichi, M. (1993). Lifetime prevalence of specific psychiatric disorders in a general medicine clinic. *General Hospital Psychiatry, 15,* 224–233.

Saunders, S.M., Howard, K.I., & Orlinsky, D.E. (1989). The therapeutic bond scales: Psychometric characteristics and relationship to treatment effectiveness. *Psychological Assessment: A Journal of Clinical and Consulting Psychology, 1,* 323–330.

Schooler, N. (1994a). Engaging families in treatment effects outcomes. *Syllabus and proceeding summary American Psychiatric Association annual meeting.* Washington, DC: American Psychiatric Association, 64.

Schooler, N. (1994b). Maintenance treatment: Drug and psychosocial effects. *Syllabus and proceeding summary American Psychiatric Association annual meeting.* Washington, DC: American Psychiatric Association, 303.

Schou, M. (1991). Relapse prevention in manic depressive illness: Important and unimportant factors. *Canadian Journal of Psychiatry, 36,* 502–506.

Scriven, M. (1991). *Evaluation thesaurus. (4th ed.)* Newbury Park, CA: Sage.

Shapiro, D. A. & Shapiro, D. (1982). Meta-analysis of comparative therapy outcome studies: A replication and refinement. *Psychological Bulletin, 92,* 581–604.

Sharfstein, S., Muszynski, S. and Arnett, G, (1984). Dispelling myths about mental health benefits. *Business and Health,* October.

Shaw, J. & Creed, F. (1991). The cost of somatization. *Journal of Psychosomatics Research, 35,* 307–312.

Skinner, H. (1990). Spectrum of drinkers and intervention opportunities. *Canadian Medical Association Journal, 143*:1054–1059.

Smith, M.L., Glass, G.V., & Miller, T.I. (1980). *The benefits of psychotherapy.* Baltimore: The Johns Hopkins Press.

Smith, G.R., Monson, R.A., & Ray, D. (1986). Patients with unexplained symptoms: Their characteristics, functional health, and health care utilization. *Archives of Internal Medicine, 146,* 69–72.

Smith, G.R., Babor, T., Burnam, A. et al. (1995). The substance abuse outcomes module. Little Rock: Centers for Mental Healthcare Research. University of Arkansas for Medical Sciences.

Sotsky, S., Galss, D., Shea, M., et al. (1991). Patient predictors of response to psychotherapy and pharmacotherapy: Findings in the NIMH treatment of depression collaborative research program. *American Journal of Psychiatry, 148,* 997–1008.

Speer, D.C. (1992). Clinically significant change: Jacobson and Truax (1991) Revisited. *Journal of Consulting and Clinical Psychology, 60,* 402–408.

Sperry, L. (1988). Designing effective psychiatric interventions, *Journal of Psychiatric Education, 12,* (2) 125–129.

Sperry, L., Gudeman, J., Blackwell, B., & Faulkner, L. (1992). *Psychiatric case formulation.* Washington, DC: American Psychiatric Press.

Sperry, L. (1995a). *Handbook of diagnosis and treatment of the DSM-IV personality disorders.* New York: Brunner/Mazel.

Sperry, L. (1995b). *Psychopharmacology and psychotherapy: Strategies for maximzing treatment outcomes.* New York: Brunner/Mazel.

Sperry, L. (1995c). The workplace psychiatrist's focus: Organizational, clinical-organizational or clinical interventions? *Academy of Organizational and Occupational Psychiatry. 4,* (2) 4–5.

Sperry, L. (1995d). Classification system proposed for workplace behavior. *Academy of Organizational and Occupational Psychiatry. 4,* (1) 4–5.

Spitzer, R. L., Williams, J. B. W., & Gibbon, M. (1988). *The Structured Clinical Interview for DSM III-R—Patient Version (7/88).* New York: Biometrics Research Department, New York State Psychiatric Institute.

Spitzer, R.L., Williams, J.B.W., Kroenkek, et al., (1994). Utility of a new procedure for diagnosing mental disorders in primary care: The PRIME-MD 1000 study. *Journal of the American Medical Association, 272,* 1749–1256.

Stewart, A.L., Hays, R.D., & Ware, J.E. (1988). The MOS short-form General Health Survey. *Medical Care, 26,* 724–735.

Stewart, W.F., Schechter, A. & Liberman, J. (1992). Physician consultation for headache pain and history of panic: Results from a population-based study. *American Journal of Medicine, 92*:355–405.

Stone, M. (1993). *Abnormalities of personality: Within and beyond the realm of treatment.* New York: Norton.

Stone, W., Rodenhauser, P., & Markert, R. (1991). Combining group psychotherapy and pharmacotherapy: A survey. *International Journal of Group Psychotherapy, 41,* 449–464.

Stoudemire, A., Hill, C., Morris, R., Martino-Saltzman, D., & Lewison, B. (1993). Long-term affective and cognitive outcome in depressed older adults. *American Journal of Psychiatry, 150,* 896–900.

Strum, R. & Wells, K. (1995). How can care for depression become cost-effective? *Journal of the American Medical Association, 273*:51–58.

Sussman, N. (1993). Integrating psychopharmacology and group psychotherapy. In H. Kaplan & B. Sadock (Eds.), *Comprehensive group psychotherapy, (3rd ed.)* Baltimore: Williams & Wilkins, 363–371.

Toffler, A. (1980) *The third wave.* New York: Bantam

Torrey, E. F. (1983). *Surviving schizophrenia: A family manual.* New York: Harper & Row.

U.S. Bureau of the Census (1993). *Statistical Abstract of the United States: 113th edition.* Washington, DC.

Van Casteren, T., Van der Veken, J., Tafforeau & Van Oyen, P. (1993). Suicide and attempted suicide reported by general practioners in Belgium, 1990–91. *Acta Psychiatrica Scandanavia, 87,* 451–455.

Vibbert, S. & Youngs, M.T. (Eds.) (1995). The COMPASS outcomes measurement system. In *The 1996 behavioral outcomes and guidelines sourcebook.* New York: Faulkner & Gray, B40–B49.

Viet, C.T., & Ware, Jr., J.E. (1983). The structure of psychological distress and well-being in general populations. *Journal of Consulting and Clinical Psychology, 51,* 730–742.

Vinogradov, S., & Yalorn, 1. (1989). *Concise guide to group psychotherapy.* Washington, DC: American Press.

Von Korff, M., Shapiro, S., Burke, J.D. et al. (1987). Anxiety and depression in a primary care clinic. *Archives of General Psychiatry, 44,* 152–156.

Vuori, H. (1987). Patient satisfaction—An attribute or indicator of the quality of care? *Quality Review Bulletin,* 13.

Ward, N. (1991). Psychosocial approaches to pharmacotherapy. In B. Beitman & G. Klerman (Eds.), *Integrating pharmacotherapy and psychotherapy.* Washington, DC: American Psychiatric Press, 69–104.

Ware, Jr., J.E. & Sherbourne, C.D. (1992). The MOS 36-item short form health survey (SF-36): I. Conceptual framework and item selection. *Medical Care, 30,* 473–483.

Watson, D., & Tellegen, A. (1985). Toward a consensual structure of mood. *Psychological Bulletin, 98,* 219–235.

Weissman, M., & Klerman, G. (1991). Interpersonal psychotherapy for depression. In B. Beitman & G. Klerman (Eds.), *Integrating pharmacotherapy and psychotherapy.* Washington, DC: American Psychiatric Press, 379–394.

Wells, K.B., Stewart, A., Hays, R.D. et al. (1989). The functioning and well-being of depressed patients: Results from the Medical Outcomes Study. *Journal of the American Medical Association, 262,* 914–919.

Wells, K.B., Hays, R.D., Burnam, M.A., Rogers, W., Greenfields, S., Ware, J.E. Detection of depressive disorder for patients receiving prepaid or fee-for-service care: Results from the Medical Outcomes Study. *Journal of the American Medical Association, 262,* 914–919.

Westreich, L. (1991). Assessing an adult patient's suicide risk: What primary care physicians need to know. *Postgraduate Medicine, 90,* 59–62.

Williams, B. (1994). Patient satisfaction: A valid concept? *Social Science and Medicine, 38*(4).

Williamson, P., Beitman, B.D., & Katon, W. (1981). Beliefs that foster physician avoidance of psychosocial aspects of health care. *Journal of Family Practice, 13,* 999–1003.

Wolpe, J. (1977). Inadequate behavioral analysis: The Achilles heel of outcome research in behavior therapy. *Journal of Behavior Therapy and Experimental Psychiatry, 8,* 1–3.

Wynn, L. (1983). A phase-oriented approach to treatment with schizophrenics and their families. In W. MacFarlane (Ed.), *Family therapy in schizophrenia.* New York: Guilford Press, 251–265.

Young, J., Zonana, H., & Shepler, L. (1986). Medication noncompliance in schizophrenia: Codification and update. *Bulletin of the American Academy of Psychiatry and Law, 14,* 105–122.

Yu, J., Chen, P.J., Harshman, E.J., & McCarthy, E.G. (1991). An analysis of substance abuse patterns, medical expenses and effectiveness of treatment in the workplace. *Employee Benefits Journal, Sept.* 26–30.

Zaslav, M., & Kalb, R. (1989). Medicine as metaphor and medicine in group psychotherapy with psychiatric patients. *International Journal of Group Psychotherapy, 39,* 457–467

Zimmerman, M. & Coryell, W. (1987). The Inventory to Diagnose Depression (IDD): A self-report scale to diagnose major depressive disorder. *Journal of Consulting and Clinical Psychology, 55,* 55–59.

Zimmerman, M., Coryell, W., Corenthal, C. et al. (1986). A self-report scale to diagnose major depressive disorder: Self-report vs. clinician ratings. *Journal of Nervous and Mental Disorders, 174,* 150–153.

Zimmerman, M., Lish, J.D., Farber, N.J. et al. (1994) Screening for depression in medical patients: Is the focus to narrow? *General Hospital Psychiatry, 16,* 388–396.

Zoler, M. (1994). Lithium-resistant bipolar patients benefit from combined treatment. *Clinical Psychiatry News,* 11 June.

Name Index

Subject Index